The Welfare State in Transition

By the same author

Voluntary Social Services (Martin Robertson/Blackwell, Oxford, 1981)
Marital Violence, Sociological Review Monograph 31 (editor) (Routledge and Kegan Paul, London, 1985)

The Welfare State in Transition

The Theory and Practice of Welfare Pluralism

Norman Johnson
Lecturer in Social Policy
University of Keele

HARVESTER WHEATSHEAF
New York London Toronto Sydney Tokyo Singapore

First published in 1987 by
Wheatsheaf Books Ltd

Reprinted by
Harvester Wheatsheaf
66 Wood Lane End, Hemel Hempstead,
Hertfordshire, HP2 4RG
A division of
Simon & Schuster International Group

© Norman Johnson, 1987

Typeset in Times 11/12 by
Input Typesetting Ltd, London
Printed and bound in Great Britain by
Billing & Sons Limited, Worcester

British Library Cataloguing in Publication Data

Johnson, Norman
   The welfare state in transition: the
   theory and practice of welfare pluralism.
   1. Welfare state
   I. Title
   361.6'5   HN17.5

   ISBN 0−7450−0157−2
   ISBN 0−7450−0238−2 Pbk

  3 4 5 93

For Ruth, Karen and David and in memory of Joyce

Contents

Tables

Acknowledgements

I wish to express my thanks to past and present colleagues at the University of Keele for their stimulation and encouragement. I am very grateful to Betty Reid Mandell and Ramesh Mishra for their helpful comments on the manuscript. Thanks are also due to Rowena Gay for typing the manuscript so quickly and accurately. Most of all, I wish to thank my wife, Ruth, for all her help and encouragement. This is as much her book as it is mine. Shortcomings, of course, remain my responsibility.

Abbreviations

AFDC	Aid to Families with Dependent Children
CDC	Community Development Corporation
CND	Campaign for Nuclear Disarmament
EEC	European Economic Community
GDP	Gross Domestic Product
GNP	Gross National Product
HMO	Health Maintenance Organisation
NACAB	National Association of Citizens' Advice Bureaux
NHS	National Health Service
OECD	Organisation for Economic Co-operation and Development
PI	Particulier Initiatif

Introduction

During the last decade there has been much talk about crisis in welfare states. Welfare states, it is claimed, are experiencing problems of crisis proportions arising from government overload and from fiscal and economic difficulties. Marxists and the New Right seem to be in agreement that the capitalist state has become over-bureaucratic and that it is unresponsive to people's needs. Eventually, the argument continues, a legitimation crisis will develop as the fiscal and economic problems become ever more serious and the welfare state loses public support.

It is certainly true that the cosy consensus of the 1950s and 1960s appears to have evaporated. But the term 'crisis' suggests a situation that is out of control, a situation in which grave problems are incapable of solution or containment. Talk of crisis may, however, be premature as there is evidence of continuing and strong public support for the principles upon which the welfare state is based.

There can be little doubt that governments have promoted the notion of crisis as a means of justifying cuts in social expenditure, which they wish to bring about for ideological reasons. The problems arise from a lack of political commitment to the welfare state and a refusal to accept that retrenchment is not the only possible response to present difficulties.

Doubts concerning the viability of the welfare state have given rise to a lively debate about possible future directions. Prominent participants in the debate have been the advocates of welfare pluralism. Welfare states, of course, have always been pluralistic in the sense that they have accommodated a variety of welfare providers: the state, voluntary agencies, private markets and informal networks. The case being made by welfare pluralists at the present time, however, is that the current predominance of the state in welfare provision is unsatisfactory. While the state should exercise a regulative role and remain the chief source of finance, its role as a welfare provider should be considerably diminished, and a correspondingly greater role should be accorded to the voluntary, informal and commercial sectors.

The welfare pluralist debate will never be wholly settled. In capitalist societies there will always be disagreement about the most appropriate balance to be struck between statutory, voluntary, informal and commercial provision; and the balance will change over time and from country to country. This book is intended as a contribution to the continuing debate, and one of its purposes is to identify and discuss some of the problems involved in transferring responsibility for welfare services from the state to the other three sectors. Some of the flaws in the welfare pluralist case will be exposed.

The book is concerned exclusively with welfare states in capitalist societies. There may be important lessons to be learned from studying the practice of welfare in non-capitalist societies, but a different set of questions is implied. It is the welfare state in *capitalist* societies that is said to be in crisis, and it is only in capitalist societies that questions relating to welfare pluralism arise.

The first chapter highlights some of the main characteristics of the welfare state. The second chapter considers the alleged welfare state crisis and the assumed disintegration of the postwar consensus. The meaning of welfare pluralism is looked at in Chapter 3. The next four chapters are devoted to an examination of each of the four welfare sectors. The concluding chapter then considers the alternative visions of the future of welfare offered by competing ideologies.

The examples used in the book are drawn mainly from Western Europe and the United States, but there are brief references to Australia, Canada, Japan and New Zealand.

1 The Welfare State

The term 'welfare state' was originally applied to Britain during the Second World War.[1] After the war the term came into more general use as a convenient shorthand way of referring to the social and economic policy changes then taking place, which according to those sponsoring them, would transform British society.

There were three groups of changes: (1) the introduction and extension of a range of social services, including social security, the National Health Service, education, housing, employment services and welfare services for elderly and handicapped people and for deprived children; (2) the maintenance of full employment as the paramount aim of policy; (3) a programme of nationalisation. It was these three strands together which constituted the welfare state. The intellectual credentials of the welfare state could be found in Keynes and Beveridge with elements of Fabian socialism. It should be noted that each of the three sets of changes implied an interventionist government.

In the 1950s and 1960s political and academic commentators seemed to assume that the welfare state was a uniquely British institution. Even Marshall, whose contribution to the study of social policy has been immense and largely analytic in character, has claimed that 'the British welfare state is unique because it was born in circumstances that were unique'.[2] In a later section of the same paper he states that although

the British welfare state of the 1940s was the culmination of a long process which began in the last quarter of the nineteenth century . . . it

3

was also the product of an explosion of forces which chance and history had brought together in Britain's unique experience in the war and in the transition to a state of peace[3]

This view was given increased intellectual respectability by British university courses in social administration, which had an entirely national focus. There have been changes, however, and the volume of comparative work in social policy has been steadily expanded since about 1970. It would be very difficult today to find a social policy specialist who would maintain that the welfare state was unique to Britain. In spite of variations in scope, scale, aims and organisational arrangements, Wedderburn's view that 'the welfare state is a common phenomenon of all capitalist societies' is now generally accepted.[4]

HISTORICAL PERSPECTIVE

The welfare state did not suddenly arrive on 5 July 1948.[5] Most of the services in the majority of welfare states evolved over very long periods. As Fraser says, 'The Welfare State was not the product of a spontaneous act of creation in 1948 but the latest stage in a dynamic process of adjustment between individual and society. The British Welfare State was not born—it had evolved'.[6] It is a similar story of gradual evolution in most of the other countries of Western Europe, in Australia, New Zealand and, over a shorter period, in the United States. For example, Forsberg writes, 'The first epoch in Swedish social welfare policy can be said to have begun in the 1880s'.[7] Kuhnle, in relation to Germany, also refers to the 1880s: 'Most writers trace the initiation of the welfare state, or at least the beginning of the present stage of development, to Bismarck's large-scale social insurance schemes of the last quarter of the nineteenth century'.[8] More generally, Flora and Alber claim that 'the take-off of the modern welfare state occurred in the last two decades of the nineteenth century'.[9] In the United States, however, the beginnings of large-scale federal involvement in welfare services came later; not until the New Deal of the 1930s, although states and localities had been involved from a much earlier date.

According to one kind of interpretation, the evolution of the welfare state is a story of continuous progress, each step in the process being seen as inevitable.[10] Fraser calls this 'the Whig interpretation of history', which sees the evolution of the welfare state as 'the unfolding of some great scheme of progress as increasingly enlightened men approached ever onward and upward a future promised land'.[11] In fact the evolution was far from even. In any one country there were periods of rapid development followed by relatively quiet periods, and there were occasional periods of retrenchment. Different countries developed services at different rates, at different times and with different priorities.

Nevertheless, by 1900 Germany already had sickness insurance, industrial accident insurance and old-age pensions. By 1911 every country in Western Europe had some form of workers' compensation scheme. In 1913 Sweden was the first country to introduce a pensions insurance scheme covering the entire population, but by that time Australia, Austria, Belgium, Denmark, France, Germany, New Zealand and Britain had already made some provision for pensions. By 1913 Austria, Belgium, Denmark, Germany, Italy, the Netherlands, Norway, Switzerland and Britain all had some form of sickness insurance which financed both cash benefits and some medical care services. Membership of the schemes was compulsory for certain categories of workers in Austria, Germany, the Netherlands, Norway and Britain; elsewhere membership was voluntary but with some subsidisation from the state. Unemployment insurance, introduced in Britain in 1911, tended to come later elsewhere; for example, not until 1927 in Germany, not until 1935 in the United States and not until 1944 in Canada.

Superficially it appears from the above discussion that most capitalist countries were moving along the same path, although at different speeds, and in a general sense there is some truth in that impression. If the welfare state is seen as a response to major, long-term changes in the political and economic structure, then the similarities in the responses of different countries would be emphasised. Thus Flora and Heidenheimer claim that although macrosociology is characterised by a variety of different views, interpretations and theoretical perspectives, there is general agreement that

the growth of the modern welfare state can be understood as a response to two fundamental developments: the formation of national states and their transformation into mass democracies after the French Revolution, and the growth of capitalism that became the dominant mode of production after the Industrial Revolution[12]

As a response to mass democracy the welfare state can be viewed as stemming from demands for greater equality and the recognition of social rights to welfare services and economic security. As a response to the growth of capitalism the welfare state may be interpreted by Marxists and others as an attempt to deal with the contradictions and problems of the capitalist system by contributing to both capital accumulation and legitimation.

However, a more detailed look at a number of countries reveals very considerable variety in their welfare arrangements. As Higgins says, 'One of the curious and fascinating questions which arises when we begin to compare social policies in different countries, or in different historical periods, is why there should be such an enormous variety of responses to what, on the face of it, appear to be similar states of need'.[13] Even this understates the diversity, since it ignores differences within countries which may be especially significant where there is a mix of ethnic and religious groups and where there is a federal rather than a unitary constitution. The best example is, of course, the United States. In a sense it is misleading to talk about the American welfare state since so much responsibility for social welfare programmes is carried by state and local governments and there is considerable regional variation.

A good deal of academic energy has been expended in attempting to explain both the similarities and the differences among welfare states. As one would expect, most of these explanations are very broad. There has been considerable debate between those who assign the major role in determining the varying forms and scope of welfare in different countries to socio-economic factors and those who assign the major role to political factors. Castles has called this 'the battle of the paradigms'.[14]

The main thrust of the argument giving primacy to socio-economic factors is that there is a direct relationship between levels of economic development and levels of welfare provision. One seemingly obvious and frequently cited connection is that the richer a country is, the more it can afford. On the other hand, there is nothing compelling a rich country to spend its wealth on social services. It might just as easily choose to spend the resources on armaments or it might leave most of the wealth in private hands. A further point of connection between economic development and welfare expenditure is that, as economies develop, the traditional supports of family, kin and local community are eroded, and other forms of provision have to be developed to take their place. At the same time, people become increasingly vulnerable because of greater specialisation, the rapid obsolescence of skills and fluctuations in the trade cycle. A final observation is that developed economies have to pay attention not only to the size of the labour force but also to its quality, and this has implications for the provision of education and health services.

Wilensky, in his earlier work, was prominent among those writers emphasising the prime importance of economic determinants. His view was that the level of economic development is much more important than the ideology or the political composition of different regimes in determining the extent and kind of welfare provision. Nevertheless, Wilensky did recognise other influences, such as 'the degree of centralisation of government, the shape of the stratification order and related mobility rates, the organisation of the working class and the position of the military'.[15]

In his later writings Wilensky takes more account of party politics. He continues to maintain, though, that leftist party dominance does not increase welfare spending: 'During the entire period since World War I or the shorter period after World War II, cumulative left power has had no effect on welfare effort or output . . . no measure of left power has any significant explanatory effect. Whatever influence left parties have is indirect and weak'.[16] The continual electoral dominance of a left-wing party may actually lead to a reduction of welfare spending. Catholic party power is much more significant in encouraging welfare output: 'In contrast to leftism, cumulative Catholic power since World War I increases welfare effort'. Only intense inter-party competition, especially with Catholic parties, will produce high-spending left governments.

As one would expect, political scientists are predominant in rejecting the notion that different levels of economic development are sufficient explanation of different levels of welfare provision.[17] Political explanations, by contrast, emphasise the role of political parties, pressure groups and the bureaucracy in policy-making. The work on political parties has stressed two factors: the competition between political parties for votes and the presence and strength of leftist parties. Competition between parties is assumed to engender a high level of welfare effort and expenditure because welfare policies and promises to spend more on them are vote winners.

We have already considered Wilensky's view that leftist political parties have an insignificant impact on levels of welfare provision. Heidenheimer, Heclo and Adams are less emphatic than Wilensky and argue 'that there is at best an unreliable and fairly weak relationship between leftist dominance and extensive income transfers relative to the economy. More striking is the fact that where socialist parties and strong labor movements are more or less absent, government transfers are consistently smaller in the aggregate'.[18] Castles agrees with the view that 'a large party of the right will tend to impede welfare state provisions',[19] but he also cites his own research results, which indicate 'a strong correlation between the growth of the welfare state and the strength of non-rightist parties in government for the period from about 1960 to the mid–1970s'.[20] Castles notes, however, that research by Alber shows that in the 1970s it was centre-right governments which took the lead in the growth of social expenditure. Alber's research agrees with that of Castles insofar as the 1960s are concerned, and it also demonstrates a strong correlation between left-wing governments and high levels of social spending in the 1950s.[21]

Traditional Marxists and neo-Marxists are sceptical about the impact of political parties in capitalist countries. Their view is that class politics is more important than partisan politics. It is working-class pressure and the strength of the capitalist class outside the parliamentary system which determine the pace, extent and direction of social change. Castles expresses the view that these two interpretations of class and partisan politics need not necessarily be in direct opposition: 'partisan control and class politics might be complementary variables for understanding diverse areas of public policy at different times'.[22]

Another political explanation of social policy variations concentrates on the activities of pressure groups in urging or resisting changes. It would be misleading to argue that pressure groups have no influence on social policy, but this influence is wielded within known parameters and any changes achieved are in the nature of slight modifications and adjustments. It is certainly extremely difficult to make a convincing case that political action of this kind, even cumulatively over many years, can account for the very big differences in social provision between one country and another. On the other hand, constellations of pressure groups, major interests such as the labour movement, for instance, may have greater explanatory potential. For example, Mishra explains the differences in the development of the welfare state in Britain and the United States in the following terms:

Our thesis is that the higher the proportion of labour force unionised the greater the chances that the state will assume responsibility for basic needs. This can best be illustrated by contrasting Britain with the United States. Both countries industrialised under middle-class dominance, yet by the First World War Britain had taken important steps towards the welfare state while in America it was not until after the great depression of the 1930s that a government programme for social security was launched.[23]

This has some affinity with the neo-Marxist view referred to earlier.

The development and growing influence of public bureaucracies constitutes another political explanation. There is little point in attempting to introduce complex systems of state welfare unless there is an effective administrative structure. By the late nineteenth century most countries in Western Europe had centralised administrative systems with

---

considerable capacity to respond to the new demands being placed upon them by the introduction of social insurance and other welfare provisions. This was particularly true of Germany and Sweden. Once bureaucracy is established it takes on a momentum of its own and it has a vested interest in extending its sphere of operations. Administrators are in a strong position to influence policy. In his comparative study of Sweden and Britain, Heclo writes, 'Forced to choose one group among all the separate political factors as most consistently important . . . the bureaucracies of Britain and Sweden loom predominant in the policies studied'.[24] He cites the examples of the development of unemployment insurance in Britain during and after the First World War and the successive adjustments in Sweden's pensions policy during the same period.

Administrators and others who participate in policy-making learn from their own experience—a process of trial and error—but they may also learn from the experience of other countries. In terms of policy innovation some countries are seen as leaders and others as laggards. The United States is usually regarded as one of the laggards, except in the case of educational services which expanded far more rapidly between 1890 and 1920 than any of the European systems.[25] Which countries are seen as leaders will vary according to both policy area and historical period. The process by which one country learns from the experience of another is known as diffusion. There is no doubt for instance that the introduction of health insurance in Britain in 1911 owed a great deal to the German example, which could be used as an object lesson on the pitfalls to be avoided and the devices to be copied.[26] Heidenheimer, Heclo and Adams make the same point in relation to Sweden at the end of the nineteenth century: 'Swedish reformers during this time were heavily influenced by the new social insurance ideas in Germany'.[27] It should be noted, however, that Flora and Alber claim that there has been too great a readiness to attribute national developments to diffusion and they conclude, 'Although diffusion processes may have affected the course of national decision making, the example set by a pioneer country does not apparently provide sufficient incentive to adopt social insurance schemes independent of internal socio-economic problems and political mobilisation'.[28] Similar developments may be no more than similar responses to similar conditions.

We have now looked at some of the socio-economic and political explanations of the varying forms and scope of welfare in different countries. For some years the academic debate proceeded as though these explanations were in direct competition. More recently, however, it has come to be recognised that the two kinds of explanation may be complementary. Castles, for example, argues persuasively for 'public policy analysis which is explicitly concerned with the interaction of political and economic structures'.[29] Heidenheimer, Heclo and Adams make the same point: 'according to the most plausible conclusion that can be drawn from the host of aggregate statistical studies, economic conditions and relatively enduring configurations of political power together determine how welfare state boundaries are drawn'.[30]

MODELS OF WELFARE

A model is a frequently used explanatory device in the social sciences. It is a conceptual framework which helps to categorise phenomena and understand the relationship between sets of variables. In some branches of social science, particularly economics, model-building is quite sophisticated; but models have value only to the extent that they help explanation and analysis, and in social policy the models are relatively simple. As Titmuss says, 'The purpose of model-building is not to admire the architecture of the building, but to help us to see some order in all the disorder and confusion of facts, systems and choices concerning certain areas of our economic and social life'.[31]

One of the most widely used social policy models is that proposed by Wilensky and Lebeaux, who identify

two conceptions of social welfare: . . . the residual and the institutional. The first holds that social welfare institutions should come into play only when the normal structures of supply break down. The second, in contrast, sees the welfare services as normal, 'first line' functions of modern industrial society.[32]

The residual system, then, implies a minimal role for the state in the provision of welfare services: the family and the private market are the 'natural' or 'normal' mechanisms for meeting people's needs, and it is only when these fail that statutory services are provided. Any services that are provided are of poor quality, and cash benefits (often goods in kind or product-specific vouchers instead of cash) are at minimum subsistence level. Eligibility for public services and benefits is based upon means tests, and stigma is used as a deliberate policy. Individualism, personal responsibility and competition are stressed, and rewards are distributed according to desert rather than need. The institutional model is almost the reverse of this, with a substantial welfare role for the state. No societies conform precisely to either of these models, but if capitalist societies are arranged along a continuum, the United States would be placed near the residual end and Sweden would be placed near the institutional end.

Titmuss used three models: (1) residual; (2) industrial achievement-performance; (3) institutional redistributive. The first and third correspond to Wilensky and Lebeaux's residual and institutional models. The industrial achievement-performance model 'incorporates a significant role for social welfare institutions as adjuncts of the economy. It holds that social needs must be met on the basis of merit, work performance and productivity'.[33] Titmuss saw his three models as providing an ideological framework. Each model was based on different value premises and implied different criteria for making choices.

In using the models Titmuss argued that it was essential to take into account the 'social division of welfare'.[34] Failure to recognise that there were three major categories of welfare would result in a distorted picture. The three categories were social welfare, fiscal welfare and occupational welfare. Social welfare comprises what are traditionally referred to in Britain as the social services: income maintenance, health care, social work and other personal social services, housing, education and employment services. Fiscal welfare comprises a wide range of allowances and reliefs from income tax, for example relief on the interest payable on mortgages for owner-occupiers; allowances on life insurance premiums and superannuation contributions; allowances in respect of elderly and disabled dependants; allowances for covenants and additional personal allowances for those bringing up children on their own. This is by no means a complete list. Occupational welfare includes the benefits derived from one's job. Again, the complete list would be very long, but a few of the more important examples are occupational pension schemes; health services and insurance; cheap loans; expenses; cars; help with children's school fees; cheap meals and sporting and social amenities.

It is important to consider all three types of welfare because, despite their different administrative arrangements, their aims are often the same and all have a bearing on the extent of inequality. In writing about the social division of welfare Titmuss took Britain as his example, but his analysis is applicable to any advanced society. Furthermore, the three categories may be particularly significant in studies comparing one country with another. A totally false picture is given if expenditure on traditional social services only is taken into account. In some countries that appear to be welfare state laggards, occupational welfare may be well developed; America and Japan are good examples.

Jones has developed Titmuss's categories.[35] She examines the welfare-capitalist dimensions of social policy. Welfare capitalism is said to be a reasonable label because it signifies a combination of competitive/exchange values and practices with compensatory/gift values and practices. The balance struck between the two varies considerably from country to country, and a continuum can be constructed with welfare *capitalism* (the accent on the second word of the term) at one end and *welfare* capitalism (the accent on the first word) at the other. Welfare *capitalism* implies the industrial achievement-performance model, which gives priority to 'society first' social policy relying upon work-related social provision, with equality of opportunity and the encouragement of competition as the objective. *Welfare* capitalism implies the institutional redistributive model which gives priority to 'individuals first' social policy, with social provision based on citizenship, the objective being a fairer and more equal society. Jones says the 'society first' social policy of the industrial achievement-performance model 'is intended, first and foremost to support and reinforce the capitalist system'. She suggests that West Germany, with high social expenditure, and the United States, with low social expenditure, fall into this category. 'Individuals first' social policy 'views capitalism as at best a necessary evil: a generator of resources for subsequent redistribution in the light of avowedly non-market or anti-market criteria'.[36] She suggests Sweden and Britain with high and low overall expenditure respectively, fall into this category. One advantage claimed by Jones for her classification is that it allows for a two-dimensional picture to be drawn using two scales, one based on levels of social expenditure and one based on welfare orientation. There are, as Jones recognises, enormous problems of method and measurement.

In an inaugural lecture in 1962 Donnison claimed that there was a marked tendency, common to both the residual and the institutional schools of thought, 'to regard the social services as distinctive institutions operating according to economic, political and moral "rules" which differed from those that apply elsewhere'.[37] Donnison, however, sees the social services as 'an integral and (in some form or other) a necessary part of our economic and social system'.[38] Mishra makes a similar point, but takes it further, when he constructs two ideal types or models which he calls the differentiated welfare state, sometimes referred to as the pluralist welfare state, and the integrated welfare state, sometimes referred to as the corporatist welfare state.

Both of these are contrasted with the neo-conservative and Marxist perspectives on the welfare state. Both may be seen as variants of the institutional model. Mishra defines a differentiated welfare state as one in which 'the social welfare sector is seen, by and large, as distinctive and unrelated to the economic, industrial and public sectors'. In the integrated welfare state 'the social welfare sector is seen as closely related to the economic, industrial and public sectors'.[39] Mishra favours the integrated or corporatist welfare state in which social and economic policy are interrelated, both emerging from bargains struck between peak associations of employers, workers and the state. Mishra takes Austria and Sweden as his examples. More will be said about the corporatist welfare state in the final chapter.

POSTWAR DEVELOPMENTS

In 1948 the United Nations Universal Declaration of Human Rights ranked social and economic rights alongside the more traditional civil and political rights. One of the most important features of the United Nations Declaration is its claim to be of universal application. The most general formulation occurs in Article 22 of the Declaration, which states that 'everyone as a member of society . . . is entitled to . . . the economic, social and cultural rights indispensable for his dignity and the free development of his personality'. More specific are the right to work and the right to free education. Most specific of all is the following:

Everyone has the right to a standard of living adequate for the health and well-being of himself and his family, including food, clothing, housing and medical care and the necessary social services, and the right to security in the event of unemployment, sickness, disability, widowhood, old age or other lack of livelihood in circumstances beyond his control.[40]

After the Second World War all capitalist countries accepted the principle of the welfare state, although to different extents and with varying degrees of enthusiasm. As already noted, the foundations of the welfare state had already been laid during the sixty years before the outbreak of the Second World War; but in the postwar years the position was consolidated as the range of state provision expanded and as existing services were co-ordinated and extended. Summing up the development of the welfare state in 1983, Heidenheimer, Heclo and Adams state:

The data are far from perfect, but the overall trends in Europe and the United States are clear and consistent for the last hundred years: A rising share of total economic resources has been absorbed by taxation and devoted to public spending. Of all public spending, a growing share (except in years of war) has gone to social programs . . . national variations within these trends are important, but the overall movements stand out as long-term themes for every developed nation.[41]

In a similar vein, in attempting to explain the present circumstances of the welfare state by reference to the past, Heclo focuses on what he calls 'the broad, widely shared features of development', and identifies three 'stages of welfarism', with some overlap between each stage.[42]

The first stage, extending from the 1870s to the 1920s, is termed the period of experimentation. The chief character- istics of this phase were argument over fundamental prin- ciples, especially over the role of the state, and frequent changes of both policy and detail. The early part of this period coincided with the extension of democracy and devel- opments in the organisation of labour. The second stage, the 1930s and 1940s, was a period of consolidation when schemes were co-ordinated and social policy became more integrated. There were fewer changes of policy than in the experimentation stage, and there was an assumption, especially in Western Europe, that government could legit- imately act to ensure security and reduce inequality. The third stage, the 1950s and 1960s, was characterised by considerable expansion of social provision based on sustained economic growth. Gaps were filled and provision extended, and there were some new policy initiatives. It should perhaps be noted that in the United States the third stage was not really reached until the 1960s.

The war put an end to social reform for the time being, although there were promises of better things to come when hostilities ceased. When the war was over most countries in Europe were faced with considerable problems of social and economic reconstruction. There had been extensive bomb damage and great loss of life. Some countries had been occupied by Germany during the war and now had to adjust to a regained independence. In contrast, Germany was split into two and became an occupied country itself. Less dramatically, industry, which had been wholly devoted to wartime production, had to adjust to peacetime require- ments and absorb the men being demobilised. Japan was faced with similar problems. The United States, Canada, Australia and New Zealand, on the other hand, faced less serious problems, requiring adjustment rather than reconstruction.

The privations of war are not evenly distributed among the population. Nevertheless, in a total war all suffer some discomfort, and there is a greater sense of solidarity so that class barriers, even if only temporarily, are reduced. Those enduring privations believe that their present sacrifices must be compensated for by a higher standard of living, full employment and the provision of more and better social services when the war is over. All sections of the population have made sacrifices, and this rough equality of sacrifice must be matched by greater equality of opportunity and greater equality of condition when peace is restored. As Titmuss has pointed out, in a total war the morale not just of military personnel but of the total population has to be maintained, and the promise of a more just society is an effective morale booster.[43] The Beveridge Report in Britain is a good example of an attempt to convince people that what they were fighting for was something worth fighting for. At a more mundane level, war accustomed people to greater central government intervention and higher rates of taxation, both of which may be required for postwar developments in social service provision.

There is another side to this picture. All countries had experienced severe unemployment in the world depression which began in 1929. Italy and the Soviet Union, with planned economies, escaped the worst effects of the economic crisis, and the lesson was not entirely lost on other industrialised countries. Another lesson of the economic problems of the 1930s was that mass, long-term unemployment and the chaos resulting from runaway inflation led to the growth of political extremism. Fascism was seen as a direct consequence of economic dislocation; and full-employment policies, improved social security provisions and better housing, education and health services were seen as one possible way of preventing the re-emergence of fascist regimes. If a resurgence of fascism was seen as one danger, the spread of communism was seen as another, especially in the United States. American foreign policy was directed towards the achievement of stability in Europe. Democratic welfare states would help to ensure stability and provide an effective barrier against the spread of communism. Thane sums this up well:

American determination to build democratic institutions in a stable Western Germany, as a bulwark against communism and a revival of fascism, led to allied encouragement of provision of extensive welfare measures. . . . Indeed, under the same stimulus, sometimes, indeed, as a condition of American loans, some variant of a 'welfare state' emerged everywhere in Western Europe.[44]

Thane's reference to West Germany is interesting, but Chancellor Adenauer and the Christian Democrat government did not need much 'allied encouragement'. They were committed to capitalism and were as determined as the Americans to resist communist influence. Proximity to East Germany and the partition of Berlin strengthened their determination.

Governments may have been concerned with what they perceived as the dangers of fascism and communism, but ordinary people were concerned with re-establishing their lives with greater security and prosperity than they had enjoyed before the war. Many remembered very clearly the hardship and degradation of interwar unemployment and the inadequate, sometimes harsh, responses of governments to it. They now wanted assurance that there would be no return to such conditions, and they voted for political parties whose promises of full employment and improved social security seemed to be the most genuine.

Social reform after the Second World War was made possible by the very high rates of economic growth experienced by all advanced industrial societies, although not all countries were equally successful.[45] However, even the less successful countries such as Britain, whose economic performance was far from sparkling, achieved some growth. In a paper examining the postwar development of public expenditure in Western Europe and North America, Kohl writes:

> The rapid economic growth of the recovery period after World War II · enabled Western democracies to increase public spending in almost all fields because of greater fiscal resources. . . . Most authors, whether conservative or radical, agree that social expenditures have been the outstanding component in the secular rise of public expenditures, accounting for the large share of general growth during past decades.[46]

At the same time as public expenditure was growing, Keynesian economics seemed to offer governments the opportunity to manage aggregate demand and thus control levels of unemployment and inflation.

Thus there were four major influences at work in the period after 1945:

(1)   The direct and indirect impact of the war and the

desire for stability in Western Europe as a defence against both communism and fascism.

(2) Memories of interwar unemployment and the unwillingness of electorates, at least in Western Europe, to return governments not committed to full-employment policies and social reform.

(3) Unprecedented and sustained economic growth.

(4) The acceptance of Keynesian economic theories.

The late 1940s ushered in a period of social reform which continued unabated until the end of the 1960s. This period may be considered the heyday of the welfare state. In the immediate postwar period every capitalist country co-ordinated and extended its social security system, and benefits were increased. In Western European countries coverage became increasingly comprehensive and universal. In the United States social security expanded more gradually than it did in Europe, and it was not until the 1960s that provision became a little less selective. Almost everywhere expenditure on health and education rose absolutely and as a proportion of GDP. Housing programmes were launched in most countries, and governments began to take a more active role in housing, usually through subsidies, loans and allowances.

But while there were many similarities, there were also differences. It would be tedious to catalogue all the minor differences of detail in the schemes of different countries; instead we will concentrate on major differences of approach. Earlier in this chapter reference was made to Jones's distinction between *welfare* capitalism and welfare *capitalism*.[47] While I would not agree with Jones that in *welfare* capitalist countries, such as Britain, the capitalist system is viewed as 'at best a necessary evil', the distinction she makes is an important one. All welfare states combine public provision and/or financing of services with a market economy, but the balance changes over time and differs between one country and another.

West Germany and the United States are chosen by Jones as representative of the welfare *capitalist* nations. The examples are well chosen. In the United States private markets predominate in health and welfare services to a degree

unknown in Western Europe, and the attachment to capitalist values is much stronger. West Germany is an interesting example of a country which combines strong support
for a market economy with high social expenditure. Indeed,
West Germany is more determinedly capitalist than most
other Western European countries. In a pamphlet published
in 1985, under the name of the federal minister of labour
and social affairs, the following statement appears:

The Federal Republic of Germany has achieved its progress and prosperity with the aid of a market economy. The decision to have a market
economy was made as early as 1948, three years after the end of World
War II. At that time, the decision was by no means self-evident. After
losing the war the country was exhausted. Many responsible people of
the time believed that the answer . . . lay in a planned economy. But the
supporters of a free market approach eventually carried the day.[48]

Rimlinger discusses the different approaches of the two
main parties: the Christian Democratic approach supports
the 'social market economy' whereas the Social Democrats
support the 'socialist market economy'.[49] The main difference between the two is that the supporters of a social
market economy wish to limit government intervention,
seeing it as a possible threat to liberty, whereas supporters
of the socialist market economy view government intervention as essential to liberty which demands the protection
of the less powerful members of the community. The social
market economy stresses private initiative and the individual's responsibility for his own welfare. The socialist market
economy stresses fraternity and the duty of the state to
secure the welfare of all its citizens. These differences in
general orientation are reflected in specific policies in
relation to social insurance. The Christian Democrats take
the view that social insurance should be based on contributions from potential beneficiaries, and that both contributions and benefits should be earnings-related. So strongly
do the Christian Democrats support the contributory principle that when children's allowances were reintroduced in
1954 they were treated as part of the insurance system. The
Social Democrats support the idea of a flat-rate scheme
relying more heavily on tax revenue.

It is partly because social insurance based on the contributory principle does not conflict with the maintenance of a free-market economy that the Christian Democratic government after the Second World War was able to press ahead with improvements and extensions to the system.

Kohl's distinction between public consumption expenditures and transfer expenditures suggests a further divergence in the paths taken by different welfare states. The distinction is between those countries which followed the Scandinavian pattern, with the emphasis on the direct provision of services by public authorities, and those which followed the continental pattern, emphasising transfer incomes.[50] Health service provision and housing will serve to illustrate the differences between the two approaches.

Britain, Sweden and Italy are the only countries that have national health services based on direct provision of services financed almost entirely from general taxation. All other European countries rely on various forms of insurance. Insurance-based health-care systems are in tune with private markets, since medical practitioners are usually paid under fee-for-service arrangements. As was noted in the case of West Germany, however, insurance arrangements are perfectly consistent with high public expenditure.

As far as housing is concerned, Britain differs from just about every other welfare state in having a large public-sector housing programme in which local authorities build, maintain and manage houses. No other European country has followed this line, preferring instead to rely on the payment of subsidies to either producers or consumers, leaving the actual building of houses to commercial enterprises or co-operative and other non-profit-making associations. The use of the latter is particularly prominent in France, the Netherlands and Sweden, and much less common in Britain, West Germany and the United States.

Again it must be emphasised that direct public provision of housing may not be associated with high levels of public expenditure. An exclusive system of producer and consumer subsidies may give governments much greater control over housing markets over a much broader front.

A final distinction that needs to be made is that between welfare state leaders and welfare state laggards. In 1975 those spending the highest proportion of their GDP on social services were the Netherlands (28.3 per cent), West Germany (27.9 per cent), Denmark (27.6 per cent) and Sweden (24.6 per cent). In contrast, social expenditure in the United States amounted to 20 per cent of GDP. However, expenditure figures are notoriously difficult to compare.

On most counts Sweden is usually regarded as a welfare state leader and the United States and Japan are regarded as laggards. Sweden is usually thought of as a country with a highly developed welfare state and a high standard of living. Furniss and Tilton write:

> For more than a generation Sweden has been both celebrated and condemned as the society most closely approximating the ideals of the welfare state. . . . Estimates of the moral worth of Swedish society clearly vary, but neither enthusiasts nor detractors doubt that Sweden is the archetype of the modern welfare state.[51]

The Social Democratic Party, which claims to be socialist, was continuously in power from 1931 to 1975; it lost power in 1976, but regained it in 1982, and it remained the largest single party after the elections of 1985.

Furniss and Tilton identify four different traditions which have produced in Sweden 'consensus upon the merits of the welfare state'. The first of these traditions is paternalism, which 'stresses the obligation of the well-to-do to succor the unfortunate'. The second tradition is that of Christian charity. A third tradition is a long-standing recognition of the economic advantages to be gained from welfare provisions. Finally, there is the tradition of Swedish Social Democracy: 'a unique mixture of the three previously mentioned traditions with the socialist ideals of liberty, equality, solidarity, democracy, economic efficiency and personal security'.[52]

In marked contrast to Sweden, the United States has frequently been characterised as 'a reluctant welfare state' or 'a welfare state laggard'. Wilensky and Lebeaux graphically describe the reluctant welfare state:

> The United States is more reluctant than any rich country to make a welfare effort appropriate to its affluence. Our support of national welfare programs is halting; our administration of services for the less privileged

is mean. We move toward the welfare state but we do it with ill grace, carping and complaining all the way.[53]

According to Wilensky and Lebeaux, the principal reasons for America's reluctance lie in the dominant cultural values of American society: individualism, private property and the free market. These three closely related values lead to a fourth—a distrust of government and a strong preference for minimum government intervention. Individualism plays down the social nature of man, holding the view that individuals should be free to pursue their own ends by whatever means within the law are available to them. People are measured in terms of economic success, which is seen as the reward for hard work, ability and initiative. Everyone can reach high positions if they try, so that failure is the result of laziness, fecklessness or immorality. The main distributive principle is desert or merit rather than need. Closely related to the value of individualism is the emphasis on private property rights; individuals should have the right both to acquire as much property as their efforts and ability allow and to use their property as they see fit. The means of production are privately owned, and there is free competition among suppliers, among individuals in the labour market and among consumers for goods and services. There is the plain implication that government intervention should be kept to the absolute minimum.

Other features of American society which help to account for its relatively underdeveloped welfare state, again according to Wilensky and Lebeaux, are racial, ethnic and religious heterogeneity and political decentralisation. The point about cultural heterogeneity is that it leads to a degree of fragmentation in American society—a kind of parochialism with strong ties with one's own group and a distrust of other groups. This cultural fragmentation is matched by political fragmentation—a strong local tradition which distrusts the government in Washington. The individual states are jealous of their powers and unwilling to surrender them to central government. This makes it difficult for the federal government to introduce comprehensive national services with something approaching uniformity of provision.

As already noted, Mishra views the strength of organised labour as being among the most important influences on the development of welfare states:

Why was residual social policy undermined in Britain while it remained 'hegemonic' in the United States? The answer we would suggest lies in the far higher density of unionisation of labour as well as in the development of a socialist political movement in Britain. In the absence of these factors middle-class social policies retained their hold much longer in the United States.[54]

The United States, then, was slow off the mark in developing its welfare services. With the single exception of education, it made its first significant move in the direction of a welfare state in 1935 in response to a severe economic crisis with massive unemployment, reaching 29 per cent in 1933, steeply falling production, the collapse of businesses and the closure of banks.

Further significant expansion of the welfare state had to wait until the 1960s when the War on Poverty was inaugurated under the 1964 Economic Opportunity Act.[55] The War on Poverty had a number of shortcomings: its objectives and methods were far from clear; it was too grandiose in conception; in relation to the problems the funding was inadequate and spread too thinly; it was poorly organised and ill co-ordinated; it misconceived the nature of poverty, assuming that its causes were to be found in the deprived localities and in the behaviour of the poor. What was thought to be required was the improvement of opportunities so that deprived people could escape from the culture of poverty. Piven and Cloward claim that the War on Poverty was not only a response to urban disorder, but also represented an attempt by the Democratic Party to strengthen its base in the cities.

Less spectacular, but probably more permanent, change in American social policy occurred in 1965 with the introduction of Medicare and Medicaid. Medicare is a medical insurance scheme for elderly people covering hospital, physician and related medical costs. Medicaid is a system designed to provide for sections of the poor. Medicare is an entirely federal scheme, whereas the funding of Medicaid is shared between the federal government and the states. Both schemes involve an element of cost-sharing in which the patient pays part of the cost of treatment, although some states exempt certain categories of Medicaid patients.

In the United States in the 1960s, then, there was a considerable expansion of health and welfare provisions, and of federal involvement in them. There were further extensions in the 1970s. In spite of these developments, however, the United States remained a welfare state laggard as compared with most Western European nations.

CONSENSUS AND CONVERGENCE

In examining the place of values in social policy, Myrdal, a Swedish economist, stated in 1972:

my experiences of research and politics have . . . led me to see a remarkable degree of accordance and even conformity in the valuations underlying social policy, arising as a result of political development—what I have called 'created harmony', in contradistinction to the liberalistic assumption of a harmony of interests basic to the thinking of natural law and utilitarianism.[56]

Myrdal argued that this consensus had arisen because the public-burden model of social policy—the view that social services are unproductive and have to be paid for in the form of lower productivity in the wealth-producing sectors of the economy—had given way to the view that social services aid and encourage economic growth. All capitalist countries now recognised, according to Myrdal, that social services had potential for increasing productivity, encouraging mobility and maintaining consumption. They increase productivity by improving the quality of the labour force— this is particularly true of education and health services. Regional policies are intended to encourage industries to move into the economically depressed areas, and labour mobility policies enable people to move to where there is work. Social services also help to maintain demand—giving cash benefits to sick, unemployed and retired people keeps them active as consumers. It should be noted that benefits are paid to groups with a high propensity to spend. Speaking in the debate on the National Insurance Bill in 1946,

Clement Atlee said that 'to allow, through mass unemployment or through sickness, great numbers of people to be ineffective as consumers is an economic loss to the country. We all now hold the view that we must maintain purchasing power, and must have a proper distribution of purchasing power'.[57] This echoes Beveridge's view that the maintenance of purchasing power was to be the major means of maintaining full employment.

This has necessarily been a cursory review of the arguments which attribute a productive role to social services.[58] As we shall see later, the opposite case can be made. The point that is being made here is that insofar as these arguments were accepted by governments, unions and employers, they constituted an endorsement of the welfare state. Both Beveridge and Keynes, whose influence in the 1950s spread well beyond Britain, were convinced that the welfare state posed no threat to capitalism, but rather supported and complemented it. It did so not only through contributing to economic growth but also by picking up the casualties of the system and thus making it more acceptable. It should therefore, be no surprise to find capitalist countries embracing the welfare state in the 1950s and 1960s.

A Dutch sociologist states that although the welfare state has had to subject the capitalist system 'to certain modifications and restrictions . . . the two fundamental elements: private property and the profit motive, it has retained'.[59] Nasenius and Veit-Wilson in a paper on Sweden are even more emphatic:

Social welfare expenditure was no longer regarded as a burden on the national economy, because it strengthened consumer demand and helped both to stimulate and stabilise cyclically sensitive production. This view, with its concomitant emphasis on full-employment policies, has for long been part of the Swedish political culture and is not seriously contested.[60]

A final illustration of the same point is one made by Rimlinger in relation to West Germany:

there has been a far-reaching reconciliation of economic and social views among the leading political parties in Germany. There has been a major movement toward a central common ground of ideas and policies, with all but the most dogmatic among the neoliberals advocating social modifications of the dictates of the market and with socialists accepting a central role for the market.[61]

By the 1960s writers were beginning to talk about 'the end of ideology'. The argument was that broad agreement now existed about objectives and about the value of the welfare state in a mixed economy, and all that remained to be discussed was the most efficient way of achieving agreed ends. In 1960 Bell claimed that capitalist countries had reached the end of ideology, a stage of development in which there is 'a rough consensus among intellectuals on political issues: the acceptance of a welfare state; the desirability of decentralized power; a system of mixed economy and of political pluralism'.[62] Five years later Marshall made a similar point specifically in relation to social policy: 'Criticism there was in plenty, and fierce argument, but the issues at stake in the sixties turned out to be less concerned with social ideology than with social engineering'.[63]

Four sets of factors contributed to the end-of-ideology thesis, apart from the simple observation that most capitalist countries were moving in roughly the same direction. Each of these will be looked at briefly.

(1) The almost complete dominance in academic social policy of Fabianism or social democracy was one factor. This was especially true in Britain, Sweden, Denmark, Norway and Holland. Other ideologies to the right and left of Fabianism existed, but they were either not concerned with social policy or were considered insignificant. In these circumstances it is hardly surprising that ideological issues seemed unimportant.

(2) Another contributory factor was the predominance in political science of group theory and pluralism, in which power is seen to be widely distributed with no individual or group in a position to secure permanent dominance. The government is seen as an impartial umpire arbitrating between competing interests. The emphasis is on consensus, adjustment and agreement, and once again ideology is pushed to the sidelines.

(3) In sociology functionalist theory was at the height of

its influence in the 1950s and early 1960s. Functionalism sees society as an organic system in which every part has a function to perform. There are several varieties of functionalism, among the best known of which is that stemming from the work of Talcott Parsons.[64] According to Parsons there are four functions which have to be performed if a society is to continue as a cohesive unit. These functional imperatives are the attainment of goals; adaptation or the devising of techniques to achieve goals; integration which is concerned with the interrelationships between social institutions and social groups, with the creation of harmony among the component parts of a system; pattern-maintenance which is concerned with the management of tension and the maintenance of particular patterns of values. Social policy is concerned primarily in the last two of these, and especially with integration. In all forms of functionalism there is a strong emphasis on consensus and stability. Little allowance is made for conflict, ideological or otherwise. There is a common set of values, and general agreement about ends leaves little room for competing ideologies.

(4) Convergence theory may be seen as a specific form of functionalism. The theory rests on two propositions: (a) that the welfare arrangements of a society are determined largely by the stage of technological development it has reached; (b) as societies industrialise they become more and more alike—they converge. What we have in convergence theory is a form of technological determinism.[65] Welfare states have developed as an *inevitable* consequence of industrialisation. As Mishra says in explanation of convergence theory:

the key determinant of the social structure of advanced industrial society, the theory argues, is neither ideology, nor class conflict, nor again culture, but technology. In the long run, argues the convergence theorist, the range of problems as well as their likely solutions in these societies is heavily conditioned by the consequences and requirements of industrial technology.[66]

Ideological differences may have some significance in the early stages of industrialisation, but they matter less and less as industrialisation advances: socialism, liberalism, conservatism and capitalism are less important than 'industrialisation'. All advanced industrial societies develop similar institutional arrangements. There is convergence at the centre which lies somewhere between complete state control and complete *laissez-faire*.

CONCLUSION

This chapter has sought to provide an introduction to the welfare state. The notion that the welfare state is an entirely British phenomenon has been rejected; it is seen instead as a feature of all capitalist societies. Welfare capitalism is an appropriate title for a system in which the impact of the free-market economy has been modified but where capitalism is still the predominant form of economic organisation.

For over twenty-five years it was assumed that welfare states would continue to refine, develop and extend their services. The ideological issues had all been settled, and we now needed to concentrate on developing more effective and efficient ways of service delivery. I will return to Myrdal for what must be one of the most confident assertions about consensus and the inevitability of welfare states:

I see the welfare state as more than an achieved solution. Dynamically it has become an almost immutable trend. Its further development can be slowed down for a time and occasionally even slightly reversed. But after such a stop it can be expected to continue its course. By doing so, whatever struggles there are about specific items of reform, one of the results of the developments is a broad national valuation consensus[67]

This statement was made in 1972: a year before the oil crisis and world recession. In the next chapter we will see that the postwar trend of increasing rates of growth in social expenditure has been halted. Some commentators do not believe that this is merely a temporary, short-term set-back.

2   The End of Consensus?

There has never been a time when the welfare state has not been subjected to critical appraisal. Even in the 1950s and 1960s there were criticisms in plenty from all quarters. There was a constant rumble from the Right. Hayek's *Road to Serfdom*, published in 1944, was still influential in right-wing circles with its vision of a totalitarian socialist Britain comparable to Nazi Germany.[1] Later, also in Britain, we had a constant flow of publications from the Institute of Economic Affairs arguing for private welfare and selective benefits. In the United States Friedman's *Capitalism and Freedom* was published in 1962.[2] In the later 1960s there was a neo-conservative reaction against what were perceived as the excesses of the Great Society and the War on Poverty. In most Western European countries there were criticisms that the welfare state had proceeded too quickly and too far. Nor was there any shortage of left-wing critics—Saville, Wedderburn, Baran and Sweezy, and Miliband being some of the best known.[3]

Less fundamental criticism came from the Fabian friends of the welfare state. In 1962 Titmuss demonstrated that the welfare state had achieved very little income redistribution.[4] In 1965 Abel-Smith and Townsend 'rediscovered' poverty.[5] The Plowden and Newsom reports showed that equality of educational opportunity had not been achieved.[6] The Child Poverty Action Group was critical of the social security system and Shelter claimed that Britain's housing was a national disgrace. These references relate to Britain, but similar criticisms of individual programmes occurred in all countries.[7]

Yet for all this criticism there was little talk of crisis or retrenchment in the 1950s and 1960s; still less was there any talk of the dismantling of the welfare state. The criticisms of the New Right and of the Marxists were not taken very seriously, and the Social Democratic and Fabian criticisms were used as arguments for improving and extending welfare provisions. However, as Doron says:

This sometimes unqualified belief in progress by means of redistributive social policies and irreversible betterment has suffered a serious set-back in recent years. The set-back is reflected in the fact that the continuous expansion of progressive social policies has at present come to an end in most industrialised countries.[8]

There is now much talk of crisis. In 1984 an influential book by Mishra, *The Welfare State in Crisis*, opened with the following sentence: 'In varying degrees and forms, the welfare state throughout the industrialised West is in disarray'.[9] It is possible to identify in current writing on the welfare state four major elements of the crisis: economic problems, problems of government and fiscal problems combining to create a legitimation crisis. Each of these will now be considered.

ECONOMIC PROBLEMS

The first sign of impending trouble for the welfare state was the oil crisis of 1973, which sparked off or intensified a world recession. Since the mid–1970s most advanced industrialised countries have experienced lower rates of economic growth, higher levels of unemployment and lower rates of investment. In short, during the 1970s and early 1980s 'the economic performance of the advanced capitalist world deteriorated sharply'.[10] This presents a stark contrast to the low rates of unemployment, the relatively high rates of capital formation and the substantial economic growth which characterised the 1950s and 1960s. It is falling investment which has led to lower rates of growth and higher unemployment, and in a comparative study of twenty OECD countries, Cameron attempts to establish whether the growth of public expenditure has been responsible for declining investment. His conclusion is tentative: 'we cannot escape the possibility that the public economy of advanced capitalism *has* intruded in some yet to be determined way upon the accumulation-investment-growth-job-creation process'.[11]

Earlier work by Bacon and Eltis is much more confident in its assertion that the growth of public expenditure (the non-market sector) has 'crowded out' industrial investment in the market sector. Between 1961 and 1974 the proportion of the working population employed in the non-market sector grew much faster in Britain than in other advanced economies of the West. The welfare state is not so much the victim of economic problems as their cause. However, the 'crowding out' thesis has its critics. For example, Hawkins, the director of the West Midlands Region of the Confederation of British Industry, rejects the Bacon and Eltis thesis because 'in an economy with as much spare capacity, under-used capital and unemployed manpower as Britain has had since 1980, and has been accumulating since the early 1970s, the prospect of resource crowding out is extremely remote'.[12]

George and Wilding review the evidence for the claim that social policy expenditure undermines economic growth. At most, they argue, 'social service expenditure may have slightly exacerbated an already adverse economic situation'.[13] Furthermore, this slightly adverse effect on growth has to be set against the evidence which suggests that certain forms of social expenditure may increase productivity.

From a completely different standpoint, O'Connor, an American Marxist, supports the view that in the long term the welfare state may reduce opportunities for capital accumulation: he writes of an 'accumulation crisis' in the United States which stems from the 'dominant national ideology' of individualism.[14] Individualism legitimates the struggle for more: higher wages and the production of consumption or wage goods as opposed to capital goods. Workers have secured a bigger 'consumption basket' with a higher 'value content'. A similar process occurs in social policy. There is a demand for more benefits and services of higher quality and thus the 'social service consumption basket' and its 'value content' are increased. According to O'Connor, 'social policy has the effect of making individuals more autonomous, not in relation to control of capitalist means of production, but in relation to access to and control of means of subsistence. Social policy thus had similar effects to the accumulation of housing, consumer durables, and so on'.[15] These processes necessarily reduce surplus value for appropriation by capital. Consequently, in the developed countries, 'average profit rates and the profit share of national income . . . declined and average unemployment and/or inflation rates increased'.[16]

PROBLEMS OF GOVERNMENT

Since the early 1970s political science has been much exercised by the problems of government growth leading to overload. Richard Rose, who has written extensively on this subject, makes the following comment:

Historically, the growth of government represents a great triumph of the modern Western state. . . . In the course of the twentieth century government's activities have expanded in scale, in subject matter and in variety. Government has grown far beyond the minimalist conception of the Nightwatchman state to become the central institution of the mixed economy welfare state.[17]

Not everyone takes so sanguine a view of big government, and indeed Rose himself has identified some of the possible problems. In association with Peters, for example, Rose considers the possibility of a slide into 'political bankruptcy', which is 'the fate that faces a government that so mismanages its economy that it loses popular consent as well as economic effectiveness'.[18] Political bankruptcy is reached in three stages. The first stage consists of overloading the political economy by expanding public expenditure and allowing take-home pay to rise beyond the capacity of the economy. The second stage occurs when this overloading forces a fall in citizens' take-home pay. The final stage is reached 'when masses of citizens realise that their government no longer protects their interests as they wish'.[19] People react not usually by armed rebellion but by turning their backs on the government—by indifference, which is a powerful threat to political authority. In another publication

Rose discusses the problems of co-ordination as government grows.[20] Nevertheless, he does not see political bankruptcy as an inevitable consequence of government growth, nor does he view some of the problems associated with big government as insoluble.

For the New Right the growth of government is an unmitigated disaster. The intervention of governments in the economy and in the provision of welfare services has been a failure. In each capitalist country a long list of deficiencies of the welfare state is compiled as evidence of this failure. The massive expenditure of resources and effort has brought little benefit and caused a great deal of harm: governments become overloaded to the point of inefficiency and ineffectiveness.

Brittan and King are the overload theorists most frequently cited by the New Right. Although their focus differs slightly, there is sufficient common ground to justify considering them together. We will start with two quotations from King which express the main thesis of both writers:

The range of matters for which British Governments hold themselves responsible—and for which they believe that the electorate may hold them responsible—has increased greatly . . . and is still increasing at a rapid rate.[21]

In so short a time has government come to be regarded . . . as a sort of unlimited-liability insurance company in the business of insuring all persons at all times against every conceivable risk.[22]

According to Brittan, the problem of overload stems from the operation of the 'political market'. Brittan says that the businessman attempts to maximise profit, the politician attempts to maximise votes and the bureaucrat attempts to maximise the size of his bureau.[23] The more government provides, the more people expect. Powerful pressure groups and the electorate generally urge governments to increase and improve provision (Brittan refers to this as 'the politics of excessive expectations').[24] At the same time competitive party politics encourages political parties to make ever more extravagant promises in an attempt to win electoral support. A gloss provided by Douglas is that the competition between parties tends 'to push the whole political/economic system towards an unduly short-run perspective'.[25]

Keynesian economic policies and Beveridge-style welfare policies were responsible in the postwar years for the growth of government. Keynes made deficit budgeting and increased government borrowing and spending respectable. The initial success of these policies exacerbated the problem of overload in the long term because it increased the prestige of government and encouraged people to believe that there need be no limit to its munificence.

A further reason for overload is administrative accretion: once programmes are initiated they gain a momentum of their own. New programmes do not always replace those already in existence, so that the functions of the government agency concerned grow year by year. In addition, bureaucrats have a vested interest in expanding their departments and resisting any reduction in its resources and responsibilities. Professional providers of services, too, have an interest in extending and improving services.

The consequences of government overload, according to King, include a serious decline in government effectiveness and an increase in the number of policy failures. There is a greater likelihood of policy failures because 'the government is being enfeebled at the moment when its reach is being extended'.[26] This raises the possibility that 'mass dissatisfaction with the consequences of our present political arrangements could grow to the point where the arrangements themselves were seriously called in question'.[27] A further problem with government overload is that as the governmental system becomes larger and more complex, the difficulties of co-ordination and control increase. Among other things, this means greater freedom from political control for administrative and professional staff. For King, writing in 1975, a final consequence of government overload may be

a quite radical change in the nature of government and in our conception of it. . . . It seems probable that the State in Britain, and quite possibly in other western countries, will have become by the late 1970s, to an even greater extent than now, merely one among a number of contenders for wealth, power and influence[28]

The other contenders include large companies, trade

unions, foreign companies, foreign governments and international organisations.

The New Right use overload theories and the extremely
one-sided evidence of policy failures to argue for rolling
back the state and returning to *laissez-faire* policies; a return
to the market-place and more reliance on families and
voluntary effort. Government intervention is said to be the
negation of freedom, a close parallel being drawn between
economic freedom in the market and freedom in general.
State-provided social services, attempts by the state to
reduce inequality and to maintain high levels of employment
are all rejected as being unattainable except at too high a
cost in terms of freedom. Friedman and Friedman write,
'A society that puts equality—in the sense of equality of
outcome—ahead of freedom will end up with neither
equality nor freedom'.[29] What the New Right is advocating,
therefore, is a welfare state based on residual principles
with government restricted to the protection of individuals
from coercion, the administration of justice and mediation
in disputes, the provision of basic amenities and compensation for external or neighbourhood effects and, finally,
the protection of those members of society who cannot be
regarded as 'responsible individuals'.[30]

Many New Right publications are polemical in character,
celebrating the virtues of free enterprise and capitalism. The
best known of such writers are Charles Murray, the author
of a book entitled *Losing Ground*, and George Gilder.
Gilder's book, entitled *Wealth and Poverty*, is a full-blooded
defence of virtually unrestricted capitalism.[31] Blewett says
that 'the political significance of this particular book cannot
be neglected. President Reagan has identified himself with
the book, and his Budget Director . . . has described it as
"promethean in its intellectual power and insight" '.[32]

It is difficult to imagine many people much further
removed from Marxism than Gilder. Perhaps it is surprising,
therefore, to realise that Marxists are in agreement with the
New Right about government overload and the problems
of democratic government. However, the Marxist interpretations of these phenomena are very different from those of
the New Right. The problems, according to Marxists, stem
from the basic contradictions within the capitalist system.

Offe, for example, argues that one of the contradictions in relation to the welfare state is that 'while capitalism cannot co-exist *with*, neither can it exist *without* the welfare state'.[33] The problem with the free-market analysis is that it fails to demonstrate that advanced capitalism without the welfare state would be unworkable. Offe writes that

the embarrassing secret of the welfare state is that while its impact upon capitalist accumulation may well become destructive (as the conservative analysis so emphatically demonstrates), its abolition would be plainly disruptive (a fact that is systematically ignored by the conservative critics[34]

Offe analyses the aetiology of the 'ungovernability crisis' in terms similar to those used by the overload theorists: the growing pressure of expectations and the diminished steering capacity of the state. However, he goes on to say that

no great interpretive effort is required to decipher the stated ungovernability crisis as a manifestation—one no longer amenable to political mediation—of the class conflict between wage-labour and capital or, more precisely, between the political reproduction demands of labour power and the private reproduction strategies of capital.[35]

There is a contradiction between the functions of the state in facilitating the accumulation of capital and its functions in relation to legitimation. Class conflict is at the base of this contradiction.

This is a point taken up by Wolfe, who restates the contradiction and locates it in the political system. The contradiction, according to Wolfe, is between liberal and democratic views of the state. Liberal political arrangements attempt to facilitate the accumulation of capital, whereas democratic political arrangements stress maximum participation by all citizens. Democracy is the means of securing legitimation and ensuring the co-operation of the working class. The power of the working class prevents a settlement in favour of the capitalist class, and the power of the capitalist class prevents a settlement in favour of labour. The result is an uneasy stalemate: 'The legitimacy crisis is produced by the inability of the late capitalist state to maintain its democratic rhetoric if it is to preserve the accumulation function, or the inability to spur further accumulation if it is to be true to its democratic ideology'.[36] Wolfe claims that the only solution is the creation of a socialist system in which the people have a real say in the decisions concerning investment and the allocation of resources and rewards.

FISCAL PROBLEMS

Both right—and left-wing commentators are agreed that the welfare state is experiencing serious fiscal problems. The New Right relate the fiscal crisis to the notion of government overload—governments are overstretching their resources by attempting too much. Marxists agree with this, but argue that the fiscal crisis is one manifestation of the contradictions in capitalism and, more specifically, the contradiction in state intervention in a capitalist system. The fiscal problems for both the Right and Left are the financial aspect of the problems of government identified in the last section.

Kohl, while not himself a member of the New Right, finds the concept of government overload useful in analysing fiscal imbalances. He argues that 'if overload is understood essentially as a problem of imbalances between basic elements of the policy process, then imbalances between public revenues and expenditures can be seen as the fiscal aspect of the problem'.[37] The fiscal problem is to try to achieve a balance between expenditure arising from attempts to satisfy citizens' demands for public goods and services and their willingness to pay for them in the form of taxes. The central argument is the familiar overload one that, as the welfare state develops, people's expectations rise and pressure groups are established to protect and promote particular interests and causes. Electoral competition between parties leads to promises of more and better services and benefits which become increasingly difficult to fulfil. Governments increase taxes in order to pay for services, and eventually there is resistance to any further increases. Governments are therefore faced with a dilemma: they are popular if they provide services and they are unpopular if they increase taxes. In the United States citizens' dissatisfaction with rising taxes led to what have been referred to as tax rebellions. The best known of these took place in California in 1978 when Proposition 13 was passed imposing tax limitations. Since then many other states have followed suit and by 1981 more than half the states had passed tax or spending limitations.[38]

A gap therefore develops between public expenditure and revenue. There are several possible responses: governments can attempt to reduce public expectations and cut services; they can borrow and budget for a deficit; or they can combine both approaches. The most dramatic example of a large budget deficit is that built up by the current administration in the United States—a deficit in 1985 of $200 billion, a sum in excess of total public expenditure in Britain. Although there are plans to reduce the American deficit to $108 billion by 1988, some commentators believe that this figure will be exceeded by about $40 billion. Kohl reports an increase in budget deficits between 1950 and 1975: 'Whereas in the beginning of this postwar period, deficits were reported for only three countries, the trend growth rates have been high enough so that by 1975, the balance has been surpassed by ten out of twelve countries'.[39] OECD statistics demonstrate that deficits have persisted into the 1980s.[40] The Secretariat of the OECD concludes that 'with large public sectors, high unemployment and a desire to cut taxation rather than increase it, these deficits could prove rather stubborn'.[41]

Kohl, however, does not believe that deficits are running at dangerously unprecedented levels or that they are out of control. In other words, fiscal *problems* do not necessarily constitute a *crisis*. This contrasts with the views of the New Right—though, interestingly, not Friedman—and with the views of Marxists such as O'Connor, Offe and Habermas. Of these last, O'Connor has dealt more fully than have the other two with the fiscal problems of the state, and, since Offe and Habermas follow broadly the same line as O'Connor, he will be taken as representative of all three. O'Connor starts from the idea that the state in capitalist society has two major functions—capital accumulation and legitimisation—which may be in conflict. The state expands social services to increase public support and to legitimate both its own activities in the realm of capital accumulation and the capitalist system in general. The state assists capital accumulation in two ways: through public expenditure on the economic infrastructure (e.g. transport, water supplies, sewage) and by meeting the costs of reproducing labour power through, for example, the provision of education, housing and health services. The state bears these two forms of costs, but the resulting profits are privately appropriated. It is this which creates a fiscal gap. The fiscal problem is exacerbated by continued pressure upon governments to spend more: 'Every economic and social class and group wants government to spend more and more money on more and more things. But no one wants to pay new taxes or higher rates on old taxes. Indeed, nearly everyone wants lower taxes'.[42]

LEGITIMATION CRISIS

It should be stressed that the economic, governmental and fiscal problems of the welfare state give rise to legitimation problems and must be viewed as an integral part of any legitimation crisis. If, because of economic, administrative and fiscal problems, the welfare state cannot deliver what it promises, or what people expect of it, then it begins to lose mass support; there is a loss of legitimacy. There is a crucially important distinction to be drawn between the existence of problems and a crisis. Problems will only lead to crisis if they cannot be contained or resolved and result in a loss of stability threatening the political and economic institutions of a society.

Habermas is one writer who attempts to integrate the different forms of crisis tendencies said to be affecting advanced capitalist society. His analysis is Marxist with a distinctive, individual flavour; his theoretical framework is that of systems theory. There are three systems: the economic, the political-administrative and the socio-cultural. Each system has its attendant crisis tendencies. The economic system is subject to output crises if it does not produce the necessary quantity of goods and if profits decline. The political system has both input (loyalties) and output (decisions) crisis tendencies. The crisis arising from output problems is termed a rationality crisis: the administrative system fails to provide the decisions required to steer the economic system. There is a contradiction between the need in advanced capitalist societies for administrative economic planning on the one hand and private ownership of the means of production on the other. Turning to political inputs, Habermas states that 'the political system requires an input of mass loyalty that is as diffuse as possible'.[43] If this loyalty is not secured, then a legitimation crisis occurs; Habermas refers to this as a 'legitimation deficit' which implies that 'it is not possible by administrative means to maintain or establish effective normative structures to the required extent'.[44]

In advanced capitalism the state becomes more active; it intervenes more in the economy in the interests of capital, providing global planning and the necessary economic infrastructure and bearing the costs of both unproductive commodities (e.g. armaments) and social service provision. To some extent, therefore, the market becomes politicised. The increased involvement of the state increases the need for legitimation. Thus Habermas says, 'the expansion of state activity has the side-effect of disproportionately increasing the need for legitimation'.[45] The state in a democracy is drawn into a spiral of increasing provision of goods and services which have to be paid for out of taxation. As Habermas says:

The state apparatus thus has two simultaneous tasks. It has to levy the necessary taxes from profits and income and employ them so efficiently as to prevent any crises from disturbing growth. In addition the selective raising of taxes, the recognisable priority model of their utilisation, and the administrative performance have to function in such a way as to satisfy the resulting need for legitimation. If the state fails in the former task, the result is a deficit in administrative efficiency. If it fails in the latter task, the result is a deficit in legitimation.[46]

We are now back to the problem raised by O'Connor of attempting to reconcile the accumulation and legitimation functions of the capitalist state. Habermas says, however, that up to this stage in his argument he has succeeded only in identifying legitimation problems, and this is not the same as proving that a legitimation *crisis* will occur. Legitimation difficulties will be sharpened into a legitimation crisis only if there are failures in the socio-cultural system which result in a motivation crisis:

A legitimation crisis can be predicted only if expectations that cannot be fulfilled with the available quantity of value or, generally, with rewards conforming to the system, are systematically produced. A legitimation crisis must be based on a motivation crisis—that is, a discrepancy between the need for motives declared by the state, the educational and the occupational systems on the one hand, and the motivation supplied by the socio-cultural system on the other.[47]

The most important motivations provided by the socio-cultural system are, according to Habermas, 'the syndromes of civil and familial-vocational privatism'. Civil privatism implies a very weak form of democracy from which genuine participation is excluded because it would expose the contradictions of the system, especially that between socialised forms of production and private appropriation of profits. Familial-vocational privatism, which complements civil privatism, 'consists in a family orientation with developed interests in consumption and leisure on the one hand, and in a career orientation suitable to status competition on the other'.[48] Civil and familial-vocational privatism rest on pre-bourgeois traditions and core components of bourgeois ideology, which are being eroded by changes in the social structure. It is this erosion which precipitates crisis. It should be stressed that Habermas does not argue that there *is* a crisis. He asserts that there are certainly legitimation problems, but that a crisis would occur only if these problems could not be solved or successfully contained. In other words, Habermas is talking about crisis *tendencies* or the likelihood of crisis. He is examining the features of late capitalism which could give rise to crisis, but he unequivocally denies the actual existence of a crisis in a paper published in 1978: 'We certainly cannot speak of a real crisis of legitimation . . . people continue to vote, and in their vast majority vote for the traditional parties'.[49]

Habermas claims that it is impossible to predict whether or not a crisis will develop in the future, but most Marxist writers believe that the problems that beset the capitalist state cannot in the long run be resolved. Welfare state policies and economic growth temporarily obscured the fundamental contradictions, but the economic recession has demonstrated the inevitable instability of the capitalist system. The only solution is the formation of a socialist state. New Right theorists also envisage the collapse of the welfare state. The only solution is a drastic reduction in the role of the state and a much firmer commitment to the principles of capitalism: individualism, private property, the free market, competition and profit. The welfare state has taken a battering from both the Left and the Right.

Right-wing writers, as we have seen, subscribe to the view that the welfare state is the cause of inflated state expenditures and the growth of government. The freedom of the individual is sacrificed in the pursuit of an unachievable equality. More specifically, the welfare state reduces incentives, stifles initiative, absolves people from personal responsibility and encourages dependence. The absence of the price mechanism and market discipline encourage inefficiency and waste.

The criticisms from the Left focus on the contradictions of the capitalist state and of the welfare state in particular. The welfare state is again seen as one of the major causes of the economic, governmental and fiscal problems in capitalist democracies. More specifically, while the welfare state has undoubtedly brought about improvements in the standard of living of working people, it has failed to bring about any fundamental change in the socio-economic structure and in the distribution of power and wealth. Since the welfare state operates principally, though not exclusively, in the interests of capital, the efforts to meet the needs of working people, partly in response to the needs of capitalism and partly in response to working-class pressure, are grudging, minimal and conditional. The welfare state is more concerned with social control than with social change. Welfare recipients are expected to display 'helpful' attitudes and to conform to particular standards of behaviour. As Offe says, 'the welfare state can be looked upon as an exchange transaction in which material benefits for the needy are traded for their submissive recognition of the "moral order" of the society which generates such need'.[50] Piven and Cloward in their analysis of the American Great Society Programme in the 1960s stress the strong element of social control—an attempt to neutralise the opposition and disarm agitators by absorbing them into the programme. This is merely one example of Piven and Cloward's general thesis that social policy developments are to be interpreted in the light of class conflict; they reflect the attempts of ruling élites to retain their dominant position. The emphasis in social policy is on the work ethic and social control, and developments occur in response to social unrest.[51] In Gough's thoughtful analysis of the welfare state he writes of 'the steady incorporation of the working class, in their trade unions and parties, within advanced capitalist societies, though this very incorporation throws up fresh contradictions'.[52]

In recent years feminist interpretations of socialist theory have been particularly productive of new ways of looking at the welfare state. Much contemporary feminist theory is socialist, and some of it is specifically Marxist. Wilson has argued that 'feminism and socialism meet in the arena of the Welfare State, and the manipulations of the Welfare State offer a unique demonstration of how the State can prescribe what woman's consciousness should be'.[53] Later in the same book she states that 'an analysis of the position of women is not marginal but central to a true understanding of the nature of the Welfare State'.[54] The subordination of women is reflected in the workplace, in the family and in the social services. McIntosh and Wilson are in agreement that the welfare state contributes to this oppression through the ideological and practical support it gives to a particular form of the family. McIntosh argues that the state plays a part in the oppression of women indirectly,

through its support for a specific form of household: the family household dependent largely upon a male wage and upon female domestic servicing. This household system is in turn related to capitalist production in that it serves . . . for the reproduction of the working class and for the maintenance of women as a reserve army of labour'.[55]

In doing unpaid housework and being largely responsible for child care, women are performing functions which are essential to the continued smooth working of the capitalist system.

Marxist critiques of the welfare state place their proponents in something of a dilemma. After one has finished examining the contradictions and failures of the welfare state it becomes difficult to defend it from attacks from the Right. Rose and Rose make this point:

Much of the new political economy of welfare with its emphasis on the functional significance of the public social services for capital accumulation and political legitimation has . . . weakened the theoretical base for even the critical defence of welfare. The critique of feminism of the coercive and patriarchal character of the social services, unless it offers a clear alternative vision, weakens their defence by women[56]

After so much fundamental criticism the question arises as to whether the welfare state is worth defending, especially since it is not seen by some Marxists as a significant step on the road to socialism. Nevertheless, despite these intellectual difficulties, Marxists and other socialists have been at the forefront of the defence of welfare, because reductions will lead to a lowering of the living standards of working people, and the gains made as a result of working-class pressure will be lost. The launching of a new journal, *Critical Social Policy*, in 1981 is indicative of the seriousness with which opposition to the New Right policies is being approached. The Foreword to *Critical Social Policy* states:

This journal will serve as a forum to encourage and develop an understanding of welfare from socialist, feminist and radical perspectives. The only collective editorial policy is a common opposition to the radical right and an awareness of the inadequacies of Fabian and other orthodox models to meet its challenges.[57]

However, Marxists are not simply concerned to defend existing forms of state welfare. In a fully developed socialist society need would be the sole criterion for the allocation of goods and services, and the organisation and delivery of services would be decentralised with a large measure of self-management. Peter Leonard writes, 'The Left must go beyond simply opposing welfare cuts and mobilising a broad alliance to that end. . . . If the Left is to be revolutionary rather than reformist, new democratic structures and new welfare ideologies must be developed and struggled for'.[58]

How has the Centre-left—Fabians and social democrats—responded to the challenge from the Right? For at least twenty years, between 1945 and 1965, Fabian reformism dominated the academic study of social policy and influenced actual policy developments, particularly in Britain, Sweden, Norway, Denmark and the Netherlands. In Britain, Titmuss, Townsend, Abel-Smith and others conducted a protracted debate with the Right and especially with the Institute of Economic Affairs. For the most part, however, the threat from the Right was not taken too seriously. The election of the Thatcher government in 1979 changed all that. The Centre-left was slow to respond, and when it came, its response was fairly weak. It is, of course, more difficult for a political party or movement to sound exciting if it is merely arguing for more of the same and for administrative restructuring.

Without doubt, a contributory factor in the Centre-left's weakness was complacency; much had been achieved, and no one saw any reason to suppose that the incremental development of the social services would come to an end. Another contributory factor, in Britain, was the weakness of the Labour Party, which was more concerned with internal disputes than with mounting a sustained attack on Conservative policies. Similarly, in the United States, the Democratic Party was also on the retreat. Atlas, Dreier and Stephens say of the candidates for the Democratic nomination in 1984: 'This crop of essentially identical Democratic candidates, however, symbolises the bankruptcy of ideas among mainstream Democrats'.[59]

Mishra makes the point that the Centre-left failed to recognise the degree to which the development of social services depended upon economic growth and Keynesian economic theories. The ending of economic growth and the discrediting of Keynesian theories have removed the two main supports of the Fabian case: 'It is not so much the attack on reformism by the radical Left . . . as the increasing difficulty of the mixed economy and the crumbling of its intellectual prop, namely Keynesianism, that has silenced the Centre'.[60] An even more serious problem is that 'Fabianism lacks an articulated theory (both normative and positive) of the welfare state'.[61] Gilbert, an American writer, makes the same point in relation to the United States:

Amelioration, accommodation and piecemeal reform do not constitute a coherent philosophy of social reform. In the absence of a synoptic vision of the welfare state and a coherent philosophy to give its development, liberal doctrine offered meager defence against the political opposition to social welfare that was gaining momentum in the late 1970s.[62]

At the same time new evidence was produced in the 1980s to show that the welfare state did not deliver what it promised. In particular, a powerful egalitarian critique of state welfare was developed in Britain and elsewhere. In 1980 the Black Report showed considerable social class inequalities in health as measured by mortality rates.[63] Townsend and Davidson, using material from the Black Report and elsewhere, state that 'despite more than thirty years of a National Health Service expressly committed to offering equal care for all, there remains a marked class gradient in standards of health'.[64]

In 1982 an even more damaging assessment of the inegalitarian nature of the welfare state appeared. This was Le Grand's influential book, *The Strategy of Equality*, which examined redistribution in health, education, housing and transport. There is insufficient space to deal with Le Grand's evidence here but his conclusion in worth stating: 'Most public expenditure on the social services in Britain (and elsewhere) is thus distributed in a manner that broadly favours the higher social groups, whether "higher" is defined in terms of income or occupation'.[65]

It should be noted, however, that O'Higgins has claimed that the egalitarian critique of the welfare state is misconceived.[66] O'Higgins's arguments will be considered more fully in Chapters 7 and 8.

REDUCED PUBLIC SUPPORT?

It is frequently asserted that public support for the welfare state has declined. The election of rightist governments pledged to cut public expenditure and taxes is sometimes cited as evidence. Such evidence is questionable, however, on a number of counts. At the time of writing, some countries do not have rightist governments: Austria, Italy, Sweden, New Zealand and Australia come immediately to mind. In 1985 rightist majorities were considerably reduced in Norway and Belgium. It is true that both Australia and Sweden had right-wing governments in the late 1970s and early 1980s, but if this is to be attributed to anti-welfare state sentiments, then the subsequent election of Centre-left governments must signify a reversal of these attitudes. The point is that people vote in particular ways for a variety of motives, not all of them mutually consistent. Even in Britain the return of the Thatcher government in 1979 and again in 1983 did not represent a welfare backlash on the part of the electorate. The Conservative Party promised to reduce waste and make government more efficient. It specifically stated that it had no intention of dismantling the welfare state. A strong point in its programme was the promise to reduce taxes, but it is by no means uncommon for people to say that taxes should be cut and services should be improved. Public opinion research by Ladd and Lipset in the United States, for example, revealed such apparently inconsistent views: 'Even as they endorse measures to restrict the growth of government spending and taxation, Americans remain extraordinarily supportive of a high level of government services in virtually all sectors'.[67] Electors are not, however, quite so naïve as this statement might lead one to believe. It is not, as some people claim, that voters do not make the connection between taxation and public expenditure, but that they believe there is considerable scope in public agencies for economies by cutting out waste

In Britain several other factors contributed to the return of the Conservative Party: a belief in the strong leadership which Mrs Thatcher was thought to offer, and the belief in the incompetence of the Labour Party with open disagreement over policies among its leading members. The formation of the Social Democratic Party and its alliance with the Liberal Party may also have affected election results. An important factor in the 1983 election was the Falklands war and the jingoism which accompanied it.

Tax revolts are also cited as evidence of opposition to publicly provided services. However, research surrounding the most celebrated tax revolt—Proposition 13 in California which cut property and sales taxes—does not support the view that people were voting for cuts in services. Over 75 per cent of Californians who voted for Proposition 13 said that they did not believe public services would be cut as a result. Lipset and Schneider say, therefore, that approval of Proposition 13 did not signify opposition to the welfare state. In the campaign debate 'waste in government' was the key phrase—voters did not believe they were getting value for money.

Proposition 13 received considerable publicity, but what is less well-known, at least outside the United States, is the rejection in 1980 of Proposition 9, which would have halved state income tax. Lipset and Schneider conclude: 'The defeat of Proposition 9 demonstrates what was true all along about the tax revolt: it was an attack not on the functions of government, but on the behavior of public officials'.[68]

Golding and Middleton, however, provide evidence of a welfare backlash in Britain. They examine media coverage of social security, public knowledge and perceptions of social security and its recipients and government creation and control of news about social security. The newspapers trivialise and sensationalise. They select individual cases of abuse and fraud, dwelling on the alleged luxurious life-style of the people concerned. It is intimated that there are many more 'scroungers' who are milking the system: the social security system is 'a soft touch' and far too generous. The social security system is attacked on the basis of biased reporting of individual cases. Criticism of the social security system, Golding and Middleton claim, is gradually transformed into a generalised criticism of the welfare state.

When Golding and Middleton turn to an examination of public knowledge and attitudes they discover a devastating combination of ignorance and punitive attitudes. Social security recipients were said to be work-shy spongers, and there was a fairly general belief that benefits were too high and too easily available. It is almost a classic case of blaming the victim. Golding and Middleton write of a 'full-scale assault on the welfare consensus' and claim that 'the crisis in the British economy has become the occasion for a social derision of the poor so punitive in its impact as to threaten very props of the welfare state'.[69] An analysis of newspapers in German-speaking countries has arrived at similar conclusions. [70]

Alt claims that hard-line attitudes towards welfare services and recipients are associated with economic decline. If individuals perceive themselves to be worse off, they are less likely to support 'altruistic' policies.[71] By contrast, Heclo claims that the sources of present disenchantment are to be found in the sustained economic growth of the 1960s, which 'gradually and indeliberately . . . undermined the premises of the welfare state that policy makers thought they were creating at the end of World War II'.[72] This operated in three ways. First, economic growth meant that most people, even in recessions, were employed. There was a belief that poverty no longer existed. Social need in an age of affluence became 'an individualized rather than a collectively shared experience'.[73] Second, since the benefits to be derived from the welfare state ceased to be regarded as a response to shared problems, they became instead a means of calculating and distributing differential gains. There was competition between groups and individuals for the benefits of the welfare state and this was 'corrosive of the social solidarity that had inspired the austerity welfare state'.[74] Finally, economic growth meant that social services could be expanded at virtually no political cost, because no one was actually worse off. The political commitment required in the early days of the welfare state was no longer necessary, and it therefore began to decline.

In relation to the United States Morris says that the welfare state has never been firmly rooted, but that in recent years public support for it has declined as a result of changes in the moral climate: the sense of obligation to help others had become weaker and self-regarding views were more dominant than ever. This has come about partly as a result of the 'democratization of welfare'; that is, the wider availability of welfare, no longer solely for the poor. According to Morris, 'the unexpected consequence may be that the old sense of civic obligation to others—especially a minority—is now competing with a more self-regarding concern for oneself and one's group'.[75]

A number of opinion polls and some empirical work done by Taylor-Gooby provide evidence which, contrary to most of the findings so far considered, indicates that support for the welfare state has not declined. It would be tedious for both reader and writer to describe in detail the results of all the opinion polls, and we will therefore concentrate on some of the general conclusions to be drawn from them. One conclusion in that public opposition to government spending cuts is growing in Britain, according to *Gallup Political Indices*. In March 1979, 34 per cent of the population wanted tax cuts even if it meant worse services. By February 1980 only 22 per cent went for the option of tax cuts and reduced services, and 52 per cent were prepared to pay more tax if that meant more government spending on health, education and welfare. In December 1984 only 12 per cent favoured tax cuts even if this meant poorer services, and 58 per cent said that public social services should be extended even if this involved higher taxes. The annual survey of *British Social Attitudes*, with slightly different questions from those used by Gallup, discovered an even smaller percentage favouring tax cuts and reduced expenditure on health, education and social benefits—only 9 per cent.[76] Quoting the results of Danish and Norwegian opinion polls, published in 1981 and 1982, Johansen and Kolberg conclude that 'popular support of the welfare state in Denmark and Norway increased significantly from about the mid–1970s'. In Norway the percentage favouring an expansion of social welfare increased from 20 per cent in 1973 to 42 per cent in 1977. In Denmark the percentage favouring either expansion or maintenance of the welfare state increased from 39 per cent in 1974 to 55 per cent in 1978.[77] These figures represent a very big shift in opinion over a relatively short period of time, and this is difficult to explain with any degree of certainty. It could be that people believe that substantial cuts have been made and that further cuts are now unnecessary. It could also be that having seen services cut, people now value them more highly. In California 73 per cent of the majority who voted against Proposition 9 said they had done so because they did not wish to see further cuts in public services.

Opinion polls frequently demonstrate that people's attitudes towards welfare are ambivalent. For example, a Harris Poll conducted in the United States in 1976 found that 62 per cent were in favour of cutting federal government expenditure. The very next question, however, asked whether respondents would support cuts in seven specific areas, and in six of these, including health, education and unemployment benefit, a substantial majority was opposed to cuts. In 1980 a *New York Times*/CBS: poll found that

54 per cent favoured smaller government providing fewer services but also wanted a comprehensive health-care system financed by national insurance with most of the money coming from taxation.

In Britain, Taylor-Gooby has published the results of research conducted among 240 residents of the Medway Towns in Kent, into popular attitudes towards welfare provision. The research indicated very strong support for services for the elderly, the sick and disabled, education and the National Health Service. Benefits for lone parents, the unemployed and the low paid were not popular. Two factors seem to be at work: a distinction in people's minds between deserving and undeserving groups and a distinction between benefits for the minority of 'undeserving' poor and benefits for the mass of the population. Taylor-Gooby is critical of some of the earlier research for failing to make these distinctions. His own review of the evidence leads him to the conclusion that 'there has been no strong shift against the welfare state . . . the main services are as strongly supported as they have been at any time since the war'.[78] Taylor-Gooby notes, however, that there is some ambivalence in people's attitudes towards the welfare state:

The dominant note is one of ambivalence along two dimensions. Support for the mass state welfare services of pensions, the NHS and education is tempered by concern at unemployment and low-pay benefits, council housing and lone parent's benefits. Perceptions of redistribution and of the welfare state as a whole show strong support for the principle of state welfare with some concern at the cost and the extent of transfer to other groups.[79]

Taylor-Gooby also questions another common assumption that support for the private market necessarily means antipathy towards the state. His research demonstrated that, people could simultaneously support both market and state provision. This appears to indicate support for welfare pluralism or a mixed economy of welfare with both public and private sectors playing a part. This view is borne out by the 1984 survey of *British Social Attitudes*. Two-thirds backed the present position in education and would not support the imposition of curbs upon independent schools; only 23 per cent believed that private health-care damages the National Health Service and 46 per cent were in favour of expanding private health services.

The level of public support for the welfare state is obviously going to vary from one country to another. Heidenheimer, Heclo and Adams, for example, refer to a study of popular support for five areas of public policy in Britain, the Netherlands, the United States and West Germany. Each country was ranked according to the strength of public support in each policy area. The authors conclude:

Neither the highest ranking—that for health care in Britain—nor the lowest—for housing in the United States—should come as a surprise . . . Agenda support in the United States was consistently below that in the European countries. While the gap was smallest in education, it was largest in the areas where the norms of free enterprise support for private initiative comes into play most directly—housing and employment.[80]

This study was carried out, however, in 1974. A more recent and more comprehensive study was carried out by Coughlin, who did a secondary analysis of all the social surveys that could be found over the last thirty years in eight countries; Australia, Britain, Canada, Denmark, France, Sweden, the United States and West Germany. Coughlin's conclusion was that the evidence did not confirm the view that public support for the welfare state had declined. There has been little change over the last thirty years, and in all eight countries there is a pro-welfare state majority. The majority is highest in West Germany, Sweden Denmark and France and lowest in the United States and Australia; the United Kingdom and Canada come somewhere in between.[81]

The true test of a legitimation crisis in the welfare state is the degree to which public support for its principles has been withdrawn. The weight of the evidence looked at in this chapter points to one conclusion: that public support for the welfare state has not diminished. It is true that recipients of means-tested benefits and some stigmatised groups, such as lone mothers, do not attract much public sympathy but this has always been the case. If the object of governments' rhetoric has been to undermine public confidence in the welfare state, then it has been singularly unsuccessful. It is interesting to note the change in tone now being adopted by the Conservative Party in Britain as an election draws near. At its Annual Conference in 1986, minister after minister expressed support for welfare provision and for a modest expansion of public expenditure.

THE 'CRISIS' AND WELFARE PLURALISM

In response to the alleged crisis, governments in all capitalist welfare states have attempted to impose more stringent controls on public expenditure and to reduce the role of the state in the provision of welfare. There have, of course, been differences in timing and scope. In France, for example, the Socialist government, during its first year in office, went against the general trend. Eventually, however, Mitterrand was forced to introduce an austerity programme, and the return of the conservative Chirac as prime minister in 1986 is likely to lead to greater retrenchment.

Sweden, which has suffered less retrenchment than most, is another country which does not fit neatly into the general pattern. Between 1976 and 1982 the Moderate (conservative) government in Sweden introduced policies designed to restrain welfare expenditure, but its Social Democratic replacement has attempted to follow a middle course between the conservative policies of Britain and America and the policies followed in the early part of Mitterrand's administration when public expenditure in France rose dramatically. This middle course has enabled Sweden to retain, and in some areas to modestly expand, its extensive welfare provision.

In most other welfare states, however, policies of retrenchment have been introduced, and although the rhetoric of retrenchment has exceeded its practical application, a change in emphasis has undoubtedly occurred. This change in emphasis finds its expression in welfare pluralism: a reduction or reversal of the state's dominance in welfare provision and an increase in the role of the informal, voluntary and commercial sectors. The meaning of welfare pluralism is considered more fully in the next chapter.

3 What Is Welfare Pluralism?

Welfare pluralism is fashionable. It has been one of the central issues in social policy debate since the late 1970s. Beresford and Croft, in a paper highly critical of welfare pluralism, state:

Most of the major debates and developments now are ones that have either been initiated or largely appropriated by welfare pluralism. This is not to ignore or underplay the major developments that have taken place in left debates on welfare over the same period, but rather to acknowledge the present predominance of pluralist thinking in welfare.[1]

Before examining the reasons for this popularity we must look at the way the term is used. The problem with the notion of 'welfare pluralism' and with alternative terms such as 'the mixed economy of welfare' is their lack of precision. Judge and Reddin claim that the concept of a mixed economy of welfare 'whilst identifying a plurality of modes of provision is "neutral" with respect to any particular balance within this plurality'.[2] This may be true in the abstract, but the interpretations of the term are far from neutral. Hatch and Mocroft, two prominent welfare pluralists, start with a relatively neutral formulation but quickly move from description to prescription:

In one sense welfare pluralism can be used to convey the fact that social and health care may be obtained from four different sectors— the statutory, the voluntary, the commercial and the informal. More prescriptively, welfare pluralism implies a less dominant role for the state, seeing it as not the only possible instrument for the collective provision of welfare services.[3]

In Britain, the Wolfenden Report on *The Future of*

Voluntary Organisations was among the first publications to refer specifically to welfare pluralism, recognising that the voluntary sector represented only one of four systems of meeting need. The Wolfenden Committee, in using the term pluralism, believed it was describing the existing position; one of its major concerns was the *maintenance* of a pluralistic system. The Committee's report was not by any means anti-statist. It wished to see the voluntary sector improved and expanded, but there was no implication that voluntary provision should *replace* statutory provision. Rather, the Committee hoped 'to encourage the strengthening and extension of collective action to meet important social needs in the provision of health care, housing, welfare, the maintenance of minimum standards of income and the protection of the environment'.[4] According to this view, increasing the role of the non-statutory sector does not imply a corresponding contraction of state provision.

Similar views were expressed at a meeting of experts organised by the European Centre for Social Work Training and Research. The purpose of the meeting, which took place in 1984, was to examine the relationship between established social services and new social initiatives. Thirteen countries were represented. The report of the meeting states that 'experts from virtually all the countries represented saw the growth of these initiatives as some kind of response to alleged failures in the operation of welfare states . . . governments are encouraging and supporting new initiatives as part of policies of welfare pluralism'.[5] The new initiatives involved substantially more participation and a greater reliance on self-help, mutual aid, voluntary and informal help with social workers fulfilling a community rather than a casework role. It is significant that participants were 'in total agreement . . . that the relationship between the initiatives and established services is not one where the former will progressively substitute for the latter'.[6] Some of the themes pursued at the 1984 meeting echoed the conclusions of an International Seminar in 1982 entitled 'Getting Back to People'. This seminar, another venture of the European Centre, emphasised the twin strategies of decentralisation and participation. Again, those taking part were careful to point out that changing structures should not be used as an excuse for reducing public spending.

It is clear, however, that some welfare pluralists do anticipate at least partial replacement of existing statutory services, producing a mixed system in which the state would be less dominant than it is at present. Pluralists who advocate such a change in the balance of provision usually begin their analysis with a long catalogue of the failures of state welfare.[7] It is, of course, relatively easy to identify failings since shortage in relation to demand is universal. It is possible to argue against this that the welfare state is to a large extent a victim of its own success. It is the success of state services which has raised people's expectations of them and created the gap between demand and supply. This consideration, however, does not deter the critics who point out that after decades of state welfare, poverty and inequality still exist, health services are overstretched, there is still too much poor housing, child abuse is at least as frequent as ever and old people still die of hypothermia. Failures are emphasised and successes ignored or given little prominence. No evidence is produced to demonstrate that any other form of organisation would have done better; nor is it recognised that it was the failure of markets and voluntary effort that led to state welfare in the first place.

The criticisms, however, are not solely that services and benefits are inadequate and of poor quality, but also that the welfare state is too-centralised, too-bureaucratic and too-authoritarian. The system is unresponsive to people's varied and changing needs, and clients have little or no control over the services: they are passive recipients rather than active participants. Hadley and Hatch claim that the centralised administrative system can be criticised on four counts: non-compliance (problems of political and hierarchical control); inefficiency and ineffectiveness; bureaucratic ossification; failure to gain public support and involvement. Hadley and Hatch obviously envisage a greatly reduced role for the state with more reliance on voluntary and informal provision. Their support for commercial provision is more hesitant. At all events they do not see private welfare markets playing a dominant role:

A system of social services dominated by the commercial sector . . . in important respects negates some of the objectives for which the social services are established. Hence the criticisms levelled at the statutory services in this book should not be taken as arguments for patterns of provision that are predominantly commercial. But there are likely to be situations in which commercial provision, when subject to safeguards to maintain the quality of service and when it does not have a detrimental effect on other sources of service, can contribute usefully to a plural system of services.[8]

Hadley and Hatch, while not averse to the development of the commercial sector, are much more interested in maximising the contribution of the voluntary and informal sectors. Welfare pluralism first arose in the context of a discussion and reappraisal of the voluntary sector. The Wolfenden Report has already been referred to. Another major contribution came from Gladstone, who argued that voluntary organisations should replace statutory bodies as the major providers of welfare.[9] An emphasis on voluntarism is also the main thrust of a major study of care and welfare in Sweden by the Secretariat for Future Studies which goes so far as to suggest community care conscription along the lines of military conscription. However, once a move down the road of welfare pluralism has been made, it may prove difficult to limit the commercial sector. We are thus brought back to the economic and social markets of Titmuss. The relationships and balance between these two, in the context of the United States, is one of the major concerns of Gilbert, who claims that:

The search for a workable balance between the economic and social markets of a mixed economy poses a crucial challenge to the future of the welfare state in a capitalist society. It is a challenge that demands sober regard for both the vitality of private enterprise and the humanity of social welfare.[10]

Two closely linked themes within welfare pluralist literature are decentralisation and participation. In several Western European countries and in the United States the process of decentralisation and deregulation has already begun. Decentralisation is seen by its proponents as valuable in reducing the power of the central state and as a prerequisite for successful participation, which is taken to mean involvement in both service delivery and policy-making. But the term 'decentralisation' in the welfare pluralist vocabulary does not simply mean a movement from central to local government. It also implies that local government, too, needs to be 'decentralised'. One means of achieving this secondary decentralisation is the patch system in which small teams of social workers serve neighbourhoods with about 10,000 inhabitants. It is expected that social workers would come to know their neighbourhoods intimately and would therefore be much more aware of informal and voluntary sources of help. Young says of the patch system:

It means that social services staff will be less remote, more accessible, that they will have more contact with the community. The focus is no longer solely on clients and problems. The carers of dependent people, the friends and neighbours who provide help, are all part of the patch team's concern. Through more of a partnership with local people, patch teams aim to provide help earlier and to focus resources on sustaining and developing the care being provided by the community.[11]

This statement illustrates very clearly the relationship between decentralisation and welfare pluralism.

Decentralisation, however, need not be given a purely geographical meaning. There is also budgetary or resource decentralisation. Challis describes this form of decentralisation as a system in which 'decisions over the precise allocation of resources are formally pushed down to a lower level than is usual, at times to the individual fieldworker, to ensure more appropriate allocation of resources'.[12] Challis is a member of the team evaluating the Kent Community Care Scheme, which attempts to provide domiciliary care for frail elderly people whose circumstances place them on the verge of admission to residential care.

For each elderly person referred to the scheme, a social worker with a smaller than usual caseload will 'construct and maintain a co-ordinated package of care unique to each elderly person from a wide range of usually fragmented sources: health, social services, voluntary and informal care'.[13] The social worker, in devising the package, works to a maximum budget of two-thirds of the cost of residential care. The scheme makes extensive use of volunteers who are paid a nominal sum. Again one can see the connection with welfare pluralism.

In welfare pluralism, decentralisation is invariably linked with participation. Only in a decentralised system will people feel able to participate. The assumption is that people want to participate or that they can be encouraged to do so. This is by no means self-evident.

Welfare pluralism implies participation in service-provision, but most welfare pluralists extend the compass of participation to include the involvement of consumers and employees of statutory agencies in decision-making. There is an obvious connection here with political pluralism, and an assumption that wider participation brings about a wider dispersal of power. In a limited way this is true: participation may give people greater control over their own lives, but involvement at neighbourhood level is unlikely to lead to the exercise of political power in national, regional or even local, contexts. Power is class-based and built into economic and social structures. Even in voluntary organisations power is held by middle-class participants. Another consideration is that participation in the provision of services may not assist the dispersal of power because time, energy and resources are diverted from political action into service provision. The creation of low-paid jobs, as in the American poverty programmes, has the same effect of diverting people from political action.

This rather pessimistic prognosis should not be construed as a rejection of participation: it is a warning not to expect too much from it. The American War on Poverty and the British Community Development Projects are evidence that participation is not a panacea. As Joan Higgins says of the poverty programmes: 'Participation alone cannot secure an overall redistribution of income and wealth or the eradication of inequalities of class, status and power. The real danger is that participation, as a means to such ends, becomes an end in itself'.[14]

The themes of decentralisation and participation have anti-bureaucratic and anti-professional implications, and this partly accounts for welfare pluralism's wide appeal. There is something in welfare pluralism for all shades of political opinion. The Right may see welfare pluralism as a politically convenient formula for dealing with the problem of government overload by reducing the role of the state both centrally and locally. It may also be seen as an opportunity to transfer statutory services to the private market, introducing what is perceived as a healthy element of competition and choice. Such a system could foster a spirit of self-reliance rather than one of dependence. Another bonus would be a regeneration of family care, a 'degeneration' being assumed to have taken place.

Libertarians of the Left will also welcome the anti-bureaucratic, anti-centralist and anti-professional implications of welfare pluralism. Private market provision would, however, be rejected as would most of the larger, more traditional voluntary organisations. The advantage would lie in a more participatory style of welfare provision which would respond more rapidly and sensitively to people's needs. Gilbert notes a perhaps surprising congruence between syndicalist socialism and classical capitalism:

It is . . . resistance to the power of the state that unites classical capitalism with syndicalist socialism on important issues of public policy. Both schools of thought share a broad philosophical perspective on the virtues of decentralization, self-help, informal mediating structures such as family and voluntary organisations, and citizen participation in community affairs.[15]

In a recent book, Walker describes *A Strategy for Socialist Welfare* which would involve decentralisation and participation, especially in planning. In such a system 'clients, claimants and other citizens would be at the centre of the planning process'.[16] The purpose of pointing out these parallels between socialist ideas and welfare pluralism is not to suggest that there are no differences—the differences in aim are fundamental. However, both groups might embrace decentralisation and participation for quite different reasons.

The theories of welfare pluralism are essentially the creation of those occupying a central political position. Beresford and Croft claim, however, that it is the traditional Fabian position that has been most threatened by recent developments. Fabianism and social democracy were dominant during the period of welfare state growth as the chief proponents of welfare statism. In a period of cuts and retrenchment the Fabian position became much less tenable, and welfare pluralism offered a lifeline. This has, however, meant a shift to the right:

> But the resurgence of fabian influence on socialist social policy we are now experiencing, is of a new more right wing fabianism. Welfare pluralism has given fabianism a new lease of life, while at the same time making traditional fabianism appear more radical by comparison. Fabianism's apparent lack of consensus, its chameleon character—seemingly able to face both ways simultaneously—may persist and remain one of its strongest weapons, but it is now rooted more to the right.[17]

However, many Fabians would take issue with the welfare pluralists over the role of private markets in welfare, and they would be unwilling to bestow upon the voluntary sector the centrally important place it holds in welfare pluralism.

The emphasis in welfare pluralism on decentralisation and participation and on informal and community networks fits in well with policies of community care. In many countries community care has been developed in opposition to institutional care. Among the reasons for community care's popularity have been the pressure on institutions and considerations of cost. Community care has frequently been interpreted as care *in* the community by paid, professional workers. Too often, however, it has meant care by families with little or no professional support. Defining community care as care *by* the community is more in line with the ideas of welfare pluralism. In this context a helpful definition is that proposed by Abrams who defines community care as 'provision of help, support and protection to others by lay members of societies acting in everyday domestic and occupational settings'.[18]

Community care is popular with governments because it is thought to be cheaper than institutional care. This is equally true of welfare pluralism. It has come to the fore at a time when the welfare state is said to be in crisis. It is very much a product of the late 1970s and the 1980s; nothing was heard of it in the period of welfare state expansion from 1950 to the mid–1970s. With the onset of the fiscal and economic crisis, it was claimed that the resources were just not available to sustain increasing levels of state welfare. Fiscal and economic problems necessitated the development of non-statutory sources of welfare. Shifting the emphasis from the statutory sector to the voluntary, informal and commercial sectors seemed to offer opportunities for cutting public expenditure. Rolling back the state was also ideologically attractive to governments who hankered after a less positive, less active state. Conservative governments, looking back nostalgically to a supposed golden age and hoping for a return to traditional values, are likely to be receptive to welfare pluralism's ideas about the roles of the family and self-help. It is important to recognise, however, that certain aspects of welfare pluralism would be less welcome. It does not advocate a minimal state, and, although the state would decline as a welfare *provider*, it would still have an active role to play. This role would include the provision of a framework within which welfare pluralism could operate and the creation and maintenance of conditions favourable to its development. The state, as the only body able to ensure equity in the distribution of resources, would be the main source of finance, and it would also have an important regulative role.

As will be seen in Chapter 7, most capitalist governments have attempted to cut public expenditure or at least reduce its rate of growth. The emphasis on private competition, self-reliance, self-help and familial responsibilities is apparent everywhere, although it is most obvious in Britain, the United States and Germany, and least obvious in Sweden. Munday claims:

European countries are revising their social policies to change both the nature and weight of the contribution to social care of the four sectors in their social welfare systems. In most cases this means finding ways of decreasing the contribution of the statutory sector and increasing that of the other three sectors.[19]

Welfare pluralism has been pushed onto the political agenda where it occupies centre stage in debates about the welfare state. In the next four chapters each of the sectors of welfare pluralism will be examined. We will begin with the informal sector.

4 The Informal Sector and Social Welfare

What is normally implied by the informal sector is the provision of social and health care by relatives, friends and neighbours. It is extremely difficult to measure the extent and importance of such care because, by its very nature, much of it must go unrecorded. Both carers and those cared for may regard their actions as 'natural' and unremarkable. Even if the number and range of contacts could be accurately recorded, there would still be problems. For example, it would be difficult to decide upon an appropriate unit of measurement which takes into account not only the frequency and duration of contacts but also their intensity and the subjective meaning attached to them by the participants.

In many countries there have been studies of family care, most frequently in relation to the elderly or children, but including some concerned with the care of mentally ill, mentally handicapped and physically disabled people. There have been fewer studies focusing on friends and neighbours, although in the late 1970s and the 1980s there has been an upsurge of interest in helping networks in social policy. This interest has been more marked in the United States than elsewhere. The following passage, taken from a book by four American writers, will help to clarify the idea of helping networks:

We have chosen to use the term 'helping networks' to describe a wide range of informal helping activities . . . we believe that emphasizing informal helping within the context of a network of relationships has distinct conceptual advantages to more traditional ways of viewing social relationships. The concept of a network in its most general form draws our attention to the *structure* of relationships among a set of actors as well as the specific *exchanges* which take place among them and the *roles* they play with each other.[1]

Although difficulties of measurement and patchy evidence make the precise quantification of the informal sector problematic, there can be little doubt that in all welfare states its contribution is considerable. In the case of elderly and handicapped people not living in institutions (and most are not in residential care) the informal system is almost certainly more important than both the statutory and voluntary sectors. Bayley claims that 'in practice statutory care is the junior partner in terms of volume of provision',[2] and Hadley and Hatch sum the position up as follows:

Most of the care that is provided for dependent people living in their own homes comes not from the state, nor from voluntary organisations, nor from commercial sources, but from family, friends and neighbours. Such everyday unofficial help has come to be referred to as the informal system of care.[3]

Hadley and Hatch are referring to Britain, but similar sentiments can readily be found in literature dealing with other countries. For example, a book edited by Pancoast, Parker and Froland examines initiatives in informal care in Belgium, France, the Netherlands, New Zealand, Quebec, Britain, The United States and West Germany.[4] In the previous chapter, reference was made to a European Expert Meeting held in late 1984 in Frankfurt on 'Established Social Services versus New Social Initiatives'[5] and to an International Seminar on 'Getting Back to People', which took place two years earlier in the Netherlands.[6]

COMMUNITY CARE

Reference has already been made to Abrams's definition of community care as 'provision of help, support and protection to others by lay members of societies acting in everyday domestic and occupational settings'.[7] Community care is thus distinguished by its agents (lay people) and the setting in which it occurs (open). Abrams rejects spontaneity as an important distinguishing characteristic of community care:

I would like deliberately and specifically to avoid any suggestion that spontaneity is a defining feature of community care . . . there is no evidence . . . that would suggest that spontaneity is in any way an important source of the type of sustained altruistic practice which community care embodies.[8]

Abrams's general view is that community care in modern industrial societies is 'typically volatile, spasmodic and unreliable',[9] but that if we are looking for a firmer basis for community care, then we must look to reciprocity. Romantic notions of selfless caring relationships in a community setting must be discarded because 'giving is a self-interested activity'.[10] Abrams writes, 'The relevant finding seems clearly to be that effective community care is almost invariably tied to perceptions of long or short-term reciprocal advantage'.[11]

Abrams's definition of community care, as he himself allows, is an extreme one, based as it is on the idea of care *by* the community. A more limited notion is care *in* the community. Walker serves as an example of this approach to community care: 'We are concerned . . . with the concept of care *in* the community, which may be provided "informally", through kinship networks, by friends, neighbours and volunteers, or "formally" by statutory social services'.[12]

In the 1960s community care in Britain was generally interpreted to mean care by statutory personnel working within the community. This is clear from the community care report issued by the Ministry of Health in 1963.[13] The fact that this report was issued by the Ministry of Health has some significance in that community care was usually assumed to concern only health and personal social services: the importance of housing and social security for community care was not always appreciated.

With an increasing interest in networks of care, and the greater importance being attached to voluntary and informal care, definitions of community care have come to be widened. In academic research and policy statements a wider range of statutory services is now embraced and the roles of the voluntary and informal sectors are recognised. Another outcome of research in this area is a recognition that different ethnic groups and social classes may have different caring strategies.

Frequently, care in the community is contrasted favourably with care in institutions; as the popularity of community care has increased, the popularity of institutional care has declined. Prominent among the factors contributing to the declining popularity of institutional care was research in the late 1950s and the 1960s demonstrating the harmful consequences of living in total institutions: the break with familiar surroundings and relationships, the humiliating admission procedures, the submission to rigid regimes, the loss of the ability to determine one's own routine and activities add up to what Goffman calls 'the mortification of self'.[14] At the same time as total institutions were being vilified, a number of studies emphasised the importance of community relationships. Indicative of the interest in community was the foundation in 1954 of the Institute of Community Studies. Much of the work emanating from the Institute was concerned with the durability and the continuing role of the extended family.[15]

Another frequently stated disadvantage of institutional care is its cost, particularly as buildings deteriorate. Hughes and Lovell, for example, claim that one of the reasons for the de-institutionalisation programme in American mental health services was that 'the existing physical plant of the public asylum system—a legacy of the nineteenth century—was rapidly approaching a state of total decrepitude that made their renovation or replacement mandatory'.[16] The same legacy was apparent throughout Western Europe, although a partial exception has to be made of the Scandinavian countries.

Community care as a policy objective is by no means new, but recent events have, of course, strengthened the commitment of governments to community care since it appears to offer the opportunity to cut public expenditure and reduce the role of the state. The Commission of the European Community in its Report on Social Developments in 1981 stated:

Throughout the Community, the tendency has for some years been to reduce the number of people in residential institutions, caring for them instead in their own homes or families with the assistance of out-patient services and day-care centres. Some governments are now in favour of speeding up movement in this direction both on humanitarian grounds and with a view to economising resources.[17]

In the following year, the Commission claimed, 'the policy of community care was promoted with increasing vigour by governments anxious to transfer the cost of such care away from their budgets'.[18] Governments, administrators, social service professionals and academics have all emphasised the superiority of community over institutional care, although it is true to say that the rhetoric has not always been matched by action and the transfer of resources. It is also true that there have been some dissenting voices, and some resistance from trade unions representing institutional workers. Nevertheless, opinion has been heavily weighted in favour of community care for such groups as the elderly, the sick, the physically disabled, deprived children and the mentally disordered.

However, if community care is to be successful, it needs to be carefully planned, and adequate resources have to be devoted to it. It is patently obvious that closing institutions without providing compensating alternatives in the community simply leaves people without any help. This has been a particular problem in the mental health field; in some countries the closure of institutions has meant that mentally disordered patients have been turned out on to the streets. Discharged patients may be helped by their families, but in many cases there are no families available or families are unwilling or unable to provide the necessary care.

This is one of the criticisms made of the de-institutionalisation programmes in the United States. Even Italy's justly admired mental health services are open to similar criticisms. Italy has gone further than any other country in the transfer of patients from institutions to the community, but the service is uneven. In some areas community facilities have been developed as institutions have been run down; in other areas resources for community care have not been made available, and patients are probably worse off than they were before.

Furthermore, a full range of community services will not necessarily cost less than institutional care. If community care means leaving people with inadequate care, or if it means privatising the finance and provision of care by transferring responsibility to families, then the only gains will be economic. As will become clearer when we have looked more closely at family care, even these gains may be illusory.

FAMILY CARE

Abrams claims that care which is identified as community care frequently proves, on closer examination, not to be based on community in the territorial sense at all, but on kinship, race or religion. Kinship is especially significant:

Perhaps surprisingly, in view of all the talk there has been of the death of the family, kinship remains the strongest basis of attachment and the most reliable basis of care that we have. This is especially true among women. Between mothers and daughters, and between sisters to a lesser degree, almost any call for help is legitimate and will, if at all possible, be satisfied.[19]

One of the problems of attempting to discuss the role of the family in the provision of care is the extent of the literature on families and the range of theoretical perspectives included in that literature. Another, more fundamental problem, is that there is a variety of family types. It is, therefore, misleading to talk of *the* family as though all families were much the same: an assumption, perhaps, that the typical family consists of two married adults with dependent children. As Campling says, 'Historical and contemporary evidence shows that the only real defining characteristic of families is their variability'.[20] This variability must be borne in mind as we look at the role of the family in the provision of care.

Empirical studies have demonstrated how important the family is as a source of care in all welfare states. The care of the handicapped and sick by nuclear family members and the system of reciprocal support between elderly people and their adult children are especially significant. Family care of the elderly is particularly well-documented. The study of elderly people in Denmark, Britain and the United States by Shanas and her colleagues described the mutually supportive relationships between adult daughters and sons and their parents. The authors claimed that:

> The traditional assumptions about the changes in the family and the disintegration of relations between the generations in modern societies have never been supported by empirical evidence. On the contrary, a number of studies have demonstrated that the generations, although preferring to live apart, maintain contact and exchange mutual services. What is found between the generations is 'intimacy' at a distance rather than isolation.[21]

Four years after the publication of this report, the National Center for Health Studies estimated that in the United States 80 per cent of home health-care services for the elderly are provided by family members.[22] More recently, the report of a seventeen-nation seminar organised by the Division of Social Affairs of the United Nations concluded that 'the family continues to play a major role in the support of its elderly members. Many assumptions of the weakening of the family support system in industrialised societies are being reconsidered as a result of systematic studies'.[23]

In recent years there has been a growing interest in the distribution of caring responsibilities within families. The unequivocal conclusion to be drawn from the various studies is that overwhelmingly care is provided by women. Finch and Groves write of a 'double equation': community care = family care = care by women:

> The cultural designation of women as carers in the family setting is reflected in the available evidence about what happens in practice: in terms of primary responsibility, wives care for husbands, mothers for handicapped children and daughters for their elderly parents or disabled siblings. Care is also provided by female neighbours and volunteers.[24]

Although male carers can be found, they constitute a very small proportion of the total. The main commitment of men is expected to be to the labour market; the primary focus for women, even when they have paid employment, is the home. It is usually the woman who takes time off work when a child is sick. It is women who are expected to give up work when elderly parents (even their husband's parents) require constant attention. Hilary Land claims 'that men are not expected to look after themselves as much as women are. . . . Neither is it assumed that they will be able to look after elderly or infirm relatives'.[25]

In Britain, the Equal Opportunities Commission, the Study Commission on the Family (now the Family Policy Studies Centre) and the Policy Studies Institute have all conducted research into the division of caring tasks within families. If there is a single conclusion to be drawn from this research it is that most of the burden of caring falls on women:

Since traditional attitudes and practices within society continue to allocate to women the primary responsibility for caring functions, the majority of 'carers' are women. Moreover, the majority of women will at some time in their lives be carers; in addition to the normal demands of children they are also likely for some period to have partial or total responsibility for the care of the elderly, the physically or mentally handicapped or the mentally ill.[26]

Gillian Parker, in a review of the literature on informal care, claims that 'at the most conservative estimate, there are 1.3 million people in Britain acting as principal carers for elderly relatives, children with disabilities or chronically sick and disabled adults'.[27] Some 20 per cent of women aged between 40 and 59 were providing such care and it is probable that half of all women will do so at some stage in their lives.

A comparison of men and women caring for dependent elderly people by Charlesworth, Wilkin and Durie found that 59 per cent of the carers were women and 41 per cent men.[28] These figures appear to indicate that men provide care more often than is commonly thought, but it should be pointed out that this finding is at variance with the results of other research. An Equal Opportunities Commission survey, published in 1980, for example, found that three times as many women as men were looking after elderly or handicapped relatives.[29] A paper from the National Council for Voluntary Organisations claimed that 'women are shouldering most of the responsibilities for care. Of all carers, 80 per cent are women. Society expects women to provide care and puts pressure on them to do so'.[30] Further-more, not only are there more female carers than male, but women also spend more time in caring. Nissel and Bonnerjea, in a study of the handicapped elderly, found that women spent on average three hours eleven minutes a day in the provision of care while husbands spent only thirteen minutes.[31]

What is true of Britain is true of other advanced industrial societies. Referring to general trends in the countries of the European Community, the Commission claimed that the costs of caring fell 'on female relatives who are unlikely to receive much in the way of compensation'.[32] Gilbert says of the United States, 'As in the past, the burdens of familial care in the foreseeable future will rest mainly on women'[33] In Manhattan, a programme working with those caring for elderly people claimed that the most common carers were daughters. An interesting finding of this research was that where the son was the primary care-giver his wife was also heavily involved in caring, whereas daughters often tried to look after older parents without involving their husbands or children at all.[34] Even in Sweden where 80 per cent of the women work and where there is greater equality between the sexes, women are still the main carers.

THE IMPACT OF CARING

It is difficult to convey the impact of caring upon the carers themselves or upon their families. Statistics cannot give any idea of the unremitting drudgery which caring often entails. An incontinent, frail elderly person will have to be toileted, washed, dressed, fed and put to bed; clothing and bedding will have to be changed and washed frequently. Care is almost constant throughout the day and frequently at night. The interrupted sleep and hard physical work lead to tiredness and possibly ill-health. Charlesworth, Wilkin and Durie say that 22 per cent of the carers in their study felt that health problems 'had either been caused or worsened by caring for the elderly person'. Slightly more women than men reported a deterioration. Nor is it only physical health which is affected: 'The largest single category of problems mentioned was depression and anxiety attributable to the stresses of caring over a long period of time'.[35]

In addition, women have to cope with tension in the home. Children and husbands may resent the presence of, for example, a frail elderly relative, particularly if the elderly person appears to monopolise the time of the mother/wife. Arguments may develop, and the woman may find herself in the middle attempting to keep the peace. In the Nissel and Bonnerjea study, family members complained of a loss of privacy, and both husbands and wives reported a deterioration in marital relationships. Some parents thought that children's school performance had suffered—yet another source of worry.

In these circumstances, it is hardly surprising that most studies report a high incidence of depression, especially among those who are confined to the home. For this group, the problems of social isolation are added to the stresses and strains of caring. Carers feel trapped with no possibility of escape and with no one to help. Charlesworth *et al.* say that 44 per cent of both male and female carers reported restrictions on their leisure time, 'although men appeared to resist more strongly encroachment on their leisure activities'.[36] If carers manage to combine paid employment and caring, then isolation is much less of a problem. Caring does, however, restrict employment opportunities. An Equal Opportunities Commission report states:

Caring inevitably restricts the type of employment that can be undertaken to work that is near-at-hand, possibly part-time, but certainly with working hours that fit into the carer's routine. Such employment is unlikely to be well paid or to offer good prospects for advancement . . . The conflicting demands of caring and employment can put carers at a disadvantage in comparison with their colleagues.[37]

Again, the disadvantages are more serious for women than for men, because, as several studies demonstrate, it is more often the woman who gives up work or who moves from full-time to part-time employment. Furthermore, men enter into caring roles at a later age than women. In the Charlesworth, Wilkin and Durie study 46 per cent of the male carers were aged 60 or more compared with 39 per cent of the women. It should be noted, too, that restriction of employment opportunities has important financial implications for families, so that the extra expenses involved in caring may have to be met out of a reduced budget.

SOCIAL CHANGE AND FAMILY CARE

In most advanced industrial countries the proportion of dependents in the population has been increasing for decades, and this trend is likely to continue beyond the end of the century.[38] This is true of both the very elderly and the physically and mentally disordered. In the United States the proportion of old people in the population rose from 4 per cent to 11 per cent between 1900 and 1979. Between 1980 and the year 2000 the number of people between the ages of 75 and 84 is expected to double.[39] In England and Wales the proportion of those aged 65 and over in the population rose from 4.7 per cent to 15 per cent between 1901 and 1981; between 1981 and 2001 there is expected to be a slight fall in this proportion, but a 16 per cent increase is expected in the number of people aged 75 and over and a 51 per cent increase in the number of people aged 85 or over.[40] In Norway, Sweden and Denmark the proportion of the elderly who were aged 80 and over in the early 1980s was 21 per cent, 19 per cent and 20 per cent respectively. By the year 2000 the proportion in Norway will be 29 per cent, with Sweden having 23 per cent and Denmark 25 per cent.[41] The trends in France, Germany, Italy and the Netherlands are similar so that a picture emerges of increasing numbers of frail elderly people. Nor is it simply a case of increasing numbers; the frail elderly are increasing as a proportion of total population and as a proportion of potential carers.

The number of potential carers has been declining because of reduced family size and the much greater participation of women in the labour market. Family size has been declining for at least sixty years in advanced industrial countries. In the United States, for example, the average household size has declined from 4.11 in 1930 to 2.86 in 1980.[42] A government report on the demographic situation in Denmark states that the birthrate has fallen from an average of 2.6 children for every woman in the middle 1960s to an average of 1.5 children in 1980. The report comments that 'this marked decrease results from more women remaining childless, fewer woman having more than two children, and the age at which they bear children being later'. Eversley claims that in Britain a typical couple married in 1920 and now turned 80 years of age has forty-two female relatives, fourteen of whom are not in paid employment. A similar couple married in 1950 reaching their eighties in the early years of the next century will have eleven female relatives, only three of whom will not be in paid employment.[43] Table 4.1 shows changes in general fertility rates between 1962 and 1980 in fifteen different countries. In every case there has been a decline. In two countries—Canada and West Germany—there was a decline of more than 46 per cent, and in both the Netherlands and New Zealand there was a fall well in excess of 40 per cent. The United States, Italy and Austria each experienced a decline of almost 37 per cent. The smallest decreases occurred in France (22.6 per cent) and Sweden (15.3 per cent). In the remaining countries general fertility rates fell by between 26 per cent and 34 per cent.

Social policy tends to be based on a traditional view of the nuclear family: two married adults, with the man as the

Table 4.1: General fertility rates in selected countries, 1962–1980

Country	1962	1980
Australia	95.4	62.5*
Austria	79.9	50.6
Belgium	74.6	51.9*
Canada	109.5	58.3
Denmark	70.4	46.8
England and Wales	77.2	57.3
Finland	74.3	51.8
France	80.8	62.5
Germany (FDR)	76.4	41.0
Italy	73.3	46.3
Netherlands	88.8	51.2
New Zealand	116.3	65.9
Norway	75.2	55.2
Sweden	60.2	51.0
United States	97.3	61.5*

*1979
Source: UN Demographic Yearbook (United Nations, New York, 1981).

chief earner, and two or three children. But this traditional view fails to correspond to contemporary reality in a number of ways. One discrepancy is the widespread participation of women in the labour market. In Britain, between 1971 and 1981, women's participation rates increased from 55 per cent to 63 per cent. There was an even bigger increase in the proportion of mothers with dependent children under 16 who worked: 41 per cent in 1971, 52 per cent in 1981. Two points should be noted about these figures, however. First, a high proportion of women, and an even higher proportion of mothers, work part-time: in 1981 the part-time participation rates were 28 per cent for women generally and 35 per cent for mothers. Second, participation rates are much lower among mothers with pre-school children: in 1981, 27 per cent of such mothers worked, but only 7 per cent worked full-time.[44] Similar changes have occurred in the United States, where 'the proportion of working-age women in the labor force in recent decades has almost doubled, rising from 27 per cent in 1940 to 51 per cent in 1980' and where 'between 1960 and 1979 the proportion of married women in the labor force with children under six years of age more than doubled from 18 to 43 per cent'.[45] The changes in Sweden have been even more striking. In 1965, 27 per cent of all women in Sweden with children under the age of 7 were in paid employment, at least half-time. By 1984 this figure had increased to more than 80 per cent. The Swedish Institute makes the following comment.

The growing number of gainfully employed women reflects a profound and still continuing change in Swedish family patterns. During the first half of the 20th century, the predominant pattern was a gainfully employed man married to a housewife. Today the predominant pattern is the two-breadwinner family, i.e. where both husband and wife are gainfully employed—with short or long interruptions when children are born.[46]

A statement by the Danish government on the demographic structure in that country refers to the greatly increased proportion of married women in paid employment and the increased level of education among women and concludes that 'the number of children must conform with

the expectations with regard to training and work participation that are now entertained by both parents'.[47]

An OECD study of women's employment, published in
1984, refers to 'the dramatic global development of female
participation in the labour market over the last 30 years'.[48]
Taking all twenty-one member countries together, the
number of economically active women increased by 74 per
cent between 1950 and 1980. During the same period the
number of economically active men increased by 25 per
cent. Only Japan shows virtually no increase in female
participation.

The study demonstrates that participation rates vary with
age: the highest participation rates usually occur between
the ages of 20 and 24 and between 40 and 44, while rates
decline between the ages of 25 and 34. There are exceptions
to this, however. In Sweden, for example, female participation rates remain at over 80 per cent over the whole of
the age range of 20 to 54, and in the United States the rates
remain at over 60 per cent for the same age range. In
Belgium, by contrast, there is a steady decline in female
participation after the age of 29.

The extent of participation also varies from one country
to another. Denmark and Sweden have the highest rates of
participation, while Ireland, Italy and the Netherlands have
much lower rates than other advanced industrial nations.
It is possible that these variations are a reflection of the
availability of part-time work. The OECD report notes that
'a fairly large proportion of the female labour force consists
of part-time workers. Their share is high particularly in
the middle age groups'.[49] There are again great variations
between countries. In Norway, for example, about 54 per
cent of economically active women worked part-time in
1981, and the figure was only slightly lower in Sweden at
46.4 per cent. In Italy by contrast, only 5.8 per cent of
economically active women worked part-time. In the United
States the proportion of part-timers was 23.7 per cent and
in Britain it was 37.1 per cent. Ermisch claims that in Britain
'all of the net increase in women's jobs since 1961 is
accounted for by part-time jobs'.[50]

It is difficult to be certain about the consequence of these
changes for caring. At the very least one can say that paid

employment, even part-time, plus housework and child care does not leave much energy or time for other forms of care.

The growth in the number of one-parent families has created a further discrepancy between traditional stereo-types of the family and the real position. The increase in lone parenthood is largely, though not entirely, the consequence of the increasing incidence of divorce. Lesley Rimmer writes; 'In all countries where there is legal provision for divorce there has been an upward move in the number of divorces and in divorce rates'.[51]

Divorce rates in selected EEC countries appear in Table 4.2. It will be seen that Denmark leads the European league with 12.7 divorces per thousand existing marriages in 1983: an increase of over 100 per cent since 1960. The United Kingdom with a rate of 12.2 in 1983, has experienced easily the greatest increase in divorce since 1960—slightly more than 600 per cent. In the same period the divorce rate in the Netherlands increased by 430 per cent. Both Luxembourg and Belgium experienced increases in excess of 300 per cent. In the United States and Sweden almost half of all marriages end in divorce. Many of those who get divorced eventually remarry.

Table 4.2: Divorce rates in selected EEC Countries, 1960/ 1983

Country	Divorces per 1,000 existing marriages	
	1960	1983
Belgium	2.0	6.8
Denmark	5.9	12.7
Federal Republic of Germany	3.6	8.1
France	2.9	7.7
Italy	—	0.9
Luxembourg	2.0	6.4
Netherlands	2.2	9.4
United Kingdom	2.0	12.2

Source: Eurostat Demographic Statistics (Statistical Office of the European Communities, Luxembourg, 1985).

To sum up, although most people will experience a period when they live in families which conform to the stereotype of a married couple with the father in employment and the mother at home, this is no longer the most typical family pattern. At any one time in Britain, for example, only 15 per cent of families are of this kind, and one child in eight lives in a single-parent family. In the United States 18 per cent of all families with children are one-parent families, the vast majority of them headed by women.

It is obvious that divorces and remarriages considerably complicate kinship networks and responsibilities, but we need to know much more about the implications of this for caring. We need to know what obligations are seen as attaching to what relationships. Our knowledge at present is minimal and there is here a rich area for research.

THE FAMILY AND SOCIAL POLICY

There are several problems associated with any discussion of family policy. One problem is that many countries do not have any clearly identifiable policy which may be termed *family* policy. Kamerman and Kahn, in a study of government policy towards families, divide the fourteen countries covered into three categories:

(1) Those with an 'explicit, comprehensive family policy' (e.g. France, Norway and Sweden).
(2) Those with an 'explicit but more narrowly focused family policy' (e.g. Austria, Denmark, Finland and West Germany).
(3) Those 'without any explicit family policy and where the notion of such a policy is rejected' (e.g. Canada, Britain and the United States).[52]

A second problem relates to ideologies surrounding the family and to the disparity between rhetoric and action. There may be strongly expressed sentiments in support of the family, but these may not be matched by positive action and resources. There may be strong resistance to state intervention in what is seen as an essentially private institution.

A third problem is that family structures are so varied and policies may affect different families in different ways. Policies may be universal in scope or they may positively discriminate in favour of particular kinds of family (e.g. single-parent families, poor families). A further source of variation is that the objectives of family policy may change. Family policy in Sweden, for example, was originally concerned to encourage population growth, but more recently it has been seen as an important element in the movement towards equal opportunities.

Finally there is the problem of deciding what exactly constitutes family policy in any one country. Kamerman and Kahn distinguish between explicit and implicit policies. The second category includes policies not specifically or primarily addressed to the family but which have indirect consequences. The difficulty with the notion of implicit policies is that there are very few social policies which do not have consequences for families.

The range of material makes selection essential. Four areas will be briefly considered: social security policies, policies designed to relieve carers, labour market policies and family impact statements.

Social Security

All social security systems were originally based on the assumption that women were economically dependent upon men. Although this aspect of income maintenance is now changing—especially in Scandinavia but also in Britain and France, for example—progress has been slow and far from complete. In the main, the effect of the changes has been to enable either partner to claim for the other.

Child benefits or family allowances and maternity benefits are available, almost everywhere on a universal basis. The United States is virtually alone in providing no child benefits, and it shares with Australia the distinction of having no maternity benefits. The nearest approach in the United States is the Aid to Families with Dependent Children (AFDC), a means-tested scheme administered by the states, although financed partly by the federal government. The benefits are aimed at poor, single-parent families or families in which one of the parents is disabled or, in about half the states, when a parent is unemployed. In some states, especially since the early 1980s, workfare schemes have been introduced. Under these schemes AFDC claimants are expected to work as a condition of receiving the benefit.

A sharp contrast to the United States is provided by

Birmingham City University - Kenrick Library
Self Service Receipt for items borrowed

Title: Mixed economies of welfare : a
comparative perspective
Item: 6131350313
Due: 15/01/2009 23:59

Title: welfare state in transition : the theory and
practice of welfare plurali
Item: 6107624158
Due: 15/01/2009 23:59

Total items: 2
27/11/2008 11:15

Week loan items CANNOT be renewed.

France, Austria and Sweden, all three of which have extensive and generous family benefit systems. In France, for
example, there are family allowances, family income
supplements, antenatal and postnatal benefits, single-parent
allowances and starting-school allowances. Family allowances, which are not means-tested, are paid in respect of
all dependent children up to the age of 20. Antenatal and
postnatal benefits, also not means-tested, are paid for nine
months and two years respectively.

In Austria there are marriage benefits for those marrying
for the first time, family allowances (payable for all children
under the age of 19), lump-sum childbirth benefits (payable
at birth and when the child reaches its first birthday)
maternity benefits (payable to working mothers at a rate
equivalent to previous net earnings). In addition, mothers
are entitled to a year's extended maternity leave without
pay during which time they will be paid an allowance to
compensate for loss of earnings. Nursing mothers who
remain at work are entitled to a minimum of forty-five
minutes a day to allow them to attend to their children. In
the early 1980s, 3.5 per cent of the gross domestic product
went towards government family-welfare provision.
According to Münz and Wintersberger, family policy since
1970 has been used as an instrument of vertical
redistribution.[53]

In Sweden the thrust of family policy differs from that of
the French and Austrian systems in that it is more concerned
with equal opportunities between the sexes. In addition to
the usual maternity and child benefits, Sweden has a system
of parental insurance which enables new parents to take six
months off work and receive benefits equivalent to 90 per
cent of gross earnings. Parents may decide how the time
shall be split between them. A further six months' leave
with parental benefit is available at any time up to and
including the child's first year in school. Furthermore,
fathers are entitled to ten days' leave of absence with
parental benefit when a child is born even if the mother is
receiving benefit at the same time.

Relief of Carers
It has already been noted that caring generally bears more heavily on women than on men and that the burden is a heavy one. The burden can be lightened by provision of domiciliary services such as home helps, meals-on-wheels, health visitors, home nursing and social work support. In most Western European countries these services are a statutory responsibility, although frequently a charge is made. In the United States such services are more often obtained from private or voluntary sources, although the Older Americans Act empowers Area Agencies on Aging to fund or provide nutrition services, homemakers (home helps) and transport. In 1979 there were more than 6,600 nutrition programmes providing more than 250,000 meals daily.[54] If the experience of Britain is anything to go by, then male carers are much more likely than female carers to benefit from domiciliary services.

Short-stay residential care, day centres and night hospitals are obviously invaluable in affording carers some respite from the daily grind of looking after frail elderly or handicapped people. The general principle whould be that if families are to be expected to provide care for elderly and handicapped people, then it is up to government agencies to support them. A recent development in the voluntary field has been the establishment of mutual-support groups for carers.

Labour Market Policies
There are those who believe that the proper place of women is in the home and those who believe that women have as much right as men to paid work. This division of opinion was very clearly illustrated in the 1985 general election in Sweden. Roland Stanbridge, reporting on the election campaign in *The Guardian*, referred to party differences on 'the key ideological question of whether women should be working or staying at home with young children'.[55] The Moderate (conservative) Party proposed the eventual abolition of all public day-care facilities for children and promised a child-care compensation payment to allow mothers to stay at home. The Social Democrats, on the other hand, take the view 'that women should have the right to work

or, indeed, that women should work'.[56] This could be achieved by increasing the number of places in crèches. The stated policy of the Social Democratic Party is to ensure that by 1991 every child over the age of eighteen months should have the right to a place in a crèche. An interesting feature of this debate is that all parties share an assumption that women have the major responsibility for child care. The provision of a place in a crèche is to allow a *woman* to work. The family policy debate was a debate about *women's* rights.

Similar debates have taken place in other countries. In the United States Gilbert has criticised President Carter's 1980 Conference on Families for attempting to take into account a diversity of family forms, for paying insufficient attention to the needs of traditional families and for recommendations designed to make it easier for women to go out to work:

> while these recommendations for family policy offer something for everyone, there is relatively little here to nourish and support the traditional nuclear family as a child-rearing unit . . . Recommendations that seem to address the family unit directly lean more toward providing incentives and support for working mothers than toward sustaining intact families in which mothers might prefer to stay at home and perform the traditional child-care and home-making functions.[57]

Gilbert suggests that the trend should be reversed by compensating full-time homemakers. He suggests a social credit scheme in which people who stayed at home as full-time housekeepers would acquire credits which could be exchanged, when children had grown up, for so many units of academic or technical training.

Child-rearing is still generally regarded as a mainly female responsibility. The provision of day-care for children is therefore a crucial element in any equal opportunities policy. Day-care facilities may be provided by employers, statutory authorities, self-help groups or commercial undertakings. In the United States commercial concerns and employer-provided schemes are prominent. In Sweden, where day-care facilities are extensive, there is some commercial provision, but most day-care is provided by local authorities: in 1982 approximately 36 per cent of all children aged 0 to 6 were in local authority day nurseries, with 10 per cent in commercial establishments and 14 per cent in other forms of day-care. A Swedish Institute publication states that 'the expansion of day nurseries is an important element in a reorientation of Swedish family policy so that it also fulfils the needs of two-breadwinner families.'[58]

Norway and Denmark also have well-developed day-care systems. In West Germany there are very few facilities for children under 3, but a high proportion of children above that age attend kindergarten. Italy is very poorly served, and Questiaux and Fournier report a severe shortage of facilities in France.[59] Land and Parker have this to say about British policy in this area:

We feel that it is plausible to interpret this pattern of day-care policy in Britain as indicating a reluctance on the part of the state to share the care of young children with mothers except where it can be regarded as falling into areas of special or professional competence like education or medicine. Care and nurture of babies and infants must usually remain the clear responsibility of the family.[60]

In Britain public child-care facilities are extremely scarce and the availability of commercial services is very uneven. Consequently, many working mothers have to rely on informal arrangements within their circle of family, neighbours and friends. A study by the Department of Employment demonstrated that most child care, even when not undertaken by the mother was done on a voluntary, unpaid basis.[61] Other policies designed to facilitate two-wage families include the encouragement of part-time work, job-sharing, flexi-time arrangements and parental leave.

Family-Impact Studies

One of the aims of family-impact studies is to focus attention on the family. Policies would be evaluated in terms of their likely impact on families of different kinds, and a family-impact statement might accompany all new legislation. Existing policies and policies in the process of implementation would be similarly evaluated and monitored. Most policies have a family dimension: social security, health services, services for elderly and disabled people, education, child care, housing, fiscal, transport and employment policies are obvious candidates for systematic family-impact evaluation. At the very least, conflicting aims and effects might be exposed.

The use of family-impact studies was one of the recommendations of the White House Conference on Families, and some experiments along these lines have been conducted in Australia. The Study Commission on the Family has also recommended the adoption of such a system in Britain. So far, however, no country has adopted the idea.

THE NEW RIGHT AND THE FAMILY

Conservatives have always been supporters of the family, frequently bemoaning its decline, which they see as the cause of declining standards of discipline among the young and, more broadly, of declining moral and religious standards throughout society. The family, when properly functioning, is seen as an effective means of socialisation and social control: it is a source of stability in the married partners, and it provides a stable background for the rearing of children who develop into well-adjusted adults. Since the family is such an important influence, it follows that many social problems will be seen as stemming from inadequate and unstable families. Parties of the Right in all countries stress the importance of the family, but it is, of course, the virtues of the traditional family, a married couple with dependent children and a non-working mother, that they are extolling. However, it is not only conservatives who attach importance to families. The White House conference on Families provides an illustration of political concern among liberals in the United States, for example. But, as Peele explains, the Conference served to highlight the fundamental differences between liberal and conservative perspectives on family policy:

Thus, if family policy for liberals entailed programs designed to provide safety-nets and support when the free-enterprise system failed to function efficiently . . . the right's understanding of family policy was very different. Conservatives wanted programs designed to strengthen traditional family relationships and to bolster parental authority.[62]

According to American conservatives, the best way to strengthen the family is to keep government out and leave families to make their own decisions. The state and the family are seen as being in direct opposition. A good example of this position in British conservatism is to be found in Mount's book *The Subversive family*,[63] which has been described by one critic as 'a classical statement in the anti-collectivist tradition of the ideological opposition between family and state' which provides 'a good deal of fuel for the rhetoric of the new right'.[64]

There has always been a strong support for the family from religion. This has been particularly obvious in Catholic countries such as Spain and Italy. The Catholic Church's strictures on divorce, contraception and abortion have been given wide coverage, and the debate need not be summarised here. Rather more interesting, perhaps, is evangelical Christianity in the United States and its crusade for a return to traditional values. Peele argues that 'the emphasis on family or social issues which characterized the new right in 1970s was in part a response to the perceived permissiveness of an earlier decade'.[65] According to the New Right it is the welfare state and social-democratic philosophy which have led to what it perceives as a decline in the family and the consequent erosion of decent moral and religious standards. An alliance of the political and the religious Right will reverse the trend by restoring the family to a centrally important place in American society. The religious Right and the political Right have been brought together, according to Peele, by 'the appearance of a set of issues on the national agenda of interest to conservative Christians'. This set of issues 'has come to be known as "family issues" or "social issues", and they are central to the activity of both the new right and the religious right'.[66] The issues Peele refers to are abortion, support for Church schools, expecially those established by fundamentalist and Baptist Churches, and a host of moral questions concerned with sexual permissiveness, homosexuality and general moral decadence. Time and again conservative writers in the

United States make the connection between family, religion and morality. Kristol, for example, claims that 'neoconservatives look upon family and religion as indispensable pillars of a decent society.'[67]

In Britain and continental Europe fundamentalist religion is not such a prominent political force as it is in the United States. It is true that Britain has Mary Whitehouse, Lord Longford, the Festival of Light and a number of born-again Christians, but they are less politically significant than are similar groups in the United States. In Britain the Church of England, described by Sydney Smith as 'the Tory Party at Prayer', probably has more influence within the conservative Party than has evangelical Christianity.

The family is seen by Mrs Thatcher as an important element in her strategy for transforming British society. Fitzgerald argues that the shift from an interventionist state to a minimum state gives a central role to the family:

It becomes clear that Thatcherism's strategy must include not only the transformation of the economic field from being that of a 'mixed economy' to that of a free market order, but the transformation of the socio-political—a transformation which shifts the key role in this field from the state to the family.[68]

In conservative parties everywhere, marriage and motherhood are regarded as the basis of the family. A report from the Conservative Political Centre describes marriage as 'the vital link which binds together the family'.[69] David claims that the New Right is trying to revive a model of the private family through 'social policies which increasingly celebrate motherhood as a crucial social activity for all women'.[70] In the traditional view of the family mothers are expected not to work. Mothering for women is seen as 'natural': since it is only women who can bear children, it is only women who can be expected to nurture them. It is a fact of biology as is a man's 'natural instinct' to provide for his wife and children. Fitzgerald describes this socio-biological perspective as 'biological essentialism', which is 'implicit in neo-liberalism'.[71]

Mrs Thatcher draws parallels between running a family and running a government. Nevertheless, it is ironic that she should be encouraging women to be satisfied with wife-

hood and motherhood when she herself is a career politician. The explanation for this apparent contradiction is
that there are some exceptional women who need the stimulation of a career.

In many ways the New Right is looking back with
nostalgia to a largely mythical golden age of the family; this
is certainly true of Mrs Thatcher's desire for a return to
Victorian values. It would be a mistake, however, to dismiss
this view as no more than nostalgia. The restoration of the
family to a pre-eminent position in society is part of a much
broader plan to privatise welfare provision. The neo-liberal
vision of the minimum state implies a drastic reduction in
the welfare role of the state and a transfer of functions
and responsibilities to other institutions. It is assumed that
families are both willing and able to take on a heavier caring
role than they accept at present. The evidence suggests that
this assumption may be unfounded.

FRIENDS AND NEIGHBOURS

The overwhelming importance of kinship ties in informal
caring is confirmed by many studies in many countries.
Much less work has been done on friends and neighbours
as sources of care. Friends have one important characteristic
which distinguishes them from kin and neighbours: one
chooses one's friends but not one's kin and neighbours.
Friends are distinguished from neighbours by their wide
dispersal, and from kin by a lack of diversity in terms of
age, stage of the life-cycle and social class.

Friendship depends on a degree of equality between
participants; it is a reciprocal relationship. A one-sided
caring relationship is not likely to lead to or to sustain
friendship. As Allan observes, friends must be capable of
contributing 'equivalent financial and emotional resources
to the relationship'.[72] Allan's conclusion, shared by other
workers in this field, is that:

While part of friendship is caring about each other to a greater or lesser
degree, caring for one another is not an element inherent in the routine
organization of friendship . . . the majority of routine friendships are not

particularly well suited for providing the sort of caring community care entails, notwithstanding the friendship ideals that might make one think they would be.[73]

Willmott reaches the same conclusion. He says that people have more social contacts with friends than with kin, but that 'in terms of help the bias is the other way . . . at the critical stages, such as old age, infirmity and when babies are born, relatives outnumber friends as sources of support in the ratio of ten to one.'[74]

There are class, gender and age differences in friendship. Middle-class people have more friends than working-class people and men have more friends than do women. Middle-class people tend to have a higher proportion than working-class people of non-local friends. The same is true for men as compared to women. Young people have more friends than older people.

Friends and neighbours may of course correspond, but close proximity can also inhibit friendship because of possible invasions of privacy. As Froland *et al.* state:

While some neighbours may come to be defined as friends, in general the relationship combines a high level of knowledge about many aspects of one another's lives with a fairly low level of involvement . . . Compared to family and friends, there are generally more defined limits on the forms of helping that are appropriate to ask for and offer.[75]

Another American writer, Gilbert, says that 'although decisive evidence on neighborly aid is unavailable, there are reasons to believe that it constitutes a shallow reservoir of social support best suited for temporary help on simple problems'.[76] Willmott refers to studies which demonstrate rather more involvement of neighbours in providing companionship for, and generally keeping an eye on, elderly people.

From the quotation given above it appears that Froland *et al.* see friendship as more important in informal relationships than neighbourliness. Abrams, in considering the relationship between friendship and neighbourliness, argues that in many traditional communities people formed their friendships within their neighbourhoods, and it was friendship within neighbourhoods which gave rise to high levels of neighbourliness. The conditions which produced friendships within neighbourhoods are now rare, and their passing, says Abrams, 'can hardly be lamented'. High levels of neighbourliness occur in localities characterised by isolation, closure and shared adversity.[77]

The services provided by both neighbours and friends are straightforward tasks implying strictly limited involvement: baby-sitting, looking after children during their mothers' temporary absence, taking in deliveries, looking after keys, shopping, sharing in transporting children to and from school, borrowing and lending. It would be a mistake to diminish the importance of such tasks, but it is quite plain that they do not even begin to form an adequate basis for the development of community care policies.

Willmott, adapting categories developed in the Dinnington Project in South Yorkshire, distinguishes four categories of informal care:

(1) Personal care, which includes washing, bathing, dressing, feeding and toileting—general attention to bodily needs and comforts corresponding to Parker's notion of 'tending'.
(2) Domestic care—cooking, cleaning and laundering.
(3) Auxiliary care—mainly less onerous tasks including those already identified as being performed by friends and neighbours, but also odd-jobbing and gardening.
(4) Social support—visiting and companionship.[78]

Willmott adds a fifth, more limited service which he calls surveillance, keeping an eye on vulnerable people.

This is a helpful categorisation of services. Insofar as it relates to informal care, personal services are performed almost entirely by kin, and this may be true also of domestic care. The last two categories and surveillance are where friends and neighbours are more prominent, although kin will also be involved.

Willmott's categories serve to underline the predominance of kin in the informal system of care. The tasks calling for long-term commitment and a considerable emotional investment fall to kin. Friends and neighbours make a contribution, but this does not alter the conclusion that community care is family care.

THE INFORMAL SECTOR AND WELFARE PLURALISM

The evidence that the informal sector provides more care than the statutory, voluntary or commercial sectors is incontrovertible. That families overwhelmingly predominate in the informal system of care is equally certain. It is beyond doubt, too, that within families women are the main carers.

The lives of carers are frequently restricted, with few contacts outside the home and with little help from voluntary or statutory services. Parker, in a review of research on informal care, comments:

The evidence we are able to glean from various sources suggests that available services are likely to have little overall effect for informal carers. Firstly, few dependent people who have informal carers appear to receive services and, when they do, such services are usually crisis-orientated rather than a part of long-term support. Secondly, the criteria by which services are allocated are often irrational (not allocated in relation to need) and discriminatory (not provided where female carers are available).[79]

Welfare pluralists are anxious to strengthen the informal system by linking it with the statutory and voluntary sectors. Some of the innovatory British projects, mainly experiments with the patch system and other forms of decentralisation, have given welfare pluralists the opportunity to evaluate different ways of interweaving formal and informal care. Bayley and Tennant in describing the Dinnington project say that 'the main aim was to interweave the help and resources of the formal health and welfare services with the informal support and help given by family, friends and neighbours, together with the contribution of the voluntary sector'.[80] They acknowledge that the informal sector is the most significant provider of care and say that 'the task of statutory and voluntary care is to support and strengthen that care, not to undermine it'.[81] They point out that this does not imply a reduction in statutory effort. Indeed, one result of decentralisation is an increase in referrals—a six-fold increase in Dinnington. Whether the supply of informal carers can be increased by the same order of magnitude may be doubted.

The decentralised, participative approach favoured by

welfare pluralists is not without its critics. Pinker in his memorandum of dissent from the Barclay Report makes two criticisms of the neighbourhood or patch system. The first is that in this system 'the most vulnerable, disadvantaged and stigmatised clients will be at greatest risk . . . since they give greatest offence to local norms of behaviour and are often rejected by their local communities'.[82] Pinker's second worry is the invasions of privacy such a system could entail:

> It is argued that in a patch system social work staff would be able to build up a detailed knowledge of the local patterns of informal care and that this knowledge will be augmented by fostering contacts with intermediaries or 'gatekeepers' including people such as publicans, corner shop-keepers, lollypop ladies, and so on . . . In some of the areas operating a patch system it appears that local commercial enterprises such as pubs and corner shops would become recognised as important sources of information.[83]

Pinker insists that a respect for persons implies respecting people's privacy and their right to confidentiality.

Glennerster also expresses some doubts. First, he is doubtful about the patches' ability to relate to the NHS, especially at regional level. Second, he believes that the patch system would hold back the development of specialist teams which he considers to have been the most productive innovation in recent years. Finally, he argues that the success of such schemes is dependent upon the commitment of a great deal of scarce management time and effort, 'which may draw people's attention and enthusiasm away from improving links between personal social services and the health service on which I think community care primarily depends'.[84]

The assumption made by conservative governments that the informal system of care can compensate for a reduction in statutory services has to be seriously questioned on the basis of the evidence. In the case of families, the assumption is probably erroneous; in the case of friends and neighbours it is probably over optimistic. This is not to deny the significance of the informal sector, but rather to doubt its capacity for absorbing *extra* work. In fact, social and demographic changes may be reducing the family's capacity to care, while at the same time the number of people requiring care is increasing. Policies which take little or no account of these changes, and many appear not to, can only be unrealistic and thus fail to meet their objectives.

When the costs of community care are calculated the social costs, in terms of physical, psychological and financial strain on families, and especially on women, have to be considered, even though it may be difficult to place a money value on them. The exploitative nature of family care has constantly to be borne in mind. It is fatuous to talk about equality of opportunity for women in employment if the sexual division of labour persists in the home. This feature of family care is not given much attention in the welfare pluralist literature. The principal objective of social policy in relation to the informal sector should not be to pressurise people into taking on extra responsibility, but to provide them with a realistic choice. In cases where people *choose* to care for frail elderly or disabled relatives, they should be given every possible support. The support they know to be available will be one of the considerations when people make their choice. Those who choose not to provide direct care should feel confident that acceptable alternative services exist. If welfare pluralism has any merit at all then it must be concerned to extend choice, not restrict it.

5 The Voluntary Sector and Social Welfare

The voluntary sector is distinguished from the informal sector by its greater degree of organisation, but within the voluntary sector itself there are different degrees of formality: small neighbourhood groups and small self-help groups are relatively informal while at the other extreme are the large charitable foundations.

The term 'voluntary sector' is vague and requires expansion and clarification before its role in welfare pluralism can be usefully examined. An important preliminary distinction is that between volunteers and voluntary organisations. Volunteers or voluntary workers, in the purest sense, are people who receive no payment for what they do, although out-of-pocket expenses may be reimbursed. In recent years, however, the term 'volunteer' has also been used to describe non-professional helpers who are paid small amounts for their services. A European Symposium on Para-professionals and Volunteers in Social Welfare reported 'differing views as to whether a volunteer should ever be paid other than expenses for voluntary work', but noted that there seemed to be 'an increasing number of volunteer schemes which include modest payment for particularly difficult or time-consuming work'[1] Voluntary workers may be used by either statutory or voluntary organisations, and voluntary organisations may employ paid workers. Voluntary organisations are not therefore to be distinguished from statutory agencies on the basis of the kind of workers they employ.

A voluntary organisation is defined most simply as a non-statutory body; it owes its existence not to an Act of Parlia-

ment but to the decision of a group of people to join together for purposes of mutual aid (e.g. self-help and co-operative groups of various kinds), to protect or promote their
own interests (e.g. trade unions and professional associations), to provide services for, and campaign on behalf of,
particular sections of the population (e.g. disabled or elderly
people, single-parent families), or to promote causes (e.g.
penal reform, nuclear disarmament, environmental
protection).

The enormous number and variety of groups will be
immediately apparent. Even though this chapter is restricted
to social welfare organisations, its scope remains uncomfort-
ably large. The following list of types of social welfare
groups gives an indication of the range of the voluntary
sector:

(1) Neighbourhood organisations.
(2) Self-help or mutual-aid groups.
(3) Organisations providing services for groups of
    'clients'.
(4) Pressure groups.
(5) Groups primarily concerned with medical or social
    research.
(6) 'Umbrella' or intermediary organisations concerned
    with the co-ordination of other groups and the
    provision of resources for them.

Even this fails to give a true picture of the variety. For
example, many groups will be hybrids of the above types
and within each type there are variations in size, structure,
sources of finance, relationships with each other and with
statutory bodies and staffing arrangements; some organisations will be entirely local; some will be affiliated to
national organisations and others will be national organisations with local branches.

So far the references in this discussion have been to the
'voluntary sector', and to 'voluntary organisations', which is
the terminology used in Britain and most Western European
countries. This terminology will predominate throughout
this chapter, but it should be recognised that American
practice is different. In the United States it is usual to
distinguish between the public sector and the private sector

and then to subdivide the latter into the business sector and the non-profit sector consisting of organisations which 'are privately controlled, usually by a volunteer board, yet do not exist to make a profit'.[2] The report of the Filer Commission referred to the non-profit sector as the third sector—after business and government.[3]

The United States is one of three countries upon which this chapter will focus, the others being Britain and the Netherlands. These three are sufficiently different to make comparisons interesting, and between them they demonstrate most of the characteristics to be found elsewhere.

NEIGHBOURHOOD GROUPS

In Chapter 4 we looked at the role of informal care provided by friends and neighbours and noted the claim made by several writers that informal neighbourliness does not and cannot provide continuous, consistent long-term care. We are here concerned with voluntary neighbourhood *groups*. The titles given to such initiatives vary, but the one thing they all have in common is their territorial basis. Abrams, Abrams and Davison suggest that ideally the areas should contain 'not much more than 2,000 households'.[4] In the United States Froland *et al.* examined nineteen neighbourhood programmes covering populations ranging from 100 to 100,000: one-third of the projects were in neighbourhoods with populations between 5,000 and 10,000 and one-third were in neighbourhoods with populations between 10,000 and 50,000.[5]

The groups are deliberately trying to recreate or cultivate neighbourliness: they are attempting to create relationships which approximate to those they imagine used to characterise informal neighbourliness among actual neighbours in traditional communities. It is for this reason, according to Abrams, Abrams and Davison, that good-neighbour schemes place so much emphasis on visiting:

The conception of a project as 'neighbourly' is embodied above all in the practice of visiting other people's homes. But Good Neighbour schemes are distinguished . . . by their specific and explicit wish to use visiting as a means to a more general end—the cultivation of neighbourliness as a strong, informal pattern of social life. . . . at the same time the organisational structure of the schemes is designed to ensure that unlike actual or natural neighbours these quasi-neighbours will be reliable monitors of need, and in some limited respects givers of care.[6]

Although visiting is here identified as the distinguishing activity of neighbourhood schemes, it is by no means the only one. The provision of transport and the operation of transport pools constitutes another common feature. Neighbourhood advice centres are also commonly found, sometimes as a focal point for a much broader range of provision. Neighbourhood centres were a prominent feature of the anti-poverty programmes in Britain and the United States. Higgins notes that many of the 1,000 Community Action Agencies in the American War on Poverty 'chose to provide a one-stop neighbourhood service centre offering a wide variety of facilities'.[7]

Other activities include the provision of day centres, clubs and neighbourhood shops. Sitting services are frequently organised for families with young children or for those caring for sick or elderly people. Many neighbourhood schemes have experimented with street or block wardens in an attempt to provide those requiring help with a known point of contact who would be expected to mobilise formal and informal resources. Some problems have been encountered in the operation of such schemes, the chief one being a shortage of people seeking help. This is a problem identified by Abrams, Abrams and Davison in some of the British good-neighbour schemes. A clue to the reasons for failure may be found in some of the American literature on 'natural' neighbourhood helpers. In many local communities there are people to whom others turn for help and advice, and before a neighbourhood scheme is established such people must be identified and their agreement to act as contacts must be sought. Froland *et al.* describe a neighbourhood-awareness project which attempted to build up a network of 'block watch' groups as a crime prevention measure. People were persuaded, sometimes against their will, to 'volunteer' their services. The scheme collapsed because people did not know and trust each other. Most schemes now attempt to identify key personnel and secure their co-operation before block associations are founded, and this has proved to be a much more successful strategy. The authors note that 'although the groups are initially mobilised around the issue of crime, contact among neighbours becomes more generalised and some groups have assumed more "neighborly" roles'.[8]

In this way, such groups begin to take on the characteristics of a residents' or tenants' association, both of which are common. In Britain, for example, associations of local authority tenants increased rapidly during the 1970s, and in 1977 a National Tenants' Organisation was formed. The associations are partly pressure groups on behalf of tenants and partly social groups. Regular consultative arrangements are usually established, and tenants become involved in the day-to-day management of their estates. Ann Richardson says of these schemes:

The actual functions of tenant participation schemes vary considerably. Some operate as *de facto* complaint forums, in which tenants raise specific problems concerning housing maintenance and other local management issues. Others involve regular discussion of broader issues, such as estate modernisation plans or proposed changes in administrative procedures. Some explicitly preclude consideration of any financial issues, such as rents, but others enable these matters to be discussed along with any other issues tenants wish to raise.[9]

The 1980 Housing Act required all local authorities to establish schemes for tenant participation in the management of their estates, but no guidance was given as to the form this might take.

Similar developments have occurred in the United States, where tenants' groups have proliferated in recent years. Atlas and Dreier sum up the American position: 'Tenant activism developed steadily during the 1970s and early 1980s. Tenant groups now exist in almost every city and many suburbs. These include building-level, citywide and several statewide tenant groups. A National Tenants Union was formed in 1980 to help coordinate the growing number of tenant activities'.[10]

Residents' and tenants' associations are also a prominent feature of housing in the Netherlands. An interesting aspect of Dutch housing policy is that grants are available 'for additional expenditure associated with certain participation procedures involved in new housing development'.[11] Reports of the procedures and of the use made of them by future occupants must be submitted for approval by the housing authorities before grants are paid.

In tenants' associations we have another example of neighbourhood groups growing up around a single, though many-faceted, issue. Through interaction on a specific issue, some groups generate more varied neighbourhood activities; some attach themselves to general-purpose community groups. In the United States, for example, many tenants' groups are attached to such organisations as the Association of Community Organisations for Reform Now, National People's Action or the Industrial Areas Foundation. Twelvetrees, in a discussion of these organisations, claims that they are adopting the militant, overtly political style pioneered by Saul Alinsky. All three employ paid organisers who 'seek to mobilise large numbers of people in poor neighbourhoods on the basis of "self interest" and "power" '.[12] The organisers attempt to recruit primary leaders indigenous to the neighbourhood by 'establishing relationships with people . . . who want power'. Abrams' notion of 'modern neighbourhoodism' also emphasises the political nature of neighbourhood groups. Abrams argues that traditional forms of neighbourhood care in intensely local, homogeneous communities are dying because the conditions which gave rise to them are dying. Modern neighbourhoodism, by contrast, is thriving:

Modern neighbourhoodism in its purest form is an attempt by newcomers . . . to *create* a local social world through political or quasi-political action. Great organisational skills . . . are often used in attempts . . . to protect amenities, enhance resources and, to a greater or lesser degree, wrench control of the local *milieu* from outside authorities and vest it in strictly local hands. Much of the driving force and most of the success of the enormous diversity of neighbourhood care projects . . . springs from these sources.[13]

The political objectives of neighbourhood groups are inseparable from economic considerations. Urban deprivation, housing and unemployment, for example, are both political and economic issues, and economic regeneration has to accompany, if not precede, social regeneration. With this in mind, neighbourhood projects frequently concern themselves with economic development and with the establishment and running of community businesses. This aspect of community action is most fully developed in the Community Development Corporations (CDCs) stemming from the American anti-poverty programmes of the 1960s. According to Twelvetrees, 'the idea behind CDCs is that the neighbourhood should control the revitalisation process'.[14] The problem of running a business in a ghetto and the lack of local commercial, management and technical expertise meant that profitable enterprises, in the early years at least, were a rarity. They are still far from common, but those CDCs which have learnt from past mistakes are now running a variety of successful businesses. Profitable enterprise undoubtedly has the capacity to increase the prosperity of a neighbourhood provided the profits go back into the community and provided the workforce is drawn from the local area, but the problems of decaying inner-city areas are so immense as to call for a massive injection of resources, and the pressure for profitable operation may mean that the social objectives of the projects are pushed to one side.

Conflicting objectives is by no means the only possible danger that neighbourhood groups have to guard against. Another is too great a reliance on one or two key people. If for some reason key personnel have to curtail or relinquish their activities, the group may disintegrate. If key personnel are paid professionals there is the danger of their being too directive. There are fine distinctions to be made between advice and guidance and direction.

An even more fundamental problem is the degree to which voluntary neighbourhood organisations are seen as offering a solution to the problems of deprived areas. Davidoff and Gould, writing of the American poverty programmes, comment, 'What these programmes have in common is an underlying strategy based on a false assumption—the assumption that because the problems of race and poverty are found in the ghettos the solution to these problems must also be found there.'.[15] Benington, the director of the Coventry Community Development Project, makes a similar comment about the British anti-poverty programmes:

Because their causes do not operate at the local level alone, many of these problems are not susceptible to solution at the local level alone. Self-help and community action may help to gain marginal improvements and some compensatory provision. But the crucial determinants of the residents' quality of life remain unaltered.[16]

As Benington's statement implies, the Community Development Projects linked a neighbourhood approach with ideologies of self-help. As attention in the next section switches from neighbourhood groups to organisations based on principles of self-help, this potential overlap must not be forgotten. Analytically, however, the two types of organisation may be treated separately. Interestingly, Pancoast, Froland and Parker argue that common interests are now becoming more significant than neighbourhood ties:

self-help initiatives at the local level reflect a greater emphasis on communities of interest rather than communities of propinquity. . . . While neighborhoods are still the base for some social bonds, the relevant ties for many . . . are developing increasingly from among disparate contacts. Out of these, a collective identity based on mutual interests can be forged.[17]

SELF-HELP

Self-help is an old idea revived and given fresh impetus in recent years. A classic treatise on self-help is that written by Samuel Smiles in Victorian England. But Smiles was writing about individuals rising from humble circumstances to achieve fame and fortune through showing initiative and enterprise, perseverance, diligence and thrift.[18] Self-help in this meaning of the term has needed very little revival. It has never been entirely absent, and it was built into the welfare state which many supposed to be based on quite different principles.

The term 'self-help' may be misleading on two counts: it is frequently associated with *laissez-faire* policies and it is very often equated with individuals' self-regarding actions. Neither of these is an essential feature of self-help.

Our focus here, however, is not so much upon individuals helping themselves, or even upon individuals helping their neighbours, as upon *groups* whose main purpose is *mutual* aid and concerted action: self-help 'at a collective rather than individual level'.[19] Self-help groups are formed by people who have a shared problem, or concern, joining together for mutual support and the provision of services to members; most will also be concerned with pressing the case of the particular social, medical or cultural group from which members are drawn.

The very rapid growth of self-help groups is one of the most obvious and significant features of the voluntary sector in recent years. Writing of the United States, Wollert and Barron say:

Self-help groups, in which members share a common concern and assume primary responsibility for both organisational direction and mutual assistance, have emerged over the last several decades as a robust social phenomenon in the United States. It has been estimated . . . that well over a half million self-help groups currently exist in this country . . . and that at least 14 million citizens are members[20]

Bakker and Karel describe a similar development in the Netherlands, although they see it as having occurred more recently:

In Dutch society in the early 1970s, many new small groups developed, people joining hands to cope with particular problems: because they suffered from an unfamiliar disease, because they were parents of a handicapped child, or because they felt alienated from society. . . . It is interesting to note that these self-formed groups are active in all parts of the welfare state[21]

Richardson describes the British scene in the following way:

Self-help groups have burgeoned in recent years, taking on not only common and familiar problems but also those of a much rarer nature. There are groups for people with all sorts of handicaps . . . for people with all sorts of diseases . . . to help people conquer certain addiction and behavioural problems and separate groups for their relatives . . . for people who face . . . widowhood, a stillbirth, infertility or bringing up a family on their own.[22]

An indication of the rapid growth in the number of self-help groups is the spread of self-help clearing houses which act as both information and resource centres. The clearing-house idea began in the United States, where clearing-houses are now widespread and firmly established. Clearing-houses are at present sprouting in most Western European countries, including Britain and the Netherlands. A clearing-house should provide a forum for the exchange of ideas and information and should be able to advise those wishing to establish self-help groups about how to proceed. Another clearing-house task is the maintenance of a directory. Even when directories exist, however, it is difficult to be precise about the number of groups in any one country, because some groups are small and local and the picture is constantly changing as some groups disappear and new ones emerge.

Wollert and Barron look at the factors favouring the growth of self-help groups in American society. They identify three sets of variables. The first set relates to pressures for extra resources arising from an erosion of traditional sources of help, weak governmental support for the development of formal programmes and the inability of the public and private sectors to provide effective services. The second group of factors refers to the importance of values, ideals and beliefs such as religious fundamentalism, democratic ideals, a belief in self-reliance and a distrust of social service professionals. The final set of influences are the benefits which people expect to gain from joining together.[23] Some of these factors relate specifically to the nature of American society and would not necessarily explain parallel developments in other countries.

The failure of statutory services to meet needs is frequently cited as a reason for the growth of self-help organisations. This is a popular theme among welfare pluralists, but the anti-state libertarian Left and the New Right also support self-help arrangements. By its proponents self-help is seen as a justified and healthy reaction against a welfare state in which bureaucrats and professionals predominate.

There appears to be widespread agreement about the anti-bureaucratic, anti-professional element in many of the self-help initiatives, and one is tempted to suggest that New Right criticisms of big government and bureaucracy have not only taken root but also borne fruit. However, as the discussion proceeds it will become apparent that this is only one facet, though an important one, in a complex interplay of influences.

The arguments relating to bureaucracy are the familiar ones of remoteness, inflexibility and unresponsiveness to needs. Rules, regulations and formal procedures are possibly appropriate in the case of standard cash benefits, but they become less so when dealing with more individual and more personal needs. Because many needs are not being adequately met, and because people feel powerless when faced with a large bureaucracy, clients and potential clients become disenchanted with statutory services and turn to self-help as a viable alternative.

Self-help is consistent with welfare pluralist strategies of decentralisation and participation. Although many local self-help groups are affiliated to national organisations, self-help is typically a local activity. By its very nature self-help is participatory, although the degree to which members wish to participate will vary, some being continuously active, some taking part from time to time and some whose membership entails little more than the payment of a subscription and the receipt of literature.

Self-help, it is claimed, can be a means of giving people more control over their lives by reducing their dependence on both statutory help and professional workers. The report of a European Symposium on Para-professionals and Volunteers included the following comment:

> There are strong indications of an anti-professions, self-help movement growing in several societies. Ivan Illich in particular has argued that in dealing with health and welfare problems we have become too dependent upon the official agencies and their professionals and many of us would benefit by doing much more for ourselves and for one another. This is not necessarily a reactionary, conservative view.[24]

Relationships between health and welfare professionals and their clients, between providers and recipients, are unequal. They are unilateral in that the client has nothing to offer in exchange for the service which therefore takes the form of a gift.[25] Clients are forced to accept professionals' definitions of problems and needs which may not accord with their own interpretations. By contrast, in self-help organisations the distinction between providers and receivers is blurred or non-existent, and it is members who control both the organisation and the definition of problems and needs. Not only do such organisations reduce stigma by reducing dependence, but they may very well produce a more accurate identification of need. People who have themselves suffered from a particular disability, for example, or those who have cared for someone with such a disability are likely to know much more than doctors or social workers about its impact and management. In a self-help organisation the combined knowledge of the membership is potentially at the disposal of all those who need to avail themselves of it. A long-established self-help group will have built up a store of specialist information much of which will not be available from any other source. Furthermore, members learn by doing, and this, together with the availability of mutual support, increases confidence, and they have the satisfaction of doing things for themselves.

There is quite obviously a powerful ideology of self-help which becomes even more marked when some of the newer, more militant groups are considered. The increasingly political nature of many self-help groups is commented upon by several writers. Pancoast, Parker and Froland, for example, writing about the United States, say that 'from the 1950s to the 1970s, a new force emerged, the increased politicisation of self-help, which is associated with the civil rights movement, the women's movement, consumer groups, and the like'.[26] Similarly, Bakker and Karel, writing of the Netherlands, identify 'the themes of social and political liberation: emancipation, interest promotion and autonomy all representing self-help as a liberating force in relation to social and political ideologies in society'.[27] Lawrence, commenting on the position in Britain, writes of groups which 'are suspicious of the centralised and highly structured state apparatus' and have developed 'collective forms of organisation which are derived from shared experiences and a common perception of their status, one which is generally at odds with the state's perception of them'.[28] It should be apparent that the organisations referred to by the writers quoted above are very different from the archetypal self-help organisation, Alcoholics Anonymous.

Women's groups have been among the most prominent of the more militant self-help organisations during the last two decades. A wide variety of such groups exists. In Holland, for example, an official publication identifies three brands of feminism, each comprising several groups: civil rights feminism, concerned with equal rights for women; social feminism 'that regards the liberation of women as being linked to the struggle against inequality between social classes': radical feminism 'which conceives of the strategy for the liberation of women in terms of the detachment of women from all social structures created by men, and the creation of a separate culture'.[29] Most feminist groups challenge existing structures, are non-hierarchical and work on the principles of self-help and self-determination. This is true, for example, of groups providing refuges for battered women.

Radical support for self-help stems from its potential as a participatory alternative to state services. It gives working-class and disadvantaged people more control over their lives and enables them to articulate demands for a greater share of resources. Insofar as these demands are met, self-help may lead to a reduction in inequality. Changes in service delivery, however, are unlikely to have more than a marginal effect on inequality. While self-help groups may give a voice to consumers, and to some extent challenge professional dominance, no great disturbance of power relationships is involved.

There are some grounds for doubting the capacity of self-help organisations to achieve even these marginal changes. As Lawrence says, 'Self help groups are not by definition radical. Indeed, the skills, time and energy required to organise such groups may result in their being either more successful and sustained in middle class areas or dominated by an unrepresentative section of their membership'.[30] Finch, in a very interesting study of pre-school playgroups in deprived areas of Lancashire, found that self-help was largely a myth insofar as working-class women were concerned. Finch argues that setting up and operating a self-help group is largely a middle-class activity, and she doubts whether working-class women can easily take on such roles. Furthermore, there is evidence to suggest that working-class women do not want this kind of provision. Finally, voluntary supervision of a playgroup for a certain number of sessions a week does not meet the requirements of women who wish to work. As a consequence, such groups tend either to collapse or to abandon the principle of self-help. Finch concludes that the promotion of self-help playgroups is essentially deceitful for three reasons:

First, encouraging the women to run their own preschool facilities rather than seek an extension of statutory resources is deceitful because it promotes a form of provision which such women cannot supply for themselves. Second, the idea of self-help obscures the fact that what is being sought are facilities on the cheap, incorporating the unpaid labour of mothers themselves . . . Third, as a form of preschool provision, playgroups make no contribution whatsoever to the needs of parents in paid work, since they both assume and encourage full-time mothering.[31]

Morgan provides an example of how governments and professionals can subvert and depoliticise self-help. Her analysis refers to the United States, but there are clear implications for other countries. In the United States and elsewhere refuges for battered women were initially established and run by small feminist collectives with the dual aim of providing a place of safety and promoting among the women an understanding of their structural position. Shortage of funds forced the refuges to seek financial help from the state. This was given, but at a cost to the groups of abandoning their political aims. The problem of wife-battering was reformulated in terms of individual pathology rather than structure. Centres became much larger, more service-orientated, more deversified and the principles of self-help were lost:

Refuges, formerly run by small collectives of feminist activists, often with a strong community base, were replaced by larger 'service' centers administered by boards of directors and staffed by professionals . . . whereas once the aim was to educate women to live independent lives, it shifted toward family reunification. Where once the impact of gender domination was raised as a way of understanding violent abuse of women, now the focus is on individual pathology . . . and the psychological profile of the victim.[32]

Governments have always been prepared to tolerate self-help organisations provided they posed no political threat. Self-help groups certainly have the potential for challenging the status quo, but, as the Finch example shows, the state may use them as a means of social control. At present governments in many Western countries are actively promoting self-help organisations as service-providers, because of the opportunity such a policy presents to reduce public expenditure and curtail the role of the state. Nevertheless, official attitudes to self-help organisations are ambivalent. This is a point made by Gerd Leene in relation to the Netherlands:

The reaction . . . to new self-help initiatives has been ambivalent, sometimes seeing them as positive in terms of community competence and self-reliance; but sometimes viewing them with suspicion because the initiatives do not always fit well within the framework of official regulations and arrangements for social welfare.[33]

PRESSURE

It should be clear from the discussion of self-help and neighbourhood organisations that voluntary agencies frequently engage in pressure group activities. For some groups pressure is their sole or main purpose, attempting to change public attitudes and campaigning for better provision of services. In Britain the Child Poverty Action Group and Shelter are good examples of groups in this category. An interesting example in the United States is the Gray Panther Movement, which 'concentrates on problems of agism . . . and its relationship to racism, sexism and other degrading forces in society'. Munday says that 'the outstanding characteristic of the Gray Panthers is that it is an organisation of old people that emphasises advocacy and rarely engages in direct services . . . they are a political and social force to be reckoned with in America'.[34]

Other groups combine service provision with pressure: many neighbourhood organisations fall into this category, but so do some of the more traditional service-providing agencies. Many of the groups for physically handicapped combine both functions. The exact balance between service provision and pressure will vary from one organisation to another: in some instances pressure will be a major concern while in others it will be peripheral to their main activities and applied only intermittently.

There are a few voluntary organisations which seldom, if ever, apply pressure. The best example of such an organisation is Alcoholics Anonymous, which 'is not allied with any sect, denomination, politics, organisation, institution; does not wish to engage in any controversy; neither endorses nor opposes any causes'.[35] Organisations, such as Gamblers Anonymous and Recidivists Anonymous, which have modelled themselves on Alcoholics Anonymous, are similarly non-political. Local branches of medical research organisations are often engaged exclusively on fund-raising and would not normally be regarded as pressure groups.

Despite these exceptions, however, pressure group activity—what Kramer calls the improver and advocacy role—constitutes one of the main characteristics of voluntary agencies. In the United States, the Filer Commission said that 'the monitoring and influencing of government may be emerging as one of the single most important and effective functions of the private nonprofit sector'.[36] In Britain, the Wolfenden Committee noted that voluntary organisations 'are well placed to act as independent critics and pressure groups'.[37] Kramer goes even further when he claims that this advocacy or improver role 'comes close to being a unique organisational competence of the voluntary agency'.[38]

The obvious aim of pressure groups is to influence policy by achieving legislative change, be securing a larger share of resources or by encouraging statutory agencies to more fully implement policies and thus improve provision. Attempts to cut expenditure and reduce provision may be opposed. Groups may also place emphasis on welfare rights, trying to ensure that potential claimants know their entitlements and how to go about obtaining them. Welfare rights campaigners will be concerned not only with the level of provision, but also with eligibility criteria and procedures.

While pressure groups in most countries work on several fronts simultaneously, they attempt to concentrate their efforts on those parts of the political system where pressure is most likely to bring about the desired results. In the United States, for example, most pressure group activity centres on Congress and state legislatures because this is where the groups' influence on legislation is most effective. At the same time, of course, groups do not entirely neglect local, state and federal bureaucracies. In Britain and the Netherlands, however, pressure groups are much more concerned to influence local and central government bureaucracies because it is in these that policies are formulated and legislative proposals are drafted. The methods used to influence a representative assembly are entirely inappropriate in dealing with a bureaucracy. Consequently, in the United States the lobby is the most common strategy, while in the Netherlands and Britain direct and private negotiations with government officials is more usual. The more public nature of the lobby also encourages much greater use of the mass media in the United States.

Pressure group activity brings voluntary organisations into direct conflict with government. In the United States lobbying by voluntary organisations is expressly sanctioned by law, but there has been much heated discussion about the right of voluntary bodies in receipt of federal funds to use them to finance lobbying. The debate has become more heated since Reagan became president, with the administration allegedly showing hostility towards radical and left-wing groups. The assistant director of the National Committee for Responsive Philanthropy, Timothy Saasta, states that 'while President Reagan has urged that private charities take over many of the Government's social welfare functions, his Administration has systematically undermined the nation's nonprofit organisations to try to silence them as advocates for the rights of the poor, women, minorities and the disenfranchised'.[39] Saasta contends that there have been persistent attempts by right-wingers to 'defund the Left'. The attempts have taken three forms. First, there have been efforts to limit the use of federal funds for lobbying, and the loss of tax-free status has been threatened. Another proposal was that lobbying would have to be carried out by separate staff in separate offices. Intense opposition caused this proposal to be abandoned. It was replaced by less draconian measures which extend the definition of lobbying so that activities which had formerly been allowed were now proscribed. Second, there have been successive attempts to limit the organisations which are allowed to participate in the Combined Federal Campaign (charitable deductions from the paychecks of federal employees). Most of these have been overturned by the courts, but a measure implemented in 1983 stated that participating organisations would not be allowed to spend more than 15 per cent of their funds on lobbying, advocacy, litigation and public education. Third, cuts in federal aid to voluntary organisations have hit housing and community development and social service agencies hardest.

It is clear that in Britain and the Netherlands, as much as in the United States, some voluntary organisations and some pressure groups are more acceptable than others. The more radical, non-traditional groups find it more difficult to raise funds, and their access to the policy-making process tends to be more limited. Governments look much more favourably upon voluntary agencies which provide direct services for approved groups.

PROVISION OF SERVICES

Salamon and Abramson say of non-profit organisations in the United States that 'though private in character, they are essentially public in function, providing a host of public goods and services as the major vehicle through which private charitable resources and voluntary efforts are brought to bear on the solving of community problems'.[40] Sugden makes a similar point about Britain,[41] and as will be seen, the Netherlands provides the most complete example of voluntary organisations serving public purposes.

Berger and Neuhaus refer to voluntary agencies, together with families, community networks and Churches, as 'mediating structures' which stand between the individual and the state.[42] Such structures, they claim, are understood by those who use them, and there is much less chance of alienation as the divide between government and the governed is mediated by structures which result in the 'empowerment of people'. Berger and Neuhaus argue that not only should public policy promote and protect mediating structures, but also that 'wherever possible public policy should utilise mediating structures for the realisation of social purposes'. This does not imply less government expenditure; indeed, Berger and Neuhaus assume that the welfare state is capable of expansion. Expansion, however, need not mean an increase in services provided directly by government; mediating structures, with government funding, should be used instead.

In Britain it is relatively uncommon for voluntary agencies to provide services on behalf of statutory authorities, although there are some agency agreements in the physically handicapped field. Of course, statutory bodies frequently give financial assistance to voluntary organisations, and more statutory funds become available through purchase of services—especially residential services. In the United States the use of voluntary agencies to deliver services is much more highly developed. Legislative changes in the 1960s and 1970s—especially Title XX of the Social Security Amendments—encouraged the purchase of services by government as an alternative to direct provision. As a result of these changes, Kramer claims, 'government purchase of service had become the principal mode of financing service delivery in the United States'.[43]

The Netherlands provides the best example of the use of mediating structures in the provision and delivery of social services of all kinds, as the following statement by the Ministry of Welfare, Health and Cultural Affairs indicates:

Virtually all the social welfare services in the Netherlands are run by non-governmental organisations of which there are many thousands. Most of them are organised on a municipal or regional basis and concentrate on one or more specific areas, such as family welfare, immigrant workers, the elderly, community development or general social work . . . practically all types of welfare work have their own national umbrella organisation—also non-governmental—which provides general services and represents their interests, for instance to central government.[44]

This heavy reliance on voluntary organisations, referred to as *particulier initiatif* (PI), stems from the religious divisions in the Netherlands and the opposition of both

Catholics and Protestants to direct government involvement in the provision of health, education and social welfare services. Each denominational group and a number of secular groups has established a complete range of social, political and cultural services for its adherents. Each of the major blocs has its own political party, trade unions, employers' organsiations, newspapers and radio and television stations, and each provides schools and universities, insurance against sickness and unemployment, health and welfare services and sporting and cultural facilities. This arrangement of a series of separate welfare systems is frequently referred to as 'vertical pluralism'. Originally the sturcture developed independently of government, but the rapid expansion of welfare provision after the war led to a growing reliance on government funds, so that currently between 95 per cent and 100 per cent of welfare costs are borne by central, provincial and municipal government.

Since the early 1970s there has been mounting criticism of PI. This criticism took official form with the report of a government consultative committee in 1974. The report expressed concern about fragmentation and lack of co-ordination, resulting in unevenness of provision, duplication, gaps and an uneconomic use of resources. More fundamentally, there have been worries about the lack of democratic accountability and about the religious dominance in the PI system in a country which is becoming increasingly secular.

The government response to these criticisms has been to try to reduce the number of separate agencies. The home-help service provides an example: in 1962 there were 970 agencies, but by 1984 the number had fallen to 242. The ministry of Welfare and Cultural Affairs states that 'a judicious funding policy, the expansion of the programme and organisational mergers are some of the factors which have combined to ensure that both the agencies and the services they provide are more evenly distributed throughout the Netherlands and more efficiently and effectively managed'.[45] This policy of 'judicious funding' has been followed in most other fields, with government subsidies becoming dependent upon two main factors: the acceptance of rationalisation and the provision of information which allows the government to introduce a measure of quality control. Brenton talks of a transition from a separatist model of PI-government relations to an incorporated model, the latter stage not yet having been reached and progress towards it being slow.[46]

If the three countries considered in this chapter are arranged along a continuum according to the proportion of service delivery entrusted to voluntary agencies, Britain and the Netherlands represent the ends of the continuum with the United States lying somewhere in between. The advantages claimed for voluntary provision include the voluntary sector's flexibility and speed of response, the opportunity for experimentation, the widening of consumer choice and the encouragement of participation. It is probably true that, as new needs are identified, voluntary organisations *in the form of new groups* can respond more quickly than government agencies. A small group of people can join together with only rudimentary organisational resources. But that this applies only to new organisations, is a point emphasised by Kramer:

Because voluntary agencies are more likely to be trail-blazers in their early stages, their high birth rate, more than their proverbial low mortality, helps ensure changes in the social services. Paradoxically, the oft-criticised 'proliferation' of voluntary agencies expresses a resurgent vitality and constitutes one of the prerequisites for the performance of the vanguard function.[47]

There is little evidence to suggest organisational flexibility in large established groups which may be no less bureaucratic than government departments. True pioneering by voluntary organisations is restricted to the margins, to the identification and meeting of new needs by newly formed groups. Long-established organisations are more concerned with the refinement and extension of existing programmes. Nor should it be assumed that statutory agencies never initiate new developments. The poverty programmes in both Britain and the United States, for example, were the result of central and federal government initiatives.

The widening of consumer choice necessarily implies an element of duplication and some over provision. For example, if there is a shortage of residential accommodation for elderly people, someone who is in urgent need will be forced to accept any available place. It must be remembered, too, that some social service clients, confused elderly or mentally handicapped people, for example, are in no position to exercise choice. For other consumers it would be necessary to assume a large number of self-referrals and the absence of geographical restrictions.

Voluntary organisations do offer opportunities for participation. This is particularly true of self-help groups; it is less true of organisations which are run by full-time, professional staff. There is evidence to suggest that participation in voluntary organisations is a middle-class preserve.

The criticisms made of the Dutch welfare system indicate some of the problems of relying on voluntary provision. They include lack of co-ordination, variable and incomplete coverage and an absence of democratic accountability. It is interesting to note that Hadley, Hatch and Jones, who visited the Netherlands on behalf of the Wolfenden Committee, concluded that 'the Dutch model is not one that could be transplanted in this country'.[48]

VOLUNTARY ACTION AND WELFARE PLURALISM

In Britain the notion of welfare pluralism first arose in the debate about the role of the voluntary sector. In 1978 the Wolfenden Report stated that one of the main benefits stemming from the voluntary sector was the contribution it made to 'the pluralistic character of our political and social institutions'.[49] A consideration of the voluntary sector's relationship to the informal, commercial and statutory sectors will bring out more clearly its contribution to welfare pluralism.

Relationships with the Informal Sector
The Wolfenden Report provides a helpful framework for looking at voluntary-informal relationships. Three roles for voluntary organisations in relation to the informal system are identified: replacement, relief and reinforcement. Replacement occurs 'where family or neighbourly arrangements do not exist, have broken down or cannot cope'.[50]

This normally involves residential care, which might just as easily be provided by statutory as by voluntary agencies. Relief involves voluntary bodies taking some of the burden off families by, for example, providing short-term residential care or day centres. Again, such provision might just as readily be the responsibility of statutory bodies. Indeed the Wolfenden Committee says that one of the characteristics of replacement and relief services 'is the large amount of resources required to run them, because most depend on full-time staff and some on substantial capital investment'.[51] Thus only statutory bodies or the larger voluntary bodies have the resources to replace or relieve informal carers.

Reinforcement refers to services which attempt to positively strengthen informal caring arrangements by 'providing psychological support, developing extra skills and motivation or offering material resources'.[52] Good-neighbour schemes and self-help organisations fall into this category. An interesting recent development has been the growth of carers' groups, which very clearly reinforce informal caring.

Relationships with the Commercial Sector

In the United States small businesses have complained about unfair competition from voluntary agencies which enjoy tax-exempt status. As voluntary bodies are forced by financial pressures to become more commercial, offering goods and services for sale, it becomes more difficult to distinguish between them and their wholly commercial counterparts.

When voluntary agencies sell services to government on a contractual basis, they may come into direct competition with small businesses. In the majority of cases, however, as Kramer notes, voluntary agencies are not reimbursed for their full costs and have to make good the deficits. It is only when the rates charged by voluntary agencies approach the true cost of providing the service that commercial enterprises move in and competition occurs.[53]

The small-business lobby in the United States is very active: it has called for more stringent criteria for the award of tax-exempt status and for tighter control of commercial activities by non-profit groups, but, as Purkis notes, it has gone further than this 'in raising basic questions about what the rationale of tax exemption is supposed to be'.[54] It is possible that similar controversies will arise in Britain as the number of small businesses, especially in the field of residential care, increase. It could pose a dilemma for governments wishing on the one hand to encourage small businesses, and on the other to facilitate voluntary provision.

Relationships with the Statutory Sector

Voluntary-statutory relationships are frequently character-ised as being a partnership, but this is not particularly informative unless the nature of the partnership is examined a little more closely. For example, Kramer says of England, 'the frequently invoked concept of a partnership between the two sectors . . . seems to imply parity and a degree of interdependence that does not always conform to reality, in which the voluntary agency is at best a junior and usually silent partner'.[55] In the United States the partnership is a little more equal 'in a social service economy that remains essentially pluralistic despite the dominant influence of government funds and policies'.[56] In the Netherlands there are some grounds for arguing that the voluntary agencies are the dominant partner, retaining a high degree of autonomy in spite of heavy reliance on statutory funding and the government's attempts at regulation.

Frequently, the role of the voluntary sector is seen as either complementary or supplementary to statutory provision: a third position is where voluntary agencies are the sole or main providers of a service. Voluntary organis-ations fulfil a complementary role when they are providing services of a different nature to those of the statutory auth-orities. Friendly visiting or the provision of social clubs for elderly or handicapped people might be examples. Self-help arrangements also complement basic state provision because they provide a qualitatively different service. Highly special-ised services may also lend themselves to voluntary provision. Services for people suffering from a particular disability are often of this kind.

Supplementation of statutory services occurs when volun-tary agencies provide additional facilities of the same sort. The most common examples are in various forms of residen-tial accommodation, but voluntary social work agencies and

voluntary hospitals fall into the same category. Supplementation is said to facilitate choice; on the other hand, it is
sometimes characterised as duplication and an uneconomical use of scarce resources. In other instances the
balance may be reversed, with voluntary organisations as
the main or sole provider of a service. This happens when
new needs arise—for example, refuges for battered
women—or where groups are unpopular and stigmatised—
drug addicts and single homeless people, for example.

This threefold model does not particularly recommend
itself to ardent welfare pluralists, because it is based on the
assumption that the state will continue to be the dominant
provider of social services. The voluntary sector has a
specific role as critic, but in the provision of services it plays
a subsidiary, complementary and supplementary role. Hatch
therefore suggests an alternative analytical framework
consisting of two competing interpretations. The first of
these 'sees the voluntary sector as essentially marginal,
useful for minor problems and in emergencies': it takes an
optimistic view of the capacity of statutory authorities to
meet most needs. The second interpretation 'sees the voluntary sector as a more integral and pervasive factor in social
provision. It rests on reservations about what the state can
do and optimistic propositions about the potentialities of
voluntary action'.[57] Hatch appears to favour an integral role
for the voluntary sector with the state providing the
necessary financial backing. The state would retain a
substantial regulatory and enabling role in setting standards,
measuring performance and attempting to ensure equity and
some degree of accountability.

This is a view shared by Gladstone who writes approvingly
of Berger and Neuhaus and their notion of mediating structures. Gladstone advocates 'gradualist welfare pluralism',
which he describes as a 'de-monopolising strategy', with a
'steadily increasing role for voluntary action'.[58] Gladstone
favours the *replacement* of statutory by voluntary action, but
like Hatch, he sees increased statutory funding as essential.

It is significant that Berger and Neuhaus, Hatch and Gladstone all emphasise the necessity for increased government
funding of the voluntary sector. In Britain, the United States
and the Netherlands government funding increased substan-

tially during the 1970s. Kramer writes of 'the rapid acceleration in public funding of voluntary agencies' in the United States.[59] In 1980 non-profit education, health and welfare organisations received over $40 billion in aid from the federal government. This was easily the largest single source of income, constituting 35 per cent of the total. An estimated $10 billion came from other levels of government. In Britain funding from central government departments has increased from £19.2 million in 1974/5 to £128 million in 1983/4. These figures exclude the sums paid to voluntary bodies by the Manpower Services Commission, which in recent years has emerged as a major source of financial support for voluntary agencies. The Job Creation Programme between October 1975, when it began, and March 1977 contributed £31.2 million to the funds of voluntary organisations; in 1983/4 the Job Creation Programme's successor, the Community Programme, contributed £285 million. Also excluded is the money distributed to housing associations through the Housing Corporation—£489 million in 1982/3. Grants from local authorities in the personal social services alone amounted to an estimated £7.9 million in 1974/5, by 1984/5 this figure had risen to £29.1 million. The figures for the Netherlands are not very meaningful. They show a very rapid expansion from 1950 to the late 1970s, but this is simply a reflection of expanding welfare provision, which every advanced industrial country experienced during that period.

A growing feature of the relationship between voluntary agencies and government is what Kramer calls 'vendorism'—the purchase of services by public bodies from either non-profit or profit-making organisations. This is much more common in the United States than in Britain. Kramer claims that in the United States purchase of service arrangments account for over one-third of governmentally financed personal social services.[60] Although vendorism is not nearly so developed in Britain, payments by local authorities to voluntary organisations in the personal social services field increased from £61.5 million in 1975/6 to £141 million in 1980/1.

Greatly increased reliance on government funding has given rise to fears about the threat this may pose to the independence of voluntary organisations. We have already noted attempts in the United States and the Netherlands to limit the activities of voluntary organisations by means of financial pressure. In the United States the dispute has mainly been about lobbying, and it is the more radical organisations which the administration has attempted to curb.

As for Britain, Brenton comments that 'it must be acknowledged that government control and influence over the future development of the voluntary sector is more than marginal, and that for some kinds of agency it may be decisive'.[61] Brenton cites a number of cases to illustrate this point. Two of these achieved particular notoriety. In 1980 MIND was highly critical of the running of Broadmoor secure psychiatric hospital, and the Department of Health and Social Security came under pressure to cut its grant. Although MIND retained its grant, the secretary of state, in commenting upon this case, said, 'if there is a body which is simply concerned to campaign vociferously for or against certain policies, then I think public authorities should be very slow to spend money on supporting them'.[62] The second case occurred in 1983. Dr Gerard Vaughan, the minister for consumer affairs, was disturbed by the association of Mrs Joan Ruddock with the Citizens' Advice Bureau in his own constituency. The cause for his concern was that Mrs Ruddock was the chairperson of CND, although why this should affect her work for the CAB is far from clear. Dr Vaughan withheld 50 per cent of the £6 million grant paid to the National Association of Citizens' Advice Bureaux, stating that the other half would be paid 'provided they put their house in order' and claiming that he had received many complaints about the growing left-wing influence in the organisation.[63] In the event, an inquiry into the affairs of the NACAB said that the charges of political bias were unfounded.

Registration with the Charity Commission qualifies voluntary organisations for valuable tax concessions, and this presents further opportunities for control. Political activities may entail the loss of charitable status, and there have been complaints over many years that the Charity Commission defines 'political activity' too narrowly. All efforts to bring about social change are excluded as, on different grounds, are self-help arrangements.

In practice it is difficult for central government to exert very detailed control and when grants are small it is not worth the expense of doing so. However, government does not have to resort to the overt political control used in the cases referred to above. There are several less direct ways in which it may influence the nature of the voluntary sector. For example, the criteria it applies to grant applications will cause voluntary organisations to tailor their applications in such a way as to enhance their chances of being successful, and this may distort their activities.

Participation in government programmes may be even more restrictive. The voluntary organisations may be purely reactive, policy and the voluntary sector's role being decided by the statutory partners. In Britain this is substantially the case in the inner-city partnerships and some of the programmes mounted by the Manpower Services Commission. Vendorism may work in a similar way in that voluntary agencies may find that the contract work leaves them no time for any other activities. The contract work itself will, quite rightly, be subject to fairly detailed control.

It is clear that the more governments use voluntary agencies as instruments of public policy the more compelling become the arguments in favour of public funding. But public funding carries a price: it entails a loss of independence and expectations of conformity.

Judging from their public statements, both the Thatcher and the Reagan governments intended shifting some of the burden of provision from the statutory to the voluntary sector. In fact the Reagan administration has done very little to enhance the role of the voluntary sector. Salamon makes the following comment on the gap between promise and performance:

In few areas did the Reagan administration enter office with a clearer sense of purpose than in its commitment to voluntarism and private action as a way to respond to national needs. Yet in few areas were its concrete achievements more difficult to discern. Committed to a new approach to public problems stressing private initiative instead of public action, the administration never managed to convert that commitment into a serious program of action.[64]

..un-profit organisations have actually done less well under Reagan. Federal aid to the non-profit sector was cut by over 11 per cent between 1980 and 1984. Excluding hospitals, which received more favourable treatment, the cuts exceeded 34 per cent. In most cases equally severe cuts have occurred at the state level.[65] The British government has come somewhat nearer to fulfilling its promise. Brenton sums up the position in Britain:

> In its public statements and in practice the government maintained its financial commitment to the voluntary sector, but its total grant allocations came nowhere near realistic levels of support for the enhanced voluntary service input it envisaged. Consequently, a dominant and concurrent theme in its policy statements centred around the potential of private sources of funding.[66]

But questions have to be asked about the suitability, the capacity and the willingness of the voluntary sector to undertake the implied extra load. Some of the weaknesses of voluntary provision have already been noted: uneven and incomplete coverage, lack of co-ordination, lack of internal democracy and lack of accountability. These are by no means minor blemishes that are easily remedied; they are major failings which can be tolerated so long as voluntary organisations play a relatively marginal role in social provision, but which demand the most serious attention if the voluntary sector is to be expanded at the expense of the state.

It is also quite obvious that voluntary organisations do not at present have the capacity to absorb extra responsibilities. Presumably some of the staff formerly employed by statutory agencies could be transferred to the expanded voluntary sector, but this would be a major undertaking. The voluntary sector cannot manage its present load without a heavy reliance on government funding, and most welfare pluralists assume that substantially more funds from statutory sources would be made available. An equitable system of distribution would have to be devised, and, since voluntary organisations would be spending taxpayers' money, problems of accountability would need to be addressed.

Provided sufficient extra resources were made available, some voluntary associations might very well welcome the opportunity to replace direct state provision. This cannot be automatically assumed, however, as the following brief account illustrates.

In 1984 the British secretary of state for social services propounded the idea that local authority social services departments would contract out services for children and elderly and handicapped people to private and voluntary organisations, and then simply hold the ring. The secretary of state promised a Green Paper on the subject in the very near future. The paper was still not published in June 1986 and, in exasperation, a consortium of over thirty voluntary organisations, the Voluntary Organisations Personal Social Services Group, published its own paper in which it rejected the notion of contracting out and argued for 'a major, continuing and expanding role for Social Services Departments of local authorities'. Social services departments would continue to be the main providers of direct services. The paper went on to say that 'squeezing local authority spending and shifting services to an inadequately funded voluntary sector is no way to plan and provide services for the most vulnerable and disadvantaged people in society'.[67]

The arguments for welfare pluralism have concentrated on the failings of state provision. The weaknesses of the voluntary sector have not been entirely ignored, but it has been assumed that these could easily be remedied. As has been indicated, the notion of welfare pluralism arose within the context of a renewed interest in the voluntary sector. But a pluralist system also implies a role for the private market, and most moderate welfare pluralists, while accepting commercial provision, are less enthusiastic about it than they are about provision by voluntary agencies. However, as we will see in the next chapter, the commercial sector is not short of influential and vociferous advocates.

6 The Commercial Sector and Social Welfare

The welfare state was never intended to completely replace private markets. Indeed, some would claim that it was specifically designed to facilitate capital accumulation through the creation of a disciplined, educated and healthy labour force, the provision of infrastructural services and the maintenance of demand. Nevertheless, the state did intervene in market relationships; in some instances it was thought sufficient to modify the free play of market forces, in other instances partial or substantial replacement of the market occurred, but there were no examples of commercial provision being completely ousted. Flora sums the position up in the following way:

> The development of the Western welfare state is not to be understood as a step on the road towards socialism. It should be interpreted instead as a complementary process in the evolution of a relatively coherent tripartite structure consisting of: capitalist market economy, democratic mass polity, and welfare state.[1]

This calls to mind the distinction made in the postwar debate about the welfare state in West Germany between a 'social market economy' and a 'socialist market economy'.

The balance between the commercial and public sectors varies from one country to another, but there are also considerable variations within countries as between one service and another, and even between different subdivisions of a single service. It is plain that private markets in the social services are much more prominent in the United States than they are in Britain and they are more significant in Britain than in Sweden. One can postulate three possible positions in relation to service provision:

(1) Private markets alongside the statutory system which remains the main provider. Education is in this position in most Western European countries. Education also provides an example of variation *within* a service. Heclo, Heidenheimer and Adams claim that 'in Europe private institutions become fewer as one ascends the educational ladder, which does not hold for the United States, with its large private university sector'.[2]

(2) Private markets as the main provider, but with a substantial role left for the state; housing in Britain is a good example of this position.

(3) Private markets as the main provider with a residual role left for the state; for example, housing and, to a lesser extent, health in the United States.

However, this categorisation oversimplifies the position in a number of ways. First, it deals only with provision and ignores the important role of the state in regulating and subsidising commercial suppliers. Housing furnishes an example of the distortion thus produced. Despite the fact that Britain has a higher proportion of public-sector dwellings than any other Western nation, public expenditure on housing is lower in Britain than elsewhere in Western Europe. The terms 'comprehensive' and 'supplementary' have been used to describe the differing scope of governmental responsibility for housing. Comprehensive policies are those in which the government attempts to control the whole of the housing programme, while supplementary policies are those in which government intervention is limited to the housing of minorities. On this basis, housing policy in Britain and the United States is supplementary while Denmark, France, the Netherlands, Sweden and West Germany have pursued comprehensive policies with extensive producer and consumer subsidies.

This illustrates a second problem with the threefold categorisation referred to above: the difficulty of deciding precisely where the dividing line between public and private activity lies, since the two sectors are interrelated in a variety of ways. This is further complicated by the incorporation of private-market practices into public-sector services: charges, the insurance principle and competition (e.g. between insti- tutions of higher education) might be thought of in this way.

A further point to be borne in mind is that private markets may take several forms. The most familiar is direct payment for goods and services, but this is less common in the social services than it is in other transactions. Nevertheless, in the United States 25 per cent of health-care finance in 1982 was raised from direct payments by consumers.[3] In France the proportion of health-care costs met by direct payments is about 20 per cent. Direct payments by consumers also feature in residential and day-care facilities and in private- sector house purchase.

An insurance-based private market system is an alterna- tive to a direct payment system. Private insurance cover is most likely to be used for high-cost services where public provision is non-existent or judged to be inferior. Outside the Medicaid and Medicare systems, health-care provision in the United States (especially hospital care) is financed in this way. Private health insurance has also been growing in many Western European countries.

In the social services private markets are often consider- ably modified by the use of subsidies, allowances, vouchers and regulation. In the health insurance systems of Western Europe, for example, practitioners are virtually private providers, paid by patients whose costs are wholly or partly reimbursed, but the payments received by practitioners are set by government. As already noted, the position in housing is similar with largely private suppliers regulated by government and the market modified by the payment of producer and consumer subsidies.

The arguments concerning the public-private mix in welfare are conducted at several levels, ranging from the comparison of intersectoral costs to the purely ideological. It is not always easy to separate the different levels as the descriptive merges into the prescriptive. Even the most pragmatic arguments concerned with technicalities have an ideological element. We will now turn to the arguments which are grouped under three broad headings: efficiency, choice and freedom and equality.

EFFICIENCY

The pressure on resources for social welfare has brought the issues of efficiency and effectiveness to the forefront of the social policy debate. The debate is still hampered by problems of definition and measurement, despite the attempts being made to devise acceptable social indicators. This is not the place to pursue this point; suffice it to say that efficiency and effectiveness are very closely related, but they are not synonymous. A working definition of efficiency might be the minimisation of costs and the maximisation of benefits. Effectiveness, however, is concerned primarily with the degree to which needs are being met.

Those who contend that market provision is more efficient than public provision argue their case on three fronts: comparisons of intersectoral costs, more general arguments about the benefits arising from competition, and claims that public provision has features that render it inefficient.

Comparisons of intersectoral costs are not common. Some have been conducted in both the United States and Britain, but the evidence at present is insufficient to form a firm judgement. In the United States there have been several comparisons of nursing-home costs, most of the evidence suggesting that private homes are less expensive. The evidence is far from conclusive, however; work by Biggs on the care of the elderly and by Slavin on hospitals suggests that contracting out may be more rather than less expensive. An interesting British study reported by Judge and Knapp compares the private and local authority costs of providing residential accommodation for elderly people.[4] Judge and Knapp conclude that 'private residential homes in England and Wales are less costly and might represent better value for money than their non-profit counterparts in the public and voluntary sectors'.[5] A weakness of this study, acknowledged by the authors, is that it takes no account of output— it was assumed that the services provided and their quality were similar in the two sets of institutions. Several reasons were advanced for the difference in costs, the most important of which was 'the traditional virtues of small business enterprise'.[6] These 'virtues' include the heavy involvement of the owners and their families in the business, often working very long hours. This allows for profit homes to employ very few people, who are usually paid less than trade-union negotiated wages. Keeping staff to a minimum and paying them low wages very obviously reduces costs, but the question arises as to how far this can be pushed without reducing the quality of the service. Furthermore, if family members work very long hours, their own efficiency may eventually suffer. A study of residential homes in Devon also identifies the small scale of the enterprise and reliance on family labour as important:

> Labour intensiveness is probably the most important factor in the viability of family firms; so long as the starting of a business requires the use of labour rather than capital there are possibilities for 'self-made' men. Care of the elderly is a highly labour intensive business; personal care is very difficult to mechanise.[7]

The implication is that facilities requiring a great deal of capital investment and relying on highly paid skilled labour do not lend themselves to operation by small business enterprises: a district general hospital, for example, is a very different proposition from a small residential home. It should be noted that Judge and Knapp urge caution in the interpretation of their findings: 'We emphatically do not mean to suggest that all service delivery agencies in the public domain . . . should be handed over to small businessmen'.[8] In many instances, they recognise, this would be impractical.

Others, less restrained than Judge and Knapp, argue for large-scale transfers of services to commercial suppliers. At this point the ideological aspects of the debate become rather more pronounced. The arguments are the familiar ones of efficiency through competition which encourages suppliers to reduce costs to the minimum and/or provide a better service than their competitors. The transfer of public services to the commercial sector, it is argued, would do much towards achieving a more dynamic economy in which entrepreneurial skills and risk-taking would be rewarded.

Rationing would be by price, and equilibrium between supply and demand would be assured. Inefficient, unprofitable suppliers would be forced out of business. The best interests of all would be served by everyone pursuing their own self-interest.

Several assumptions are built into these arguments. The most fundamental is that welfare markets will be characterised by perfect competition—or something approaching it—which depends upon a large number of competing suppliers with no impediments to free competition among them. It also relies upon knowledgeable consumers with free access to services. Such conditions are rare, however. Every advanced industrial country has granted monopolies to certain professional groups. This is most obvious in the health-care services. Maynard, for example, argues that because of the uncertainty associated with health-care markets, and because of the need to protect ignorant consumers from unprincipled and unqualified practitioners, 'the State, in all Western countries, has given the medical profession considerable monopoly power to influence the quantity and quality of its services and its own remuneration'.[9] Trade-union activity within most health services is also an impediment to unfettered competition. Maynard claims that the monopoly power of doctors may lead to great inefficiency in private markets.

If he (the doctor) pursues goals such as income and 'empire building', rather than the health interests of his patients, he may be able to generate demand for his services and misuse the scarce resources of society: there is good US evidence . . . that this happens and that an increased supply of doctors, other things being equal, can lead to increased levels of activity and higher fees.[10]

The potential for the exploitation of patients is obvious. By lengthening the treatment or by recommending more expensive treatments the doctor may increase his income. He may be even more likely to do this is he knows that an insurance company will foot most of the bill. Friedman argues that impediments to free competition should be removed; this would involve the removal of professional monopolies.[11] Doctors, however, are an extremely powerful group, and any attempts to reduce their monopoly, and therefore their income, would be fiercely resisted.

Nor can it be assumed that consumers are knowledgeable and discriminating and have unrestricted access to services. Many studies indicate that consumers of social services are not particularly discriminating. On the whole they tend to express satisfaction with services even when expert opinion and the application of a variety of criteria indicate a number of inadequacies. Browne, in an interesting American study, examined children's day-care facilities provided under a variety of different auspices. She found that consumers did not exercise 'a high level of discrimination'. She comments:

One of the theoretical advantages of the mixed economy of day care derives from competition among providers seeking to attract well-informed consumers. To the extent that consumers lack the knowledge, skill and, perhaps inclination to discriminate among day care provisions of different quality, the mixed economy of care operates with a low degree of internal regulation.[12]

This is not to suggest that parents and other social service consumers are unintelligent – it is more related to a lack of experience of alternatives and a desire not to appear ungrateful.

Two further points about consumer access and competition between suppliers need to be raised. The first is that consumers are restricted by distance and the availability of transport. Parents, for example, may very well believe that a primary school fifteen miles away from where they live is better than the one down the road, but they may also believe that fifteen miles is too far for a young child to travel. The second point is that it is becoming increasingly common, especially in the United States, to use third-party purchase of service contracts, which usually cover the agency's cost plus an addition for profit. Once the contract is awarded, the agency does not have to compete for customers, and the consumer has no choice unless the contract is divided among several competing suppliers.

A further source of private-market inefficiency is identified by Laming, who says that although private medicine in the United States may provide a good standard of service for the individual patient, 'the fragmentation seems to make the system both expensive and inadequate'. According to Laming, the system is expensive *'because hospitals are in competition with each other*, so that they each seem to feel the need to have the full range of the latest high tech equipment, mirco-surgery, organ replacement services etc. and this results in a great deal of duplication' (emphasis added).[13]

Another assumption underlying the private-market case is that the sum total of individual purchasing decisions will result in a sufficient quantity of the good being produced to satisfy 'social' requirements. The point here is the existence of externalities which occur when the purchase of a benefit by an individual also results in benefits to others. Purchasers will consider only their individual gain. Education is an example of a service which confers benefits upon society at large over and above those conferred upon the individual. Another example is preventative health services, which may stop the spread of infectious diseases.

A final assumption made by those who support market provision is one challenged by Titmuss in 1966: 'that social services in kind, particularly medical care, have no characteristics which differentiate them from goods in the private market'.[14] Titmuss identified thirteen ways in which medical care differed from goods normally purchased in the open market. All of them are related in some way to uncertainty and unpredictability and the vulnerability of consumers. Once again we may note that the idea of the knowledgeable, discriminating consumer choosing freely among a range of services does not accord with reality. We will return to this point when we come to examine choice and freedom.

Many of those who advocate market provision of welfare services are, of course, fully aware of the market imperfections briefly touched upon above. Their response would be that the imperfections could be rectified or modified and that even imperfect markets are superior to public provision. As Friedman says, 'Perfection is not of the world. There will always be shoddy products, quacks, con artists. But on the whole, market competition, when it is permitted to work, protects the consumer better than do the alternative government mechanisms that have been increasingly super-imposed on the market'.[15] The supporters of commercial provision, then, are claiming that the state system is less efficient than the market system. One of the problems is, of course, that if you apply the criteria of the private market to the public system, then obviously the latter will be found wanting. Public provision, it is argued, is inefficient because it lacks the discipline of the market-place. Bureaucrats have no incentive to reduce costs because they are not constrained to make profits. Consumers have no incentive to restrict demand when goods or services are provided at zero cost or are heavily subsidised. In this situation demand invariably outstrips supply, and in the absence of rationing by price, other forms of rationing have to be adopted (waiting lists and queues, for example). It must be understood, however, that third-party payments (by government or insurance companies) to private providers do not put any pressure on consumers to reduce demand. Unless some form of cost-sharing is introduced, the consumer still receives the service at zero cost. Furthermore, the public system has its own checks and balances: notably political accountability and the possibility of participation. Neither of these is as fully developed or as effective as it might be, but at least the potential is there.

At the same time, though, efficiency and cost *are* important, and public authorities have a duty to attend to them. In this they might be able to learn from the private market. Rather than attempting to increase the role of the market at the expense of public provision, it might be preferable to seriously consider how some of the more desirable attributes of the private market might be introduced into the public sector.

CHOICE AND FREEDOM

The debate between Titmuss and Lees in the early and mid 1960s was primarily an argument about choice in welfare.[16] Lees claimed that the ballot box was the only choice open to most welfare consumers. This was unsatisfactory since the ballot box allowed choice only between rival programmes or packages of measures. The vote was too insensitive an instrument for registering choices between specific services.

Lees argued that the only way in which consumers could express their preferences was through participation in private markets. Through being required to exercise choice consumers would become more knowledgeable and more discriminating, and this would lead to better services.

Titmuss's response was to ask: choice for whom? Presumably for those who could afford to pay. Markets respond to demand rather than need, and demand is effective only if it is backed up by the ability to pay. Choice might very well be enlarged for those with sufficient income, but it would be correspondingly reduced for poor people. Furthermore, some social service clients are in no position to make choices—mentally handicapped people, those with psychogeriatric problems and deprived children, for example. But choice is also restricted for people who do not fall into these especially vulnerable groups. It is restricted first of all by lack of knowledge or, more precisely perhaps, by inequalities of knowledge. Most people believe that the teacher, the social worker, the health visitor or the doctor knows best. How *do* people make choices between competing neurologists when they have no experience on which to base their choice? How do people know whether they are receiving good care or bad care? The truth of the matter is that consumers do not make choices, professionals do. It is the general practitioner, for example, who controls access to hospital and specialist services, and it is the consultant who controls the use of hospital resources. Private markets are unlikely to alter this siutation significantly—working-class consumers, in particular, are not going to be more inclined to question a professional's judgement simply because a service is being paid for.

The New Right equate freedom in the market-place with freedom in a general sense. By freedom they usually mean freedom *from* government intervention. Friedman makes the link between economic and political freedom:

Economic freedom is an essential requisite for political freedom. By enabling people to co-operate with one another without coercion or central direction, it reduces the area over which political power is exercised. In addition, by dispersing power, the free market provides an offset to whatever concentration of political power may arise. The combination of economic and political power in the same hands is a sure recipe for tyranny.[17]

But if individual freedom depends on the ability to participate in the market, what of those who are excluded through lack of resources? Political freedom must have a hollow sound to those who cannot pay school fees or doctors' bills or who can afford only substandard accommodation. The freedom to do without essential services is a freedom that most people would happily forego. Freedom is more than an absence of government intervention. Indeed, government intervention is essential to the freedom of the poor, the unemployed, the chronically sick, deprived children and the homeless.

EQUALITY

In discussions of welfare provision, the principles of equality, equity and efficiency are frequently invoked. Equality and equity are not, of course, synonymous: equity is concerned with distributional fairness or justice, whereas equality is concerned with giving people the same opportunities and the same access to resources and services. In order to produce equality of outcome, people who start from unequal positions must be allocated different quantities of resources. Equality may not be thought equitable because fairness and justice are seen as requiring unequal rewards for unequal skill and effort.

Equity and equality are sometimes seen as being in opposition to the principle of efficiency. It is quite feasible to argue, though, that equity, equality and efficiency are all served when need is adopted as the main distributive principle. Distribution according to need may result in the most efficient use of resources, because each unit of resource received by those with low command over resources produces more welfare than the same unit received by someone who is relatively well-off. Nevertheless, the demands of equality, equity and efficiency may not always coincide, and when they are in conflict, choices have to be made.

The use of the term 'need' poses a number of conceptual

problems. It is more difficult to define and measure than demand, which is measured by a customer's ability and willingness to pay the price. There is also the problem of whose needs we are talking about (individuals, families, groups or whole communities) and whose definition of needs is to be accepted. It has to be remembered, too, that needs are relative, varying from culture to culture and over time, and that they are to a considerable extent socially determined. But although the concept of need is beset with problems of interpretation and measurement, its use in social policy is remarkably persistent. At a simple, practical level, it does make sense to talk about people's housing, health, educational and financial needs, and it does make sense to talk of the needs of elderly and disabled people or deprived children.

It is certainly instructive to contrast need, however imprecisely defined, with alternative distributive principles such as desert and demand. The allocation of social service resources according to need results in a greater degree of equality than either of the alternatives. In the welfare state the principles of need and desert co-exist. Had the welfare state unequivocally embraced the principle of need it would have achieved a much greater degree of equality than is presently the case.[18] However, there is every reason to believe that a purely private-market system would result in greater inequalities. Private markets respond to demand; if you cannot pay the price, you do not receive the service. Since people's initial resources vary, some will be able to purchase more than others so that scarce resources will go disproportionately to those who can pay the most. The poor and disadvantaged are the losers.

The answer to the dilemma, according to the marketeers, is not to provide people with services in kind, but to give them the means of purchasing services from the private market. Ideally, this should be in the form of cash, perhaps through a system of reverse income tax, but vouchers might be used to ensure that the extra resources are spent on specific services. Vouchers will be looked at in a little more detail later, but for the moment it should be noted that, as compared with cash benefits, they deny choice, which is one of the main advantages claimed for private markets.

However, marketeers' attitudes towards redistribution are ambivalent, since the market system depends upon unequal rewards. Maynard explains this ambivalence:

Another complication in the liberal-market model is that it regards incentives as the engine of economic growth and moral well-being. Any redistribution by fiscal measures will reduce the incentives to save, to work and to take risks. The more significant the redistribution that takes place the more the liberals enter into conflict with their own ideology[19]

Inequality is not a major concern of those proposing commercial provision of social services. They assume that most people will be able to afford adequate provision either out of income or through private insurance arrangements. The latter is regarded as particularly significant in health care. Private insurance companies, however, do not accept poor risks such as elderly people, the chronic sick or people with a poor work record. Such people would become the responsibility of a poor-quality residual state system. To say the least, this is socially divisive.

Resources would be attracted to those areas where the profit margins are likely to be higher. The operation of the market, therefore, would lead to greater unevenness in social provision. This would apply to:

(1) Geographical areas, with the better-off areas having better facilities.
(2) Patient groups, with the elderly, the chronic sick and mentally disordered people receiving minimal care.
(3) Prevention, which obviously is not profitable for private agencies. It is possible, too, that community care would suffer if the profit margins were smaller or less certain than in institutional care.

The final consideration concerning inequality is that the private-market solution disregards the social *causes* of problems and the social *costs* which arise from technological, industrial and economic changes. Walker discusses this aspect of privatisation, citing evidence that social costs fall most heavily on the working class. Walker extends the notion of social costs to include the social consequences of government policy (for example, unemployment in Britain), which are 'borne disproportionately by already disadvantaged groups'. Walker concludes that 'the case for privatisation resolves into an argument for forcing individuals to bear the cost of socially created problems and deprivations'.[20]

THE INCREASING ROLE OF THE COMMERCIAL SECTOR

In recent years the term 'privatisation' has come into use in several different contexts. One use of the term is to describe the sale of public assets—the transfer of nationalised industries to private ownership. Within the social service field privatisation refers to a greater reliance on private markets and on the informal and voluntary sectors in the provision and financing of welfare; it may also imply a reduction in the regulatory role of the state. In this chapter we are concerned with the commercial sector, and our attention now turns to the ways in which private provision has come to play a more prominent role in the welfare state. Consideration will be given to both occupational welfare and private markets.

Occupational Welfare

One of Titmuss's three social divisions of welfare was occupational welfare.[21] In spite of the fact that Titmuss identified this form of welfare in 1956, very little attention has been given to it since. Its importance, however, cannot be doubted.

Occupational welfare schemes can be initiated by employers, trade unions and professional associations or by both jointly. The incentive for employers to initiate schemes is that they may help in the recruitment and retention of staff, although this applies more in times of labour shortage. Health insurance allows the employee to choose a time for treatment which is least disruptive of his work. Trade unions have a long tradition of offering friendly benefits to members. This may partly be a matter of solidarity, but it may also be seen as a way of attracting members.

Occupational pensions are a feature of all industrial countries, although the relationship between occupational and state pensions varies considerably. Coverage of occupational pension schemes is usually uneven, with male workers receiving more benefits than females, and non-manual workers more than manual. In a number of welfare states, most notably in Britain and West Germany, there has been a considerable growth in occupational pension schemes in the last decade, and especially in the 1980s. Wilkinson claims that pension scheme tax relief in Britain increased by 106 per cent between 1979–80 and 1983–84.[22] It became clear during the review of the social security system that the government had every intention of abolishing the State Earnings-related Pension Scheme (SERPS). Contributors to the scheme (mainly lower-paid manual workers) would be expected to join a suitable occupational scheme or make private arrangements.

Because of a public outcry, SERPS was retained but in a much truncated form which will mean lower benefits and lower government expenditure. The less attractive SERPS becomes, the more people are likely to choose occupational or entirely private pensions. In addition, the white paper, *The Reform of Social Security*, offers further financial inducements for people leaving SERPS to join private schemes.[23]

There is unevenness of coverage in occupational health insurance schemes. In the United States, for example, there are wide variations between industries and in the protection afforded by the thousands of plans.[24] Even in countries such as Britain, with a reasonably comprehensive National Health service, private health insurance has been growing, although the rate of increase has declined from 26 per cent in 1980 to slightly less than 2 per cent in 1983. Almost 50 per cent of those covered in 1983 had become members as a result of company purchases of group schemes and 25 per cent were members through arrangements negotiated by their trade unions or professional associations.

Other occupational benefits include day-care facilities for children (connected with the increased rate of employment among women), sports and social amenities, and many companies now employ welfare officers. Weddell notes that 'a number of professional social work programmes in the United States now include industrial social work as a specialisation in their curricula, with the prospect of growth in this professional field of practice'.[25]

Occupationally based services are more common in the United States than in Western Europe and more common still in Japan, where 'occupational benefits are generally operating as the "normal" and "first-line" provision for Japanese workers and their dependents'.[26] McNerney, quoting data from the US Chamber of Commerce published in 1980, writes:

Employee fringe benefit values now equal 37.1 per cent (including legally mandated programmes of Social Security, Workman's Compensation, and Unemployment Compensation) of salary in many companies and are growing faster than salary increases. If the trend continues for five years, benefits will be prohibitively expensive. Already several large companies are significantly above the average.[27]

Evidence suggests, however, that business corporations in the United States are now cutting back on fringe benefits.

In Japan most employees remain with the same company throughout their working lives and remain associated with it during retirement. Apart from the usual pension and health insurance programmes, many Japanese companies also provide housing, comprehensive medical care, educational benefits, cultural and sporting facilities and holidays. The Public Information and Cultural Affairs Bureau states:

This employment system, coupled with the traditional tendency in Japan to attach great importance to human relations, results in businesses undertaking a range of non-obligatory welfare programs for their employees that is quite extensive in both scale and variety. . . . In 1978, Japanese manufacturing industries spent ¥8908 ($42.32) a month per employee for non-obligatory welfare programs in addition to their obligatory contributions to health insurance, unemployment insurance, employees' pension, etc. which amounted to ¥17,778 ($84.47) a month.[28]

It must be remembered that welfare provision is limited mainly to larger companies, and many of the new jobs being created are in small firms. Since wages are generally lower in small firms their employees may be more in need of welfare benefits than those working for the big corporations.

Even in Japan it is apparent that those not employed by a large corporation are much less well catered for than are those employed by the bigger firms. Furthermore, employers looking for ways of cutting costs in a recession may find welfare benefits a tempting target.

Private Markets

In this section we are concerned with the growth of private welfare markets; the buying and selling of welfare goods and services. As part of the drive towards privatisation, purely commercial arrangements have come to play a more significant role in welfare provision and finance in recent years. The mechanisms of the shift of emphasis from state to market may include the following:

(1)   A general expansion of commercial provision, and the closure of statutory facilities.
(2)   The sale of assets (e.g. council houses in Britain and the sale of hospitals and schools).
(3)   Contracting out either entire services, as in the United States under the social security legislation, or parts of a service; for example, the catering and laundry facilities in the National Health Service in Britain.
(4)   A reduction in public funding through cost-sharing, charges or reduced subsidies.
(5)   Fiscal and other financial measures designed to promote private provision.
(6)   The use of more stringent eligibility criteria for the receipt of statutory benefits or services.
(7)   Deregulation: freeing markets from government intervention and supervision.

Changes of this kind have occurred in nearly all welfare states, although Sweden, and to a lesser extent Austria, have experienced only minor modifications. Centre-right or right-wing governments in Britain, Canada, Denmark, Holland, the United States and West Germany, in their support for competition and private enterprise, provide the necessary ideological background. In 1986 the French elections produced a conservative prime minister, and it remains to be seen what accommodations can be achieved with a

Socialist president. The expansion of commercial services has been most obvious in Britain and the United States, and for reasons of space the rest of this section will be concerned exclusively with these two countries.

The most dramatic changes in both countries have occurred in the provision of residential accommodation, especially for elderly people, and in the health-care services. In the United States the private market has always played a major role in the provision of residential accommodation for elderly people not requiring nursing care. In Arizona, for example, private developers have built entire cities specifically designed for the elderly—Sun City has a population of 49,000 and Sun City West has 32,000 with plans for further development.[29] However, the chief growth area in private provision for the elderly has been in nursing homes. Gilbert reports that 'between 1960 and 1970 the number of nursing home facilities increased by 140 per cent and the number of beds tripled.[30] Over 80 per cent of the facilities in 1980 were commercial enterprises. More recent evidence is provided by Laming: 'The growth of the nursing home business in the United States has been spectacular. I had contact with one nursing home chain which in 1984 acquired or opened new homes at the rate of one every five days, and some of those homes had 200 or more beds'.[31] Laming quotes the report of a Senate Committee, published in 1983, which found that 'the average return on equity for Texas nursing homes was 33.8 per cent, a rate higher than oil, banks and fast food franchises.'[32]

In Britain there has been very rapid expansion in private-market provision of three types of accommodation: residential homes, sheltered housing and nursing homes. Phillips and Vincent cite evidence which shows that the number of private-sector old people's homes almost doubled between 1975 and 1982. They claim that 'by mid–1985 this number has all but doubled again.' In 1982 there were 36,000 elderly people in private residential homes in *England alone*: by 1984 the number had risen to an estimated 50,000.[33] Supported by high-powered advertising, sheltered housing has also boomed. There are now about 100 British firms providing 10,000 units a year: about one-third of these units are produced by one supplier, McCarthy and Stone.[34]

Almost half of the elderly people in nursing homes are in private establishments and the number is expected to grow by about 45 per cent between 1985 and 1990.[35]

As far as health services are concerned, the United States and Britain could hardly present a greater contrast. In Britain 93 per cent of health service expenditure comes from government sources, whereas in the United States public expenditure on health services was just over 41 per cent of the total in 1983. Health services in the United States have always been, and remain, a predominantly private system: 12.5 per cent of the population were covered by Medicare and 9.3 per cent by Medicaid in 1982.[36]

In both countries there has been increasing emphasis on private markets in the 1980s; this has been especially obvious in the hospital services. A report in the *Boston Globe* in 1985 had this to say:

For-profit medicine is on the rise. . . . The new competitive environment has spawned fast-growing for profit hospital chains like Humana, Hospital Corporation of America and American Medical International. Together they now own 15 per cent of US hospitals. The corporations have moved aggressively to invest in a wide range of related health ventures besides hospitals . . . some analysts envision a few conglomerates or 'supermeds', controlling the entire health care industry.[37]

The same report refers to a 'frenzy of advertising' with extra-cost deluxe services to attract wealthy patients. Competition is certainly becoming fiercer: insurance companies are vying with each other to offer a bewildering variety of plans, and the insurance companies themselves are facing competition from new initiatives in health-care provision. The most successful of these new initiatives are the Health Maintenance Organisations (HMOs): prepaid group schemes which usually offer a full range of medical services for a fixed annual fee. In some cases doctors are employees of the HMO, in others they are under contract to an HMO. In 1984 membership of HMOs increased by nearly 40 per cent, reaching 16.7 million people, or 6 per cent of the population.[38]

The growth of private medical insurance in Britain has already been referred to. The expansion of private hospital provision has been very rapid. In 1979 there were 153 private hospitals with operating theatres in the United Kingdom containing 6,736 beds; at the end of 1984 there were 202 hospitals with 10,126 beds.[39] There is a heavy concentration of private hospitals in London and the South-East. In 1984 there were six American companies, six British companies and two Arab-financed groups operating in Britain. In 1986 serious consideration was being given to a proposal to use £7 million of National Health Service money to build a psychiatric hospital in Birmingham which would be run by an American company, Community Psychiatric Centres – one of several corporations developing chains of hospitals and other facilities for mental patients.

Cost-sharing, in which the consumer pays a proportion of the costs, has become a more prominent feature of both the American and the British health-care systems since 1979. NHS charges have increased dramatically: in 1986 the prescription charge was £2.20 an item as compared with 20p an item in 1979, and dental charges more than doubled in real terms during the same period.[40] Charges perform several functions. They introduce market principles into public services; they reduce state subsidies; and they make private provision relatively more attractive. In the United States both Medicare and Medicaid patients are being expected to shoulder a larger proportion of treatment costs and the number of people eligible for Medicaid has been reduced.[41] The Rand Corporation has conducted research in the United States into the effects of cost-sharing on the demand for health care. The conclusion reached was that cost-sharing did reduce demand. Some commentators have assumed that the demand thus curtailed must have been unnecessary in the first place. This is an unwarranted assumption, especially in the case of poor people.

Charges and cost-sharing obviously have the potential to reduce the take-up of services by poor people. In the United States the situation is made even worse by the growing reluctance of private hospitals to accept Medicare or Medicaid patients. Once such patients are accepted, they may be offered shorter periods or lower standards of care. This has occurred because of changes in the reimbursement system that have had the effect of reducing the amounts received by hospitals for treating Medicare and Medicaid patients.

The introduction of Diagnostic Related Groups has worked to the disadvantage of Medicare patients. This system involves the payment of a flat rate for specified diagnoses. Irrespective of the patient's need for further hospital treatment, he or she is discharged at the end of the time allotted to the diagnosed condition. A further diagnosis is required before the patient will be allowed to remain in hospital.

Another major policy area which is being increasingly privatised is housing. Although funding for housing has been drastically cut in both the United States and Britain, in one respect at least, the changes have been more pronounced in Britain. The Housing Act of 1980 required local authorities to sell their houses at very considerable discounts to any sitting tenants who wished to purchase. Between 1980 and 1983 over 547,000 houses were sold.[42] More recently whole estates have been sold to private companies and responsibility for urban renewal is being transferred to private developers. Local authorities have been given greater powers to force tenants to vacate their houses so that they can be sold with vacant possession. By the middle of 1986 about eighty estates had been sold to private developers by over forty local authorities.[43]

Furthermore, mortgage interest tax relief increased by 28.6 per cent between 1979–80 and 1983–84, and there was a substantial increase in the number of improvement grants. Robinson sums up the changes in British housing as follows:

Clearly the sale of council houses programme, the increases in improvement grant allocations and the growth of mortgage interest tax-relief all form part of the Government's privatisation policy on housing. This aims to encourage the expansion of the private sector, especially home ownership.[44]

One consequence of these changes and changes in the arrangements for paying housing benefit is the transformation of public sector housing into 'a residual, welfare sector catering only for low income households and those families with special needs'.[45]

We have now looked at the growth of private markets in three major areas. But residential accommodation, health and housing are not by any means the only areas to be affected. In the United States, for example, private practices are being opened by an increasing number of social workers; a similar development is occurring in Britain, although on a very small scale. Meals-on-wheels, home helps, hospital catering and laundry services, school meals and day-care facilities are also being transferred to independent contractors.

THE COMMERCIAL SECTOR AND WELFARE PLURALISM

Alternative welfare state strategies might serve to encourage or deter the development of a vigorous commercial sector within welfare pluralism. In an earlier chapter, reference was made to Kohl's analysis of public expenditure trends in which he distinguishes between public consumption expenditure (expenditure on direct service provision) and transfer expenditures (for the redistribution of cash incomes). Two basic patterns can be discerned: the Scandinavian pattern, followed by Denmark, Finland, Norway, Sweden, Britain and Ireland, which emphasises direct service provision, and the continental pattern, followed by most other countries in Western Europe, but especially Belgium, Italy, France, the Netherlands and Luxembourg, which emphasises transfer expenditure. Kohl relates these patterns to two different approaches to social policy:

The Continental pattern emphasises the redistribution of cash income relegating final consumption decisions to individual preferences. While this may be an effective way to achieve income maintenance or greater income equality, cash transfers encourage reliance on the market provision of social services and thereby reinforce private modes of producing and delivering such services. . . . The Scandinavian pattern, on the other hand, favors the public provision of services whereby collective choice more directly shapes the structure of supply and the mode of control.[46]

This helps to explain why private marketeers prefer cash benefits rather than services in kind and why they prefer subsidising consumers rather than suppliers. Another way of achieving the transfer of resources, although it affords rather less choice than cash benefits, is by means of vouchers. In the United States vouchers are used in housing, the Food Stamp programme and, to a limited extent, in higher education. The Reagan administration wanted to extend vouchers to virtually every social programme, but this has not so far happened. Vouchers are by no means a new idea. As early as 1970 a long-term research programme into the use of vouchers in housing was launched. It attempted to compare vouchers with unrestricted cash transfers and with direct housing provision. After considering the evidence from this research, Bendick concluded that, although vouchers did not increase recipients' spending on housing by as much as had been anticipated, and did little to ensure an adequate supply of low-income dwellings, they were nevertheless worthwhile because they were less costly than direct provision and less prone to abuse than cash transfers.[47] Experiments have been conducted in both America and Britain into education vouchers, but so far they have not been generally introduced.[48] In the United States food vouchers are also used in the Women, Infants and Children programme.

In many respects the movement towards private markets is a response to what are perceived as escalating costs and the wish to reduce public expenditure. As Walker says, 'Privatisation is a euphemism for cuts in the total amount of public expenditure devoted to the social services'.[49] It must be remembered, too, that private suppliers rely very heavily on state support, for the payment of residential fees, for example, and for a supply of personnel trained at the state's expense. There is an ethical issue involved here. Is the use of public funds to support profit-making enterprises justifiable? What is involved is a redistribution from the taxpayer to those offering for-profit services.

Frequently, arguments about the role of the commercial sector assume that the issue is simply concerned with who should *provide* welfare services. Le Grand and Robinson, however, point out that there are at least two other questions to be addressed. The first relates to the method of financing a service: the balance between public and private finance and the degree to which the state *subsidises* provision. The second relates to *regulation* of the quantity, quality and price of a service.[50] Extreme free-market liberals would support the replacement of state provision by market provision, the reduction of statutory finance to an absolute minimum and the sweeping away of all but the most basic regulations.

Welfare pluralists, however, are less sanguine about private markets. Although they believe that the market has a role to play in welfare provision and finance, they recognise its limitations and the need for safeguards. Because of the market's potential for abuse and exploitation, welfare pluralists support a regulatory role for the state. As Klein argues in relation to the National Health Service, 'the growth of the private sector is likely to create more demands for public regulation, whether in the interests of the individual consumer or in the collective interest of all health care consumers'.[51] Decisions, of course, have to be made about the level of regulation. One of the advantages claimed for private markets is that they tap reserves of entrepreneurial flair. Too much regulation might smother this. Too little regulation, on the other hand, gives too much opportunity for abuse and exploitation. Another problem is that of trying to devise an effective system of inspection which is not at the same time cripplingly expensive. Within these limitations and qualifications, however, most welfare pluralists would argue that the role of the market could be expanded.

One problem for welfare pluralists is that powerful private markets might very well constitute a danger to voluntary organisations. This could happen either by direct takeover— for example, some health companies have bought up voluntary hospitals, clinics and rehabilitation facilities—or through the diversion of funds. In the American context Gilbert writes, 'Once an almost exclusive preserve of voluntary nonprofit organisations . . . the private sector of social welfare has been penetrated by an increasing number of proprietary agencies dedicated to service at a profit'.[52] Furthermore, the pursuit of profit may encourage self-interest and selfishness, which are the reverse of the values of altruism and service to others on which charitable action is based.

Qualified support for markets leads welfare pluralists to adopt a largely pragmatic approach. Judge and Knapp, for example, state, 'We certainly take the pluralist view that services can be produced and delivered in a variety of ways and that the most efficient mix should be chosen on the basis of evidence rather than rhetoric'.[53] Gilbert argues in a similar vein: 'The essential issue is not to determine the universally superior form of organisation, but to understand the particular conditions under which profit or nonprofit-oriented agencies may be the most suitable provider of social services'.[54] Gilbert suggests for *practical* considerations which might influence the choice between public and private provision:

(1) The degree to which the service is standard-ised—standardised services are easier to cost and monitor and the consumer can more easily evaluate them.
(2) The degree of competence of the average client and their vulnerability to exploitation.
(3) The degree of coercion in the service—a service invested with coercive powers is not suitable for private provision.
(4) The degree to which the service is amenable to regulation.[55]

These are stringent conditions which may rarely be found in combination in the social services. Gilbert suggests that meals-on-wheels programmes, transportation services for the elderly and handicapped and home-help services might meet the criteria for private provision. Significantly, the private market is already heavily involved in these services in the United States. Laundry and catering services in hospitals, refuse collection and school meals also appear to meet Gilbert's conditions. In view of Gilbert's point about coercive services, it is interesting to note the development of private prisons in the United States and the proposal for a similar development in Britain. Another example is the private provision of protective services for abused and neglected children in the United States.

There is a possible danger in Gilbert's approach. It implies a piecemeal, service-by-service approach, and the problem of deciding the 'right' overall balance may not be faced. Rudolf Klein, for example, argues that there is a point beyond which the growth of the private sector would 'threaten the survival of the NHS as a viable institution'.[56] The New Right's position is clear: they see no reason for retaining the NHS except as a residual service. Welfare pluralists, on the other hand, have to decide what value they place on current public services and regulate the growth of the private sector accordingly. Klein notes 'the dangers of drifting by inadvertence into a situation where the essential nature of Britain's health-care system had been transformed as a result of public non-policy'.[57]

In this chapter we have been considering the strengths and weaknesses of commercial provision and financing. Before any conclusions about these can be reached, however, the advantages and drawbacks of statutory services have also to be considered. We need to know what we stand to lose by transferring resources to the commercial sector. It is to the statutory sector that we now turn.

7   The State and Social Welfare

THEORIES OF THE STATE

In the space available there is no possibility of attempting anything more ambitious than a brief sketch of different theories of the state. There is a vast and growing literature on this topic, much of it complicated and closely argued. Three schools of thought on the state will be discussed: pluralist, corporatist and Marxist.

Pluralist Views
The principal components of pluralist politics are elections, representative democracy, political parties and pressure groups. The state, if it is mentioned at all, consists of the formal institutions of government. References tend to be to 'the political system' rather than to 'the state'.

Power is widely distributed among a plurality of interest groups, each of which seeks to mobilise political support. Power is defined in terms of decision-making by asking which groups or individuals participated in the decision-making process and whose view prevailed? In this view of politics the government is a mediator, an impartial umpire concerned with the 'authoritative allocation of values'.[1] The whole system rests on an underlying consensus on what are seen as central values—democracy, the rule of law and respect for private property, for example.

This perspective has been criticised on several grounds. Mills, for example, claimed that power was not widely distributed, but concentrated in the hands of interrelated élites who use power for their own ends.[2] Concentration on

150

the apparatus of democratic politics served to cloak this. Bachrach and Baratz also criticised the pluralist view of power, arguing that non-decisions were as important as decisions. The power to keep items off the political agenda was crucial.[3] Lukes, while acknowledging the contribution of Bachrach and Baratz, claimed that their formulation of power is deficient in two respects: it fails to take account of the structural element in power, and it does not recognise that power may be exercised when there is no conflict. It is a significant exercise of power to prevent conflict arising in the first place. This is done by manipulating people into believing that the power-holders are acting in everyone's best interests. People acquiesce in actions which are not in their real interests but only in their interests as defined by the power-holders.[4]

Corporatist Views

Corporatism emphasises the importance of key or peak associations in negotiation with the state. In advanced industrial capitalism the competitive pressure groups posited by pluralism are partially replaced (the degree depending on the country concerned) by corporate groups which 'are defined by their location in the social and economic division of labour: their identity is given by the *function* that their members perform in society and the economy'.[5] Cawson, in a book which is a model of clarity, explains the main characteristics of corporatism:

One of the most important features of corporate representation is that the organisations are involved in negotiation with the state not simply to press their demands, but to act as agents through which state policy is implemented . . . In a corporatist model of policy-making, representation (of demands) and implementation (of policies) are fused with a mutually dependent bargaining relationship in which favourable policy outcomes are traded for co-operation and expertise.[6]

Corporatist arrangements are most frequently found in the economic field in which tripartite discussions take place between both sides of industry (in Britain the Trades Union Congress and the Confederation of British Industry) and the government. Such discussions do not have to be tripartite, however. For example, the Joint Commission in Austria has four participant organisations.[7]

Marxist Views

Marxism has been particularly rich in theories of the state. There are innumerable variations, but the common core is that state power in capitalist society is based on class; that political power and class power are closely linked, and that the state to some degree serves the interests of the dominant class, or at least facilitates capital accumulation. Marx himself held the view (shared by most present-day Marxists) that the state has a dual role of serving the long-term interests of capital, but also, to a degree, serving the interests of the community as a whole. This apparent paradox is one of the contradictions of the capitalist state.

Among contemporary Marxists it was Miliband who in 1969 rekindled interest in the state. Miliband contended that:

The most important political fact about advanced capitalist societies . . . is the continued existence in them of private and ever more concentrated economic power. As a result of that power the men . . . in whose hands it lies enjoy a massive preponderance in society, in the political system and in the determination of the state's policies and actions.[8]

The state, then, is largely the instrument of the dominant class, whose members own and control the means of production. Those who occupy the top positions in industry, the media, the universities and the state, are drawn from the same dominant class. Furthermore, the state is dependent upon the capitalist class for its resources.

Poulantzas questioned Miliband's approach of establishing who occupies élite positions, claiming that this was irrelevant. Poulantzas argued that it was the structure of capitalist society and the balance of power among classes within it which determined the class bias of the state. One of the features of the capitalist state was that the dominant class was not unified but split into fractions. The state needed to be 'relatively autonomous' from the specific interests of particular fractions if it were to be in a position to protect the long-term interests of the capitalist class.

Offe departs from both Miliband and Poulantzas in postulating a quite different relationship between the state and the capitalist class. The state is not allied with specific classes: 'While it does not defend the specific interests of a single class, the state nevertheless seeks to implement and guarantee the *collective* interests of all members of a class society *dominated by capital*'.⁹ The state itself is excluded from accumulation, but it depends upon the accumulation process for the revenues it needs to further its political ends. It is therefore in the state's *own interest* to create the conditions most conducive to capital accumulation. It must conceal its dependence on capital accumulation, and this is achieved by the democratic process of elections which gives the state its legitimation.

The three writers chosen to represent Marxist views by no means exhaust the range of Marxist theories of the state. Furthermore, the three writers themselves have been treated too briefly to do them justice. Readers interested in pursuing their ideas in greater depth are advised to go to the original texts.

THE MINIMAL OR LIMITED STATE

Anarchists hold that the state is immoral because it uses coercion to enforce rights and violates the absolute rights of life, liberty and property. The state, the main source of injustice, should be replaced by decentralised, non-hierarchical, communal institutions and assemblies. The centralised state would disappear. Classical liberal theory is less extreme, supporting the notion of a Nightwatchman state limited to the enforcement of contracts and the protection of its citizens from theft, fraud or violence.

The most interesting and influential arguments for a minimal state in recent years have been those propounded by Nozick in *Anarchy, State and Utopia*.¹⁰ As the title indicates, the book is divided into three parts, but the main argument is contained in the first two parts, and we will concentrate on them. In the first part Nozick argues against the anarchists that a minimal state is possible without infringing anyone's rights. The minimal state would develop out of a state of nature. In such a state most would behave according to moral principles, but nevertheless disputes and abuses would occur. In these circumstances people would begin to set up private protection associations. Eventually one of these would become the dominant protection agency, which would acquire a monopoly of force within a geographical area and be responsible for protecting everyone's rights within its territory. At this stage a minimal state will have emerged without anyone having taken a specific decision to form it. Nozick borrows Adam Smith's notion of 'the invisible hand' to explain these developments.

In the second part of the book Nozick argues that a minimal state is *all* that is justified. Any state which attempts to be more than minimal necessarily violates individual rights. To argue this point Nozick develops a novel theory of justice based on entitlement theory. People are entitled to what they have so long as its acquisition did not involve the infringement of anyone else's rights. Any attempt by the state to interfere with entitlement would be illegitimate. Redistributive welfare state policies are to be deprecated because they damage entitlement rights. There is no moral justification for taking from A (who is wealthy) to give to B (who is poor). Furthermore, people are under no obligation to help those less fortunate than themselves. Nozick sums up his views as follows:

Our main conclusions about the state are that a minimal state, limited to the narrow functions of protection against force, theft, fraud, enforcement of contracts, and so on, is justified; that any more extensive state will violate persons' rights not to do certain things and is unjustified. . . . Two noteworthy implications are that the state may not use its coercive apparatus for the purpose of getting some citizens to aid others, or in order to prohibit activities to people for their *own* good.[11]

This is an alarming philosophy with considerable appeal to the New Right. It is a philosophical indictment of the welfare state, providing the ammunition to those who wish to roll back the state. The New Right's views logically lead to a minimal state.

Some of the neo-conservatives are much less extreme in their attitudes towards the state than are Nozick and the New Right. Kristol, for example, who calls himself a neo-conservative, says that neo-conservatives do not seek to dismantle the welfare state, but to reshape it. By reshaping it, however, he obviously means cutting it back, since he asserts that 'the welfare state, over the past 25 years, lost its original self-definition and became something more ambitious, more inflated, and incredibly more expensive'.[12] Nevertheless, although he believes that 'the last hope for humanity at this time is an intellectually and morally reinvigorated liberal capitalism',[13] he distances himself from the New Right: 'Neoconservatives, though respecting the market as an economic mechanism, are not libertarian in the sense, say, that Milton Friedman and Friedrich A. von Hayek are. A conservative welfare state—what was once called a "social insurance" state—is perfectly consistent with the neoconservative perspective'.[14]

THE INTERVENTIONIST STATE

The growth of state intervention after the Second World War has already been outlined in Chapter 1. This occurred whichever party was in power; parties of the centre, right and left seemed to be in agreement. Keynes and Beveridge provided ample justification for state intervention in both the economic and social spheres. Even more significant, perhaps, was that neither Keynes nor Beveridge saw increased state intervention as being inimical to capitalism and the market economy. Indeed, they would be more efficient. Nevertheless, political conservatives have always had an ambivalent attitude towards state intervention, and in recent years the dominant attitudes within conservativism have moved from reluctant acceptance to hostility.

Social-democratic and Fabian views have been much more welcoming of state intervention, believing that the socialist values of liberty, equality and fraternity were not capable of achievement in an unregulated market economy. Government intervention was both necessary and desirable to ensure that public purposes were pursued and that needs were met. The state rather than being the enemy of freedom and the potential violator of rights was the only institution capable of promoting the freedom of all and protecting everyone's rights. For theorists of a Fabian persuasion, as for other socialists, equality and freedom are interdependent. Freedom without some measure of equality is meaningless. Economic subordination is as objectionable as political subordination, and since unchecked markets produce gross inequality, not only in income and wealth but also in status and power, they also reduce freedom. As Weale points out:

> The accumulation of resources in private hands, which may be used for controlling the conduct of others, in principle poses as great a threat to individual liberty as government power. For this reason there is no general inference to be drawn to the effect that the protection of individual liberty requires *laissez-faire*.[15]

Weale also provides an interesting perspective on the relationship between economic security and liberty, indicating at the same time the need for government involvement. The central idea is that of autonomy, of which Weale writes:

> There is one overriding imperative to which government action ought to be subject in the field of social policy, and that is the principle that the government should secure the conditions of equal autonomy for all. . . . This principle of autonomy asserts that all persons are entitled to respect as deliberative and purposive agents capable of formulating their own projects, and that as part of this respect there is a governmental obligation to bring into being or preserve the conditions in which this autonomy can be realised.[16]

Autonomous action is the product of deliberation in which the individual makes choices from among a range of options. There will be constraints, but these should not be so confining as to deprive the individual of autonomy. Economic deprivations result in a loss of autonomy, because alternatives are absent or strictly limited. Economic security, then, is necessary if the principle of autonomy is to be observed, and this implies that it is the state's responsibility to provide a comprehensive system of income maintenance. Furthermore, if people are to make full use of their autonomy, they need to acquire basic social and intellectual skills. Weale concludes that the state therefore has a responsibility to provide 'high-quality mass education up to the standard school-leaving age, with the aim of equipping all children with the cultural resources necessary for them to become autonomous social agents'.[17] It might be possible to construct a similar case in relation to other social services—health and personal social services, for example— although Weale does not do so.

The principle of autonomy guarantees only that minimum needs will be met. Distribution above the minimum, in Weale's analysis, relies on a contractarian argument. The most widely known modern variant of the contractarian perspective is that developed by Rawls. The theory begins with an imaginary original position in which men and women are equally free and rational. They are also equally ignorant about their own and others' abilities and about the positions they are likely to occupy in any future society. Rawls refers to this as 'the veil of ignorance'. The next step in the argument is to ask what distribution of resources and roles would men and women in the original position choose. Rawls claims that two principles would govern people's choices: (1) that rights and duties would be equally distributed and (2) 'social and economic inequalities . . . are just only if they result in compensating benefits for everyone, and in particular for the least advantaged members of society'.[18] This second principle, called the difference principle by Rawls, obviously has distributional implications. Weale claims that people's decisions behind the veil of ignorance would depend upon their level of risk aversion: the more averse they are to take risks (e.g. the risk that their abilities will land them at the bottom end of society), the more they will favour an egalitarian distribution of resources.

THE ADVANTAGES OF STATUTORY SOCIAL SERVICES

Welfare pluralists frequently begin their analyses with a catalogue of the deficiencies of statutory services. There can be no doubt that some of their criticisms are justified. Nevertheless, it must be remembered that one of the reasons for the development of state welfare in the first place was the inadequacies of other forms of provision. What then are the advantages of statutory provision?

One of the most important potential advantages is the opportunity afforded for broadly based social planning. The state is in a position to take an overall view of the direction of social policy and to set priorities for its future development. It is difficult to see how the individual priorities of voluntary and commercial providers can be co-ordinated or regulated to serve public policies or purposes. Nozick's invisible hand would be replaced by a visible one.

'Planning', at present, is not the most popular word in the English language and it is anathema to welfare pluralists. It may be true that centralised plans do not always work out in the way their originators intended, and it may be true that too little account is taken of local variations and people's expressed needs, but these weaknesses can be remedied. Walker, for example, describes a form of social planning which would involve decentralisation and the participation of those whose lives are affected by the plans and those who are responsible for implementing them.[19] The alleged weaknesses of past attempts at planning in Britain and elsewhere do not constitute an adequate reason for abandoning planning altogether; we need to look for ways of overcoming the drawbacks by devising procedures which make planning more responsive to people's needs. The alternative is to deny the necessity of defining social priorities. The search for equity, for example, is more likely to be achieved through social planning than it is through the unplanned activities of thousands of suppliers, none of which is particularly concerned with equity. Redistribution will not just happen, it has to be deliberately planned.

Gladstone uses the term 'dirigiste' to deride social planning.[20] Dirigism is meant to imply highly centralised and fairly rigid bureaucratic planning. Webb and Wistow, however, question the use of the term in relation to Britain:

Is it the case that what has been labelled as dirigism is in fact associated with state social services only because the state has become the guardian of equity and that the pursuit of equity has required a considerable degree of centralist control of resources and of forward planning? In other words, can the non-statutory system provide mass-produced services, preserve equity, and at the same time avoid dirigism?[21]

In another publication Webb states, 'In practice, references to dirigism have become a fashionable stick with which to beat recent social planning: we are witnessing the use of a pejorative epithet as a means of legitimating state disengagement'.[22]

One advantage of a specific plan is that it can be questioned and evaluated. Those responsible for it can be held accountable. Accountability is enhanced when there is citizen and community involvement and where this involvement does not exclude the poor and disadvantaged. Accountability is a feature of state services generally and this is an advantage they have over services provided under other auspices. The problem of accountability has been much discussed in relation to the voluntary sector: we noted in Chapter 5 that the lack of democratic accountability was one of the main criticisms of the Dutch system. Although there is a degree of accountability when statutory agencies secure the provision of services through third-party agreements, the chain of accountability is lengthened. Accountability is a prime requirement because public money, extracted compulsorily from taxpayers, is being handed over to non-elected bodies. Although accountability in state services may not work perfectly, it is nevertheless a useful safeguard, and there are usually opportunities for registering complaints and appealing against decisions.

One feature that the voluntary, statutory and informal sectors share is that they may be seen as responding to need. This is not to suggest that meeting need is their sole purpose, but it does point up a contrast with the commercial sector which responds to demand—the ability to pay. Although the statutory, voluntary and informal sectors are alike in that they respond to need, the statutory sector is the only one which can guarantee rights of access and rights of use, procedural rights and substantive rights. There are no such rights in the other sectors, and this constitutes a very powerful argument for statutory services.

There has been considerable debate in recent years about the degree to which statutory services help to promote equality. Criticisms that the welfare state does little to bring about equality were referred to in Chapter 2.

An interesting contribution to this debate is that of O'Higgins who takes a much less pessimistic view of the redistributive impact of social policy. He argues that it is income distributed through the market which is the major determinant of inequality. Transfer incomes (cash benefits) counteract, but are not powerful enough to outweigh, the inegalitarian consequences of market incomes. O'Higgins claims that 'cash benefits are, overall, highly redistributive towards lower income groups'.[23]

The social security system is concerned with what Rae calls global egalitarianism, which attempts to achieve a more equal distribution of resources by allocating goods and services unequally, giving most to those at the lower end of the income scale. Global egalitarianism is contrasted with marginal egalitarianism, which is achieved when a service is made equally available. Health and education services are more concerned with this form of egalitarianism. O'Higgins claims that 'the NHS and most of the education system are generally marginal egalitarian in their impact', and concludes that 'in terms of restricting inequality, welfare services are performing as well as might reasonably be expected in achieving the somewhat confused aims set for them'.[24]

O'Higgins's analysis of the redistributive effect of cash benefits is rather more convincing than his treatment of the NHS and education. There is a voluminous literature on the various inequalities besetting education and ample evidence demonstrating inequalities of access and use in the NHS. However, it is one thing to demonstrate existing inequalities, it is quite another to demonstrate that non-statutory forms of provision would achieve a greater degree of equality.

The state can ensure wider and more even coverage than either the voluntary or the commercial sector. By definition, it is the one institution which covers the whole of the nation. There is never of course complete uniformity of provision: there will be urban/rural, class, gender, age, ethnic and religious divisions. There may be even more variation when states are federal or highly decentralised. Nevertheless, state health insurance or income maintenance schemes, for example, offer the same or broadly similar terms to all citizens, which is very different from the actuarial basis of commercial insurance. Voluntary and commercial agencies

are also more unstable than most states in Western democracies so that continuity of provision by the latter is more
assured. Webb identifies uniformity as one of three facets
of mass-produced services: the other two are 'a scale of
need which merits or requires national provision of service'
and 'the possibilities of economies of scale'. He suggests
that 'where each of these features of mass production is
appropriately present, it may be extremely difficult, or
unproductive, to replace the state as the provider of such
services'.[25]

It is difficult to see how commercial agencies could
adequately deal with preventative services. Indeed, prevention is likely to work against their commercial interests by
reducing the number of customers. Voluntary organisations
might adopt preventative strategies in the personal social
services, although successful prevention requires a co-ordinated, co-operative approach which is not a marked characteristic of voluntary provision. Primary prevention is
concerned with urban renewal, improved housing, a heal-
thier environment and attempts to deal with deprivation
and inequality. These are programmes which require such
massive resources that extensive state involvement is almost
inevitable. At the same time, it is true that urban renewal
in many Western countries is now being carried out by
private enterprise, and inner-city policies are co-operative
ventures involving the voluntary, statutory and commercial
sectors.

Participation occurs in all four sectors. In the informal
sector most people are part of a network of neighbours,
friends and kin, with the last, and especially the nuclear
family, particularly important in service provision. The
extent and form of participation in the informal network
depends upon gender, age and one's position in the family.
Participation in the market system is based on payment—
one participates as a customer in exchange relationships.
The encouragement of participation is frequently identified
as one of the strengths of the voluntary sector. Participation
in voluntary organisations may take the form of administrative tasks, fund-raising, service provision or membership
of a self-help or neighbourhood group. Opportunities for
participation in the statutory system are much more exten-

sive than is commonly realised. For example, one may participate as a voter, as an elected representative, as a co-opted member of local government and other committees, as a member of an advisory committee, as a member of a political party, as a member of a pressure group attempting to influence government policy, or one may assist statutory authorities in the provision of services. The statutory services offer much more scope for participation than commercial services, and they offer more scope for *political* participation than voluntary services.

In his book, *The Gift Relationship*, Titmuss argues that the public social services enlarge our freedom by allowing for the expression of altruism. This could also be said of the informal and voluntary sectors, both of which involve gift relationships, but the distinguishing feature of statutory services is that they generalise altruism, allowing us to behave altruistically towards *strangers;* Titmuss refers to this as 'anonymous helpfulness'.[26] This rather metaphysical point is expressed in the following quotation:

> the ways in which society organises and structures its social institutions—and particularly its health and welfare systems—can encourage or discourage the altruistic in man; such systems can foster integration or alienation; they can allow the 'theme of the gift' . . . —of generosity towards strangers—to spread among and between social groups and generations. This is an aspect of freedom in the twentieth century which, compared with the emphasis on consumer choice in material acquisitiveness, is insufficiently recognised.[27]

This brings us back to the socialist notion of fraternity and co-operation, which is in direct opposition to the market principles of competition. Social policy focuses on community, and public social services 'create integration and discourage alienation'.[28]

CURTAILING THE ROLE OF THE STATE

Although governments' responses to the alleged crisis in the welfare state exhibit considerable variety in points of detail and in the severity of the action taken, there is a broad similarity in the aims being pursued: the restraint of public expenditure, cutting out waste and reducing levels of service.

At the most general level all governments have taken action to reduce or control deficits by setting 'global norms'.[29] This may take three forms: (1) stating an upper limit for the deficit as a proportion of GDP, (2) setting an upper limit for public expenditure as a proportion of GDP and (3) setting an upper limit for public sector borrowing. Within these global norms particular areas of government activity are the subject of expenditure restraint, sometimes in the form of across-the-board cuts, but much more usually on a selective basis.

Changes in social expenditure in OECD countries can be seen in Table 7.1. The third set of columns compares the annual growth rates of social expenditure in the period 1975 to 1981 with the rates between 1960 and 1975. What is clearly demonstrated is that social expenditure continued to grow but at a much slower rate after 1975. By far the biggest change has occurred in the Netherlands with a decrease of 8.8 percentage points. Australia has the dubious honour of having the second biggest reduction of 7.2 percentage points. However, there is an important difference between these two countries. In the Netherlands social expenditure in 1981 still amounted to 36.1 per cent of GDP. In Australia, by contrast, social expenditure in 1981 amounted to merely 18.8 per cent of GDP—only Greece, Switzerland and Japan having lower figures.

Since 1981 there have been some changes, however. In France, for example, a socialist president was elected in 1981, and one commentator claims that 'within a few months the Mitterrand government had gone on a spending spree of unprecedented proportions'.[30] The budget deficit in 1981 was in excess of 200 billion francs, the social security budget alone having a deficit of 16 billion francs. In 1982 Mitterrand was forced to reverse these policies and a stringent austerity programme was introduced. The 1986 elections produced a conservative majority in the Assembly with M. Chirac as prime minister. Chirac has promised spending cuts, increased privatisation and lower taxes. In 1981 Reagan was in his first term of office as president of the United States. In successive budgets since then domestic budgets have been

Table 7.1: Social expenditure in OECD countries 1960–81[a]

	Expenditure share		Annual growth rate of real GDP (%)		Annual growth rate of deflated social expenditure (%)		Decrease in the annual growth rate between 1960-75 and 1975-81 (%)	
	1960	1981	1960–75	1975–81	1960–75	1975–81	Real GDP	Deflated social expenditure
Canada	12.1	21.5	5.1	3.3	9.3	3.1	1.8	6.2
France	13.4[b]	29.5	5.0	2.8	7.3[b]	6.2	2.2	1.1
Germany	20.5	31.5	3.8	3.0	7.0	2.4	0.8	4.6
Italy	16.8	29.1	4.6	3.2	7.7	5.1	1.4	2.6
Japan	8.0	17.5	8.6	4.7	12.8	8.4	3.9	4.4
United Kingdom	13.9	23.7	2.6	1.0	5.9	1.8	1.6	4.1
United States	10.9	20.8	3.4	3.2	8.0	3.2	0.2	4.8
Average of above countries[e]	13.7	24.8	4.7	3.0	8.3	4.3	1.7	4.0
Australia	10.2	18.8	5.2	2.4	9.6	2.4	2.8	7.2
Austria	17.9	27.7	4.5	2.9	6.7	5.0	1.6	2.7
Belgium	17.4	37.6[c]	4.5	2.2[c]	9.3	7.9[c]	2.3	1.4
Denmark	-	33.3[d]	3.7	2.2	-	5.4[d]	1.5	-
Finland	15.4	25.9	4.5	2.9	7.5	4.8	1.6	2.7
Greece	8.5	13.4[c]	6.8	3.5	8.4	9.4[c]	3.3	-1.0[b]
Ireland	11.7	28.4	4.3	3.5	9.1	7.1	0.8	2.0
Netherlands	16.2	36.1	4.5	2.0	10.4	1.6	2.5	8.8
New Zealand	13.0	19.6	4.0	0.4	5.5	3.5	3.6	2.0
Norway	11.7	27.1	4.3	4.1	10.1	4.6	0.2	5.5
Sweden	15.4	33.4	4.0	1.0	7.9	4.7	3.0	3.2
Switzerland	7.7	14.9[d]	3.4	1.7	7.6	2.7[d]	1.7	4.9
OECD average[e]	13.1	25.6	4.6	2.6	8.4	4.8	1.9	3.8

Notes: (a) Or latest year available, (b) excluding education, (c) 1980, (d) 1979, (e) unweighted average.
Source: Social Expenditure 1960–1990 (OECD, Paris, 1985).

reduced and defence spending increased. In 1982 Paul Schlüter became Denmark's first conservative prime minister since 1901, and his centre-right coalition government has introduced successive austerity budgets. Germany, too, has a conservative, market-oriented government intent upon restraining the growth of public expenditure. Cost-cutting programmes under conservative governments have also been introduced since 1981 in Belgium, Britain and Norway.[31] In terms of the political party holding power, Australia and Sweden have moved in the opposite direction. In Sweden the Social Democratic Party was returned to power in 1982 with 'a strategy which it presented as "the third way"—to distinguish it from the recovery models which had been adopted elsewhere in Europe'.[32] This 'third way' steered a middle course between the 'contractionist' model of Britain and Germany and the 'expansionist' model initially adopted by Mitterrand's government in France. The neo-conservative Australian government of Fraser has given way to a Labour government with initially a less extreme attitude towards public expenditure. In the budget of 1986, however, the Australian Labour government announced an austerity programme involving substantial cuts in public expenditure on health, education and social security.

Table 7.2 shows changes in expenditure for four major social policy areas. The growth rate of pensions has held up better than the other three programmes. The growth rate of expenditure on unemployment compensation declined very sharply in the United States and Australia. The British position is an interesting one in that unemployment in Britain rose more quickly in the period from 1975 to 1981 than it did in most other OECD countries. It is ironical that the government's anti-inflation policies cause unemployment to rise and thus frustrate efforts to reduce public expenditure despite cuts elsewhere. However, unemployment compensation is by no means the only explanation for the failure to reduce public expenditure: a falling GDP between 1979 and 1983 and increased spending on the police and defence are also partly responsible.

The growth rates of health and education expenditure fell in every country in the later of the two periods, but Britain and New Zealand are the only countries in which

Table 7.2: Annual growth rates of real social expenditure (%) 1960–75 and 1975–81

	Education		Health		Pensions		Unemployment Compensation	
	1960–75	1975–81	1960–75	1975–81	1960–75	1975–81	1960–75	1975–81
Canada	8.4	1.0	13.0	3.0	8.3	6.8	10.7	0.5
France	-	1.0	10.9	6.3	7.7	8.7	15.9	19.3
Germany	7.2	1.6	6.6	2.1	6.3	2.1	23.9	4.7
Italy	4.6	3.9	6.7	0.1	9.6	7.7	11.4	10.1
Japan	5.7	4.1	12.2	6.6	12.7	13.7	12.7	1.8
United Kingdom	5.0	-2.0	3.4	2.0	5.9	4.5	10.3	14.2
USA	6.1	0.4	10.3	3.8	7.2	4.4	8.3	-9.5
Australia	8.9	1.2	9.1	-0.5	8.5	4.0	24.3	4.8
Finland	3.0	1.7	11.9	3.9	11.1	5.5	31.7	20.5
Ireland	7.4	4.5	7.7	6.3	8.2	6.6	14.3	4.4
Netherlands	4.3	1.1	11.4	4.4	10.3	5.2	13.2	7.5
New Zealand	5.2	-0.9	3.5	0.9	5.2	7.7	21.5	41.3
Norway	6.9	3.6	9.0	5.2	12.1	4.6	2.6	20.8
Sweden	3.4	2.1	11.3	3.4	8.7	6.9	7.0	14.5

Source: Social Expenditure 1960–1990 (OECD, Paris, 1985)

educational expenditure actually declined between 1975 and 1981, and Australia is the only country in which health-care expenditure declined.

A major service omitted from the OECD figures is housing. In most of the countries of Western Europe housing budgets have been subjected to moderate cuts, but in Britain and the United States housing has been the most severely cut of all the services. In Britain housing expenditure has been cut by 57 per cent, and further cuts are planned by 1987/88.[33] In the United States the cuts in housing expenditure are even greater. According to Hartman the intention of the Reagan administration was 'virtually to end all programs that directly add, through construction and substantial rehabilitation, to the stock of housing available to lower-income households'.[34] To this end the 1984 budget proposed a 94 per cent cut in the level of new budget authority for housing.

The figures in Tables 7.1 and 7.2 tell us little about the specific changes made, and perhaps a few examples would be useful. One method employed to reduce costs is simply to reduce the benefits payable. In West Germany, for example, the 1982 Budget reduced maternity allowances, children's allowances and unemployment benefits. In the Netherlands all social insurance benefits were cut in both amount and duration in 1984. But Goudswaard and de Jong claim that cuts occurred even before 1984. They state that total cuts 'amounted to about 3 per cent of GNP from 1977 to 1983, when compared with the situation that would have prevailed if policies had remained unaltered'.[35] By 1986 further cuts of 2 per cent of GNP were planned. Goudswaard and de Jong say that 'the measures planned for 1984 and beyond entail an unprecedented change in the structure of the social insurance scheme and a sizeable reduction in generosity'.[36] In the United States income security benefits were cut. Storey comments that 'viewed as a one-time budgetary action, the administration's attempt to reduce income security spending was amazingly successful'.[37] Action in the 1982, 1983 and 1984 budgets involve almost a 10 per cent cut in social programmes, as compared with prior policies, by 1986. Expenditure on food stamps, child nutrition, Aid for Families with Dependent Children

(AFDC), unemployment compensation, student loans, compensatory education, housing benefits and employment and training services has been severely curtailed. The biggest expenditure cuts were experienced by the child nutrition, food stamps and AFDC programmes. Retirement, Disability and Survivors' Insurance benefits and veterans' benefits were treated more generously. It is significant that the most vulnerable programmes are those targeted on the poor, while programmes available to the whole population receive greater protection. The Social Services and Community Services Block Grants (payable to the states) have been drastically cut. Medicare and Medicaid suffered cumulative expenditure reductions between 1982 and 1985 of 5 per cent and 4.5 per cent respectively.[38] Bawden and Palmer describe the views and policies of President Reagan as 'a coherent ideological attack on the principles that have governed social policy in this country for the last half century'.[39] In France, changes to unemployment compensation in 1982 and 1984 had the effect of reducing benefits to some categories of recipient and relating the duration of compensation to the period worked before unemployment.

Increasing benefits by less than the rate of inflation has the effect of reducing the real value of payments. This is a tactic used in Britain in relation to unemployment, sickness and child benefits. Many of the cuts were subsequently reversed, but in the meantime claimants suffered loss of income. In addition, short-term benefits became taxable and earnings-related supplements were abolished. In 1980 the link between long term rates of benefit and earnings was broken. Changes in indexation procedures involving a reduction in the real value of benefits have occurred in Australia, Belgium, Denmark, Holland and Norway. The Danish government froze the indexation of welfare benefits for the whole of 1982.

An effective method of reducing public expenditure is to raise eligibility criteria so that fewer people qualify for the service or benefit. During the 1980s most welfare states have followed this course. It would not be profitable to detail all the changes since they are numerous and technical. The United States is probably worthy of special mention because it appears to have gone further than other countries in restricting eligibility. Palmer and Sawhill make the following comment:

Lower-tier safety net programs were generally cut by imposing tighter income eligibility limits and offsetting benefits more fully for earnings and other sources of income. The result has been to exclude many of the working poor and near-poor from government programs . . . to greatly reduce benefits for others, and to target a higher percentage of the reduced funds on the poor.[40]

As a consequence of these changes an estimated 400,000 to 500,000 lost AFDC eligibility, and for most of these families loss of AFDC eligibility also entailed loss of Medicaid benefits. About one million or more people no longer qualified for Food Stamps.[41]

A development which harks back to the English Poor Law is the workfare programme which has now been adopted by over half of the states, although most of the programmes are limited to a few counties. A *Panorama* television programme (broadcast on 7 April 1986) gave several examples of workfare policies. The common feature of all of them was that AFDC claimants were expected to find work rather than rely on public benefits. Some programmes waive the work requirement for women with pre-school children, but Oklahoma, which has one of the most draconian schemes, is an example of a state which forces even women with young children to seek work. The philosophy seems to be 'either you work or you starve'. Some states, Virginia was the example chosen by the *Panorama* presenters, rely on public employment, while others, San Diego for example, expect claimants to seek jobs in the private sector (after being given training in how to go about gaining employment).

Another strategy is the transfer of costs to the recipients of services and benefits. This can be achieved by introducing or increasing waiting days before benefit is paid, as has been done in the Netherlands and Denmark, for example. A similar effect is achieved by means of charges and cost-sharing arrangements. Prescription charges in Britain provide a notable example of this, having increased by 1,100 per cent (over 600 per cent in real terms) between 1979 and

1986. Similar examples of the increased use of charges can be found. Johansen and Kolberg, for instance, report that 'since 1980 several important services of the Norwegian welfare state have become more expensive for individuals. Fee-for-services has been introduced/increased concerning medical consultations, laboratory tests, drugs, physiotherapeutic treatment, travel expenses and home help for the aged'.[42] In West Germany there have also been increases in charges—notably in the health insurance system. Charges for prescriptions and dentures were introduced under legislation of 1977. In 1981/82 both of these were increased and charges were introduced for spectacles, medical appliances and hospital care. Another good example is provided by Medicare in the United States. An editorial in the *Boston Globe* in 1985 made the following statement:

The Reagan Administration has proposed $16.3 billion in Medicare reductions through freezes on payments to providers (hospitals and doctors) and increases in the elderly's share of medical costs. Under the Administration's proposal, America's 38 million Medicare recipients would pay higher monthly premiums, pay more toward hospital stays and doctor visits and begin to pay for home care. The average additional costs to recipients is estimated at $600 over the next five years.[43]

Because public services tend to be labour intensive, relatively small percentage cuts in staff can produce substantial savings. Japan, Belgium, Finland and New Zealand have all used personnel ceilings and freezes. In the United States the numbers of federal, state and local employees were slightly reduced in 1981 and 1982. Although the reduction amounted to only 1.8 per cent it nevertheless constituted a reversal of an almost continuously upward trend since 1960. The staff reductions coincided with an increase in contracting out and a consequent weakening of the public service trade unions. The Conservative government in Britain has been especially active in attempting to reduce staffing levels. The prime minister appointed Sir Derek Rayner, managing director of a large and profitable chain of retail stores, to examine management efficiency in the public services. Rayner reported directly to the prime minister and was given wide discretion. In every area which Rayner examined, staff savings were recommended. In 1976 there were slightly less than 750,000 civil servants. By January 1983 the number had fallen to 625,000. By April 1985 there had been a further reduction to 606,000, and the planned total for 1988 is 590,000.

One way of reducing central government staffing levels is by decentralising, although any savings made may be compensated for by increases at the more local levels of government. Thus, while decentralisation does not of itself reduce public expenditure, it does reduce the responsibility of central government. Decentralisation to local units of government has been a major theme in Denmark, France, Germany, Italy, Norway, Sweden and the United States. In America President Reagan makes much of what he calls 'new federalism', which represents 'a major political and philosophical departure from the prevailing view and practice of federalism as it has evolved since the 1930s'.[44] The main features of new federalism are the removal of federal regulations relating to state and local governments; the separation of functional and financial responsibility between the federal, state and local governments (sometimes referred to as 'dual federalism'); the transfer of some federal functions to states; reduced federal grants; and the replacement of specific categorical grants by block grants. France, one of the most highly centralised nations, has also embarked upon structural change with increased independence being granted to departmental and communal councils. In Britain, although there has been much academic debate about decentralisation, in terms of practical policy central control of local government has been considerably intensified since 1980.

Frequently, decentralisation is coupled with the idea of self-help and participation. In Italy, for example, two pieces of legislation in the late 1970s sought 'the complete reorganisation of the social welfare and health care sectors'.[45] Responsibilities for health and social welfare services were transferred to the communes. This policy was designed 'to ensure a management more in keeping with each local situation, and to encourage participation by local people, bringing the political forces and adminstrators closer to them'.[46]

SOME EFFECTS OF THE STATE'S DIMINISHED ROLE

In spite of what has been said about expenditure restraints and cuts, their effects on total public expenditure have been marginal. Even Mrs Thatcher has failed to reduce public expenditure, which was actually higher in 1986 than when she took office; it could of course be argued that it would have been even higher if different policies had been followed. But why is it that the rhetoric of cuts exceeds actual achievements? There are several possible reasons:

(1)   Governments wishing to make cuts may have to trim their plans in the face of opposition from either representative assemblies or civil servants or because of public disquiet. The separation of powers in the United States means that Congress may thwart the president's budget plans. President Reagan has achieved only about 50 per cent of the cuts in domestic expenditure he was seeking. The same is true in the Netherlands, West Germany, Denmark and Norway. Le Grand suggests that there may be considerable middle-class opposition to cuts in education and health services.[47]

(2)   Rising and high levels of unemployment mean that unemployment insurance and means-tested income-support payments both increase.

(3)   Demographic changes—especially higher proportions of elderly people—mean more demands on health and social services.

(4)   The cuts in social expenditure may be more than balanced by increased expenditure elsewhere—especially on defence, but also on law and order.

As already indicated, Britain may be taken as an example of a government intent on cutting public expenditure, but not managing to do so. The rate of increase has slowed down since 1979–80, but public expenditure has continued to rise: by 1984–85 public expenditure in real terms was 9.4 per cent above its level in 1979–80.[48] In 1984 the government published a green paper that attempted to look at the prospects for public expenditure into the 1990s. The paper made it clear that one of the main purposes of curbing public expenditure was the scope it gave for tax cuts.[49]

The government's inability to bring public exenditure down is partly to be explained by its emphasis on defence and law and order, both of which have benefited from increased expenditure. Robinson, in an analysis of public expenditure between 1979–80 and 1984–85 says that 'it is changes in the composition of expenditure—rather than its overall scale—which represents the major policy change of this period'.[50]

Social expenditure has experienced rather mixed fortunes. Housing, as we have seen, suffered drastic cuts. The National Health Service has been treated rather more favourably. According to Robinson, expenditure on health and personal social services increased by 17 per cent in real terms between 1979–80 and 1984–85.[51] In more recent years increases have been at or marginally above the rate of inflation. In 1986–87, for example, expenditure plans allowed for 1 per cent growth over and above the rate of inflation, assuming pay rises were held to 4.5 per cent.[52]

However, most of the extra expenditure is accounted for by demographic trends, especially the increase in the number of frail elderly people. Technological changes, because they are more costly than traditional medicine, have also contributed to the increase. In 1984 the House of Commons Select Committee on the Social Services claimed that spending on the NHS in the last five years had barely kept pace with increased demand.[53]

Demographic factors have worked in the opposite direction in education. There has been a slight fall in total expenditure on education, but this is more than compensated for by a reduction in the school-age population between 1979–80 and 1984–85. Robinson estimates that there has been a *per capita* increase in educational expenditure of 10 per cent.[54]

Social security expenditure increased by more than 28 per cent in real terms between 1979–80 and 1984–85. The main reason for this rise is the vastly increased number of people who are unemployed. A subsidiary reason is the increased costs of retirement and supplementary pensions. The government is obviously anxious to reduce the huge cost of cash benefits, and this is undoubtedly one of the reasons for Fowler's review of social security and the package of reforms contained in the 1985 white paper.[55] It is not only the British government that has failed to match action to rhetoric but none of this should be taken to mean that the cuts in programmes, combined with tax changes, have not had a significant impact. It would be nonsense to suggest that this was the case. Danziger and Smolensky, introducing a cross-national symposium on income transfer policies, have this to say:

A political revolution now under way among Western countries may have drastic repercussions on the poor. For most of the post-war period, government programmes designed to raise the income share of the poor proliferated and expanded. In the wake of the world-wide slow down in economic growth following the first oil embargo in 1973, critics argued that the gains from redistributional programmes are far outweighed by adverse side-effects that reduce work and savings. These arguments have been taken with increasing seriousness. In the United States, England, Germany, and even in the Netherlands and Scandinavia, public income transfer policies have been or are being cut back.[56]

O'Higgins, analysing the British experience, says that it is through the tax changes—reductions in the standard and top rates of income tax and increases in value-added tax—that programme changes have had the greatest impact. Increased expenditure on law and order and defence has reduced the redistributive effect of government spending, while higher spending on health and social security work in the opposite direction. O'Higgin's analysis demonstrates that inequality has increased since 1976 and that the increase has been more marked since 1979. The main factors contributing to this change are a less equal distribution of market incomes and tax changes. The most significant cause of low income is unemployment and the unemployed have now replaced the elderly at the bottom of the income distribution. O'Higgins states that 'the social transfer system has been important in restricting the degree to which increased market income inequalities have been translated into gross income inequalities.' He notes that the nature of income transfers has changed significantly, with greater reliance on means-tested benefits.[57]

Tax expenditures, tax reliefs to particular categories of

tax payers, are a regressive feature of the British system; they have increased substantially since 1979. Wilkinson calculates that the cost of relief to private pension schemes increased by 106 per cent between 1979–80 and 1983–84, whereas the cost of statutory retirement and supplementary pensions increased by only 12.3 per cent and 22.8 per cent respectively.[58] In the same period, the subsidies paid in respect of public sector housing were reduced by 21.5 per cent, but relief on mortgage interest payments increased by 28.6 per cent. Wilkinson concludes that tax allowances are inequitable, inefficient, beyond the control of government and difficult to change because of the danger of losing votes.[59]

Danziger, Gottschalk and Smolensky claim that in the United States poverty increased by 2.2 percentage points between 1980 and 1983, a bigger increase than has occurred in any other presidential administration. In explaining the causes of the increase in poverty the authors assign equal importance to unemployment and social programme cuts, but they stress that 'while the increased poverty due to the higher unemployment rate will be mostly reversed by the end of 1984, when the unemployment rate will have returned to its 1980 level, the effects of transfer programme changes are likely to persist'.[60] This statement is given greater point by the fall in the number in poverty from 35.5 million in 1983 to 33.7 million in 1984.[61] The fall is to be accounted for by reductions in the number of people unemployed.

Danziger and Smolensky sum up the experience of the six countries represented at the conference on income transfer policies:

The poor are measurably worse off than they would have been under any reasonable projection of past policies in the United Kingdom, the United States and the Netherlands. In Switzerland and Italy there have been no retrenchments; in France, programme changes were in the direction of greater social spending, until the balance of payments difficulties and inflation led to a broad retreat—indeed some would say reversal—of the trend.[62]

THE STATE AND WELFARE PLURALISM

In earlier chapters attention has been drawn to the relationship between the statutory and the other sectors of the welfare system. In this chapter we have considered some of the advantages of statutory provision and some of the consequences of reducing the role of the state. This section will, therefore, be relatively brief.

Central to the neo-liberal ideology is a deep suspicion of the state and bureaucracy which is perceived as the enemy of individual freedom and enterprise. The virtues of individualism, self-reliance, entrepreneurship and competition are extolled. Inequality is both inevitable and desirable, and incentives need to be increased, principally by reducing taxes. The combination of tax cuts for the better-off and reduced benefits is a recipe for greater inequality. This vehemently anti-statist stance leads to a complete reversal of the present pluralistic balance, the state being reduced to a residual role catering for those excluded from private markets. Clearly the neo-liberal position is not a pluralist one since the dominance of the state is replaced by the dominance of the market.

Welfare pluralists share the Right's dislike of centralised bureaucracy and they characterise statutory services as being ineffective, inefficient and unresponsive. The role of the state as service-provider should, therefore, be reduced and the delivery of statutory services should be entrusted to community-oriented structures. There are, however, several ways in which the position of welfare pluralists differs very substantially from that of the Right. The most fundamental difference is that welfare pluralists do not necessarily argue for a reduction in government expenditure, but for a redistribution of it in support of voluntary and informal provision. The state would cease to be the main provider of welfare but would continue as the main source of finance, and its regulatory role would increase. Thus welfare pluralists see the state as having rather more than a residual role. However, the state they have in mind is a decentralised one, and they would approve of the decentralisation currently taking place in many parts of the world.

In the final chapter we turn our attention to a consideration of competing patterns of welfare provision and finance. One of the major differences among the identified alternative models is the role which each of them assigns to the state.

8 Alternative Futures

Since the mid–1970s the welfare state has been under attack from several directions. The welfare state's supporters were slow to respond. In the early 1980s, however, several publications, seeking either to defend the welfare state or to restate the issues and suggest ways forward, have appeared. One of these, *The Future of the Welfare State* (edited by Glennerster), is dealt with more fully later in this chapter.[1] Two other books have been particularly influential in Britain: *In Defence of Welfare* (edited by Bean, Ferris and Whynes)[2] and *The Future of Welfare* (edited by Klein and O'Higgins).[3]

Neither of these publications arose out of a desire to defend the traditional welfare state. Bean, Ferris and Whynes argue that 'the unquestioning belief that the welfare state as it is presently constituted represents the embodiment of all that is good can be as detrimental to the cause of welfare as can the opposite.'[4] Nevertheless, the idea for the book stemmed from 'the circumstances created by the change of government in Britain in 1979'.[5] The writers claim that 'within the space of a few years it had become evident that the new administration was committed to what some of its more extreme supporters termed "rolling back the welfare state".'[6]

The book provides a theoretical defence of welfare, countering the assertions of the New Right. The first section of the book addresses the moral and ethical principles of welfare; the second section examines the workings of the market in the context of welfare provision; the third and final section applies the principles to current trends in British social policy.

Klein and O'Higgins advocate a strategy of 'purposeful opportunism'. This implies the setting of broad objectives and then devising policy options 'which are consistent with our objectives but which do not necessarily involve long-term commitments'.[7] To cope with uncertainty, and to avoid catastrophes resulting from over-optimistic assumptions, policy options must be flexible and reversible.

Both of these books address basic issues concerning the nature and scope of welfare policy and provision. A fundamental element in any reappraisal of the welfare system is the debate on welfare pluralism: it provides a framework within which specific issues (for example, the position of women, employment and unemployment, law and order, drug abuse) may be considered.

The balance between the four sectors is continually shifting, and people with different ideological predispositions will have different views about the most appropriate balance. The remainder of this chapter is concerned with the alternative futures presented by competing views. There is, of course, always a risk in attempting to categorise different views under broad headings of presenting too tidy and consistent a picture. The reader should be aware that social policy is seldom tidy and that the dividing lines between categories are not clear cut.

A NEW RIGHT/NEO-CONSERVATIVE FUTURE

The distinction between neo-conservatism and the New Right is clearer in the United States than it is in Europe. One of the best discussions of the distinction is to be found in Peele's book *Revival and Reaction*.[8] The neo-conservatives, of whom Kristol, Bell and Moynihan are among the best-known examples, are frequently former members of the Democratic party who believe that the Great Society programmes of the 1960s went too far. On the whole they 'operate at the level of intellectual debate and policy research, rather than at the level of day-to-day political organisation'.[9] They believe that although capitalism has its faults, it is infinitely better than any of the alternatives. Their attitude towards the state is distrustful but not paranoid; they wish to see the state's role reduced, but they recognise that it has a part to play in social policy. Peele maintains that the New Right is 'a very different phenomenon' from neo-conservatism.[10] The New Right engages in day-to-day politics, it is aggressive and strident and it is vehemently anti-statist. Its pet hates appear to be socialism, the women's movement, abortion, divorce, sex education and general moral laxity. Its most favoured items would include capitalism, the family, fundamentalist religion, populism and what it terms 'traditional American values'.

Levitas, more concerned with the New Right in Britain, identifies two strands: neo-liberalism and authoritarian conservatism.[11] The neo-liberal strand is represented by Friedman and Hayek: the key words in this strand are freedom, competition, accountability and efficiency. The key words in authoritarian conservatism are authority, allegiance and tradition, and the key institution is the family. Levitas suggests that the two strands are inconsistent. Neo-liberals want a minimal state whereas exponents of authoritarian conservatism, such as Scruton, wish to see a strong state intervening in the interests of control rather than social welfare.[12]

In terms of social policy the New Right's position is unequivocal. Principally, the state's role in social service provision and financing would be greatly curtailed, and bureaucratic and professional power would be reduced. Health, education and the provision of residential accommodation would certainly be entrusted to the private market, and the same might also be true of day-care and the personal social services. Cash transfers (possibly in the form of a reverse income tax) and vouchers would replace services-in-kind. A great deal would obviously hinge on how generous the transfer payments were, but since the market system *depends* upon inequality, the assumption must be that they would not be particularly generous and that there would be a considerable gap between recipients of state aid and the lowest-paid workers. For those unable to participate in the market there would be few, if any, rights, and desert would replace need as the main distributive principle.

Inequality and social division would inevitably increase. The market and the family would be the main sources of welfare provision, supplemented by voluntary organisations and charity. The burden placed on families would considerably increase and women would be expected to remain in the home.

As indicated already, American neo-conservatives share some of these New Right views—for example, the belief in the central importance of the family—but they envisage the state taking a rather more prominent role. They have their counterparts in European conservative parties. Although they believe the modern state is mistakenly paternalistic, their views about its role are less extreme than those of the New Right. Kristol, for example, writes:

There is no more chance today of returning to a society of 'free enterprise' and enfeebled government than there was, in the 16th century, of returning to a Rome-centred Christendom. The world and the people in it have changed. One may regret this fact; nostalgia is always permissible. But the politics of nostalgia is always self-destructive.[13]

Kristol favours social insurance, universal children's allowances and universal health insurance. The emphasis on universal benefits may seem surprising, but he supports them on the grounds of solidarity and fraternity. In spite of this, however, the neo-conservative view of the welfare state is that its role should be strictly limited. To arrive at a position of which they would approve would entail, even in the United States, an overall reduction of social expenditure. In Europe even more severe cuts would be implied.

A WELFARE PLURALIST FUTURE

Welfare pluralists are not given to producing blueprints. It is part of the welfare pluralist philosophy that each locality must work out for itself what particular balance of services most nearly meets its needs. Hadley and Hatch, two prominent British welfare pluralists, constantly refer to 'more decentralised and participatory structures', and they describe a number of small-scale experiments. They are aware of the difficulties of developing these initiatives into a comprehensive system of social care, but their prescriptions are of the most general kind; for example, that the government must clear spaces for community initiatives. They do, however, recognise that 'the instrument for formulating a strategy must necessarily be the state, and the statutory sector must provide a framework through which priorities and standards can be maintained'.[14]

Decentralisation and participation are key features in the welfare pluralist strategy. Community-oriented services can be developed only in relatively small localities. Only in small units do people feel able to influence policies and service delivery. The fuller development of neighbourhood councils, as in parts of the United States, would provide opportunities for participation, but the direct involvement of clients and employees in statutory decision-making bodies would also be encouraged. One of the main advantages of the voluntary sector, according to Gladstone, is 'the greater scope it offers for participation'.[15] He claims that this is particularly important because 'people who have a say in the decisions affecting their lives are more likely to be responsible and constructive citizens'.[16] In terms of participation, self-help organisations are especially significant.

The voluntary sector in a welfare pluralist model would be considerably, although gradually, expanded. Its growth would be at the expense of the statutory sector, and there would be a very definite shift in the present balance in education and in the personal social services provided for handicapped and elderly people and for deprived and delinquent children. Hadley and Hatch concede that the state would retain its dominance in social security, and Gladstone sees some problems in expanding the voluntary sector's role in certain areas of health-care provision: hospital services for the acutely sick would remain a statutory monopoly, and the government would have important roles in the allocation of resources and in prevention. Although the importance of the statutory sector as a source of service provision would be diminished, it would expand its standard-setting and regulatory functions. There may be something of a contradiction here: regulation of a pluralist system may entail more rather than less bureaucracy.

The informal sector would also be expected to take on

greater caring responsibilities. As has been noted, informal care means care by families, which means care by women. Welfare pluralism relies heavily on the unpaid work of women, not only in the family but also in voluntary organisations, where they constitute a high proportion of the voluntary labour force. In contrast to the free-market liberals, however, the welfare pluralists would not simply leave the family to get on with the job of caring for its members; statutory and voluntary agencies, unpaid and professional workers, would be concerned to reinforce the informal sector. Hadley and Hatch criticise current policies in relation to the family in Britain:

In sum, both nationally and locally the policies of the statutory social services towards the informal sector appear to be haphazard, piecemeal and half-hearted. It seems there is a long road to travel from the tangible certainties of bricks and mortar of the old people's home and the hospital to the less visible but often more effective services provided in the community.[17]

Gilbert, an American advocate of welfare pluralism, is more explicit about the need to encourage women to stay at home. He contends that current family policies in the United States do not support the traditional family with the woman as a full-time homemaker and he suggests policies which might make remaining at home more attractive.[18]

Welfare pluralists tend to be less enthusiastic about the private sector. Although Gilbert, for example, claims that the 'social market to some extent can accommodate to and benefit from an infusion of competition, choice, profit, self-interest and other methods and incentives of the market economy', he counsels caution: if the market system is given too much emphasis it might 'undermine the broad values of the social market'.[19] Beresford and Croft, in commenting upon Hadley and Hatch's guarded acceptance of a regulated commercial sector, state:

The problem is that welfare pluralists seem to overestimate the capacity of the state to regulate the slice of the welfare market the commercial sector takes and the quality of its provision, once the state sector and state controls are reduced in accordance with welfare pluralist philosophy. More fundamentally, and central to the essentially regressive nature of welfare pluralism, despite their protestations, arguments and intentions to the contrary, welfare pluralists . . . cannot escape opening wider the door to privatisation by the support for the commercial sector inherent in their advocacy of a plurality of sources of welfare.[20]

The welfare pluralist debate seems to have led to precious little expansion of the voluntary sector, but to a very rapid expansion, in nearly all welfare states, of the commercial sector.

The four sectors of welfare are intended at the local level to be interwoven. As far as Britain is concerned, the notion of interweaving services first arose in the mid–1970s, but with the growing interest in welfare pluralism in the 1980s, the idea gained wider acceptance. Hadley and McGrath describe several innovatory schemes based on the patch system.[21] One of the claimed strengths of interweaving is that it is community based; it enables an intimate knowledge of the locality to be built up and it makes full use of community resources. It provides a framework for, and it reinforces, informal care. It should be noted, however, that most of the innovative schemes have been initiated by statutory authorities. Very little would have happened without the impetus given by the state.

Welfare pluralism has close connections with political pluralism, although participatory modes of operation are not necessarily congruent with representative democracy. Furthermore, contracting out to voluntary and profit-making agencies would mean contractual accountability replacing the more usual hierarchical accountability typical of representative democracy.

A CORPORATIST FUTURE

Cawson describes corporatism as 'a pattern of articulation between the state and functional interests in civil society which fuses representation and intervention in an interdependent relationship'.[22] In a corporatist system power is dispersed 'among groups whose contribution to the economic and social product is indispensable to society, or at least recognised as such in bargaining'.[23]

Mishra, drawing upon the examples of Austria and

Sweden, argues for a corporatist approach to welfare: this, he claims, represents a middle way which 'does not reject the mixed economy and the welfare state'.[24] The result is what he calls an integrated welfare state in contradistinction to the differentiated welfare state based on Keynes and Beveridge. Mishra distinguishes between the two models in the following way:

As used here, the differentiated welfare state refers to the notion of a set of institutions and policies added on to the economy and polity, but seen as a relatively self-contained, delimited area set apart from them. The integrated welfare state suggests that social welfare programmes and policies are seen in relation to the economy and polity and an attempt made to integrate social welfare into the larger society.[25]

Mishra describes corporatism as a system of 'centralised pluralism' in which major economic interests (capital and labour) recognise their interdependence and the need to negotiate on the issues of productivity, wages, employment policy and social welfare. Bargaining and trade-offs are the means of securing consensus. For example, labour might agree to higher productivity, new working practices and moderate wage demands in return for 'reasonable' wage rises, greater security of employment and improvements in social welfare (the social wage). The essential point for Mishra is the integration of social and economic policy.

Austria and Sweden have dealt rather more successfully than other welfare states with the economic problems beginning in 1974. Both countries managed to sustain reasonable levels of economic growth, maintain low levels of unemployment and avoid the drastic cuts in social expenditure which were experienced elsewhere. Sweden faltered a little in the late 1970s and early 1980s, but the return of a Social Democratic government in 1982 has meant the maintenance of high levels of social expenditure since then. Between 1974 and 1981 Austria was even more successful than Sweden in meeting its social and economic objectives. However, Münz and Wintersberger, writing in 1984, claim that since 1981 'the economic situation has also been deteriorating in Austria, the unemployment figures are rising, it is becoming increasingly difficult to improve, or in some cases, to maintain the social and welfare standards achieved since the post-war period'.[26]

The comparative success of Sweden and Austria in retaining their welfare states virtually intact is attributed by Mishra, at least in part, to their corporatist systems. Mishra does, of course, recognise that other factors were at work, but he is not alone in attaching significance to corporatist arrangements in the retention or development of welfare states. Wilensky, for example, links corporatism with Catholicism and low tax visibility as 'sources of strong welfare effort'.[27] In a study of twenty-three OECD nations, Schmidt includes corporatism in a list of factors which, he claims, favour 'a pattern of balanced economic development, a relatively good labour-market record with low unemployment and a further expansion of the welfare state'.[28]

Corporatism in Austria makes no attempt to change the balance between labour and capital, between wages and profits. The hope is that economic growth will increase the amount to be shared out while the proportions remain the same. In Sweden, however, there is a greater concern with reducing inequalities. Among the other countries of Western Europe, the Netherlands is the most corporatist; most of the remainder contain elements of corporatism, but there is nothing which could be described as a system. Britain has experimented with corporatism, especially during periods of Labour rule. In the 1960s, for example, the Wilson government created the Department of Economic Affairs, which was responsible for producing the ill-fated National Plan. The same government established the National Board for Prices and Incomes. Between 1974 and 1979 the Labour government introduced the National Enterprise Board and collaborated closely with the Trades Union Congress in the operation of a 'social contract': this included voluntary wage restraint and negotiations over price control, investment policy, employment policy and social expenditure.

Mishra claims that strong social-democratic and labour movements are conducive to the development of corporatism. The converse of this is also true, so that 'countries in which the labour movement is weak and there is no social-democratic politics, notably the USA, have been the

furthest from the corporatist path'.[29] Mishra also claims that
a large communist party, as in France and Italy, may also
discourage the development of corporatist structures,
because a strong anti-capitalist thrust makes class collaboration impossible. O'Connor argues that there has been
some, but minimal, corporatist development in the United
States, but that it has been at the micro-level (in the workplace) and at the local or regional level rather than at
national level. Micro-corporatism is concerned with group
methods of work, work teams and quality circles, and local
or regional corporatism is concerned mainly with transport,
land-use or town planning. O'Connor claims that it is the
'ideological climate of national individualism' that has
prevented the emergence of corporatism at the national
level. Other contributory factors have been the lack of a
radical labour movement and weak federal bureaucracy.[30]

It should be noted that corporatist methods bypass the
normal representative bodies. Important decisions are being
taken by tripartite or bipartite agreements which also partly
displace competitive pluralism. This feature of corporatism
makes Winkler's distinction between democratic and
undemocratic or authoritarian corporatism all the more significant.[31] Democratic corporatism comes about gradually
through agreement and is based on voluntary collaboration.
Undemocratic corporatism is imposed from above and
'collaboration' is compulsory. Fully developed corporatism
replaces competitive group politics or reduces it to minimal
significance. In other circumstances a competitive group
sector and a corporate sector will exist side by side. Cawson
makes the important distinction between the state's
consumption or allocative functions and the state as
producer of goods and services. When the state is distributing resources, as in the social security system, then the
competitive group model applies. Allocative policies can be
administered by the bureaucracy and can thus be made
subject to 'normal' democratic procedures. When the state
is producing goods and services (as in education and health)
the corporatist model becomes more appropriate because
collaboration of professional producer groups is involved.[32]

Relationships within corporatism are by no means
symmetrical. For example, capital is stronger than labour,

especially when matters affecting capital accumulation are being negotiated. It is when such policies are being discussed that class interests become most obvious and when the comparative weakness of labour becomes most apparent. Marxists argue that the trade-union movement becomes incorporated and that class conflict becomes institutionalised and neutralised. The owners and managers of capital get their way with a minimum of opposition. Harrison suggests that corporatist strategies may 'facilitate low-visibility control of resources on behalf of the privileged'.[33] In this way, Harrison argues, corporatism 'can be a means of substantially reducing the threat posed to capital accumulation by the rise of participatory democracy'.[34] Cawson agrees that trade unions are the junior partners in negotiations concerning investment policy, industrial relations, regional policy and incomes policy. He asserts, however, that this 'does not mean that they are merely incorporated— swallowed up—and become no more than an arm of the state, for they still possess autonomous sources of power and can withdraw their collaboration'.[35]

In the social policy field, class divisions, while they still have an important bearing on negotiations, are less clear cut. Relationships are again asymmetrical, resulting in the dominance of professional producer groups who protect and promote their own interests rather than those of consumers. Harrison argues that in applying corporatism to an analysis of the welfare state the emphasis needs to be switched from labour, government and management to 'consumers, government and institutions and professions involved with services and finance'.[36] Harrison says that our understanding of corporatism needs to be widened to include consumers. Some groups, ethnic minorities, unskilled workers and the deviant, for example, will be marginalised or excluded from the incorporation process, and their needs will be ignored. As Harrison writes:

Incorporation is by no means universal, since full recognition of needs is far more readily accorded for higher-status groups, and organisations that cater for the middle classes may well be admitted more directly into the bargaining process. Certainly a 'relatively unincorporated' group remains unlikely to have access to the full range of developing fiscal and occupational benefits . . . their access to state support is often seen in terms of a 'public burden' concept, rather than an incorporation of recognised and deserving consumer interests.[37]

Harrison uses Titmuss's threefold social division of welfare—occupational, fiscal and social—which he considers a good basis for analysing the extent of welfare coporatism and the processes of incorporation and exclusion.

Held and Krieger believe that the appeal of corporatist theory lies in its amalgamation of some of the central concepts of both Marxist and pluralist theory. From pluralist theory corporatists 'adopt the basic understanding that policy outcomes are determined by the competitive claims of interest associations . . . that competition among disparate groups tends to result in state policy equilibrium, with no shifts towards labor or capital which would force a fundamental revision of the structural arrangements of capitalism'.[38] From Marxist theory comes the idea that class conflicts underlie corporatist arrangements and that 'beneath the apparent indeterminacy of policy lie activities which are designed to reproduce class relations'.[39] It is doubtful, however, whether either Marxist or pluralists, each of whom denies the validity of the other's assumptions, welcome their enforced proximity.

SOCIALIST FUTURES

There are many variants of socialism, and frequently adherents of the different brands eye each other with deep suspicion. The two socialist variations with most relevance for social policy are Marxism and Fabianism. It is important to stress, however, that while these may be convenient labels, there are as many differences within each category as there are between them. Although there are some similarities in the two approaches, the points at which their views widely diverge are usually given more prominence. The main similarity is their acceptance of the basic socialist values of equality, liberty and fraternity. Among the differences are the following:

(1) The different emphasis which each gives to theory and prescription. Marxism is strong on theory and

weak on specific proposals. Fabianism is weak on theory but strong on prescription.

(2)   Traditionally, Fabians have emphasised state centralism, while Marxists foresee the eventual withering away of the state. However, the two are closer together on this issue than they at first sight seem. Many Fabians have now lost faith in the centralist state and, while Marxists hold that the state would wither away under communism, the intervening socialist society would be governed by a powerful centralised state.

(3)   Many Fabians believe that the welfare state can co-exist with the market economy with social policy modifying the free play of market forces. Marxists wish to see capitalism completely overthrown: only in a communist classless society can welfare be given priority. However, Deacon, a revolutionary Marxist, contends that in the socialist period between capitalism and communism markets might still persist and there would be 'a complete mix of provision'.[40]

(4)   Fabians are more enthusiastic than Marxists about the welfare state, which they see as a considerable achievement; for some it is an end in itself, for others it is one step along the road to socialism. Marxists, while recognising that the welfare state has to some extent benefited the working class, claim that capitalists have been the main beneficiaries; the welfare state aids capital accumulation and legitimates the capitalist system.

(5)   Fabians still believe in the inevitability of gradualism—the evolution of socialism achieved through parliamentary means. European communist parties now claim to be committed to winning power through the electoral system, but Marxists put much more emphasis than do Fabians on the class struggle and some, Deacon for example, do not shirk from recommending insurrection in certain circumstances.

We noted in Chapter 2 that the Fabians seemed unprepared for the cuts in welfare expenditure and that they failed to provide an adequate theoretical defence of the welfare state. More recently, however, the Fabians have begun to stage a revival and to re-examine their position via-à-vis the welfare state. In 1983 a book written for a Fabian Society seminar attempted a reappraisal of the assumptions on which the welfare state is based. Glennerster in the introduction to the collection of essays says that the contributors 'begin from the belief that all is not well in the welfare state as we know it—and not just because of Mrs Thatcher's cuts'.[41] The assumptions requiring re-examination include (1) economic assumptions about full employment and growth; (2) social assumptions concerning the family and social minorities; (3) intellectual assumptions concerning the ability of social policy to bring about social change, in particular its ability to substantially reduce inequality; (4) a failure to face the problems of bureaucratic and professional power and (5) value assumptions which imply a reasoned defence of the welfare state against the attacks from the Left, the Right and the 'new voluntarists'.

Glennerster says that the common theme of all the papers in the Fabian collection is 'that the whole notion of citizenship now needs to be extended and enriched'.[42] Such an enrichment would include (1) considerable decentralisation to a new low tier of political control so that local people would become involved in local issues; (2) greater independence for local government; (3) action to ensure greater equality of rights for women and for discriminated-against minorities; (4) greater equality in the workplace; (5) a more equitable distribution of resources; (6) machinery for setting national and local priorities; (7) a more progressive tax system; (8) an incomes policy including minimum and maximum incomes and (9) a renewed commitment to full employment. Since this is a Fabian-inspired book it can be assumed that it is a representation of what Fabian social policy might look like. Most of the items in the list are traditional Fabian concerns, re-examined and reformulated in the light of changed circumstances.

Marxists are much less specific in their formulation of socialist social policy. Most of their contributions have been to theory rather than to the practice of welfare. Deacon makes a rather more serious attempt than most to spell out the implications of Marxist ideas for social policy. He distinguishes between socialist and communist social policy. This is something of a problem since most of the really radical changes have to await the arrival of communism, and there are no communist societies to act as exemplars at present.

It is Deacon's contention that socialist and communist societies would give greater priority to welfare. Under socialism more resources would be devoted to welfare services. In communist societies goods and services would be distributed according to need, and high expenditure on specialist welfare services would therefore be less necessary. The control of services in a socialist regime would be in the hands of a centralised state, but there would be gradual progress towards a communist mode of operation involving self-management and democratic workers' control of welfare institutions. In communist society, 'the local community will predominate in providing services for itself';[43] the state and the market will become insignificant as allocators of goods and services. In a socialist system the informal, voluntary, statutory and the commercial and occupational sectors would all play a role, although some progress towards the communist ideal would be expected. Users and providers of services would be equals in communist society; socialist societies will move in this direction but hierarchical professional structures will persist for some time. In a communist system goods and services would be plentiful and distributed according to need; there would therefore be little or no rationing. In socialism the work-income connection would be maintained, and the benefit and wage system would need to be so structured as to motivate people to work. Finally, Deacon foresees the abolition of the sexual division of labour in communism and some movement towards this in socialist societies.

Interesting though it is, there are one or two problems with Deacon's analysis. One is the gap between socialist and communist social policy and the indeterminate length of the socialist period. It is not suggested that a specific time-span can be allotted to the socialist phase, but if present socialist countries are anything to go by, the period will extend over several generations. Another problem is that in just about every aspect of Marxist theory Deacon identifies two or more opposing views. This may be a tribute to the richness of Marxist debate, but often the opposing views have quite different implications for social policy.

We have now looked, very briefly, at Fabian and Marxist views. The Fabian agenda is more specific than the Marxist one, and it is certainly socialist in content. It does, however, have some serious shortcomings. Most serious is the lack of a social-class analysis. In the index to the book of Fabian papers the only mention of social class refers to the Introduction, where the Marxist notion of class struggle is being criticised. The assumption is that the Labour Party can be persuaded to adopt what is a radical new agenda, and there is insufficient recognition that powerful class forces may line up against the proposed changes, even supposing that a Labour government is prepared to give them priority. Socialists cannot just ignore class conflict, which according to Gough, is essentially 'between the labour movement and the capitalist class'.[44] Gough explains that 'the core of the "labour movement" in all advanced capitalist countries consists of the unionised, predominantly manual, working class'.[45] Class conflict has been partially absorbed into the political system by the development of labour, social-democratic and some communist parties as the political wing of the labour movement. Working-class struggle and influence have been important in securing gains in the past, and they are still essential if gains are to be made in the future.

A class analysis might give the Fabian agenda greater coherence. Another unifying theme is the concept of equality which is probably the chief, and most widely accepted, socialist value. What is required is a thorough examination of strategies to reduce inequality and a wider view of inequality to include racial discrimination and sexual discrimination both at work and in the home.

It would take up too much space to describe in detail the policies required to achieve greater equality in all spheres of life, but one or two points need to be stressed. One is that a narrow concern with *social* policy will not lead to the development of successful strategies to combat inequality. Economic and fiscal policies are probably more important in this context. The artificial division between social and economic policies needs to be broken down.

The second point concerns the relationship between transfer incomes and incomes distributed through the market. In Britain it is frequently claimed that the post war social legislation and subsequent social service developments have not promoted equality. Le Grand, for example, states:

> Equality in public expenditure, final income, use, cost and outcome has not been achieved . . . Overall it is difficult to avoid the implication that the strategy of promoting equality through public expenditure on the social services has failed. It has failed to achieve full equality of whatever kind for most of the services reviewed (health, education, housing and transport).[46]

O'Higgins, on the other hand, says that the egalitarian critique of state welfare has a number of weaknesses. He claims that transfer incomes are markedly more egalitarian than income distributed through the market.[47] The conclusion is that the egalitarian effects of transfer incomes are swamped by the inegalitarian market system, and a substantial reduction in inequality therefore 'requires either a reduction in the role of the market or a reduction of inequalities within it'.[48] The extension of unmodified private markets would increase inequality. Two points flow from this: (1) private welfare markets must be actively discouraged—this could be achieved by removing all tax advantages and making people pay the full cost of the services; (2) inequality needs to be attacked at its source, and for this an incomes and prices policy is absolutely essential. Fiscal policies also have a role to play; indirect taxes such as VAT, which is regressive, should be abolished so that all taxes are levied on incomes and profits. The tax system would be more progressive and a wealth tax would be introduced. Income tax relief on mortgages and other tax expenditures would be reduced or abolished.

A third point that needs to be stressed is the impact of unemployment. Unemployment is a major cause of inequality, not least because it significantly reduces working-class power. Sinfield argues that it is 'difficult, if not impossible, to achieve other basic socialist goals or even maintain the limited advances that have been gained by people dependent on their labour *without* reversing the shift in power and income brought about by sustained high unemployment'.[49]

A final point concerning equality as a socialist objective is the implication it has for participatory policies. Real participation can only occur in local neighbourhoods. One of the failings of Fabian socialism in the past has been its over-reliance on a centralist state. However, strategies of decentralisation and participation are not the monopoly of welfare pluralists. As Beresford and Croft argue; 'there is no lack of alternative socialist proposals for decentralised social services and for the general decentralisation and democratisation of local services available to, and indeed under consideration by some progressive local authorities'. Some of these initiatives (in Walsall, Islington and Sheffield, for example) have been described within the pages of *Critical Social Policy* and elsewhere, and there is no need for further analysis here.[50]

Developments such as those proposed in *The Future of the Welfare State* are unlikely to be implemented with any degree of coherence unless they are included in some form of social plan. Although the Fabian collection contains two papers on planning, a more radical and interesting treatment of the topic is provided by Walker, who sees social planning as 'a strategy for socialist welfare'.[51] He contrasts structural social planning, which he favours, with bureau-incrementalism (a contingent and piecemeal form of planning) and rational-comprehensive planning (centralised national planning). The form of structural social planning recommended by Walker has the following characteristics:

(1) It would be specifically socialist, pursuing socialist goals and encouraging discussion of socialist issues. Walker says that 'the essence of socialist social planning is the democratic pursuit of equality and the promotion of a socialist way of life based on fellowship'.[52]

(2) Policies would be transformative rather than ameliorative.

(3) It would attempt to integrate social and economic policy.

(4) It asserts that economic policy and planning should be subordinate to social policy and planning; this is a reversal of the usual position.

(5) Need thus becomes the guiding distributive principle.

(6) It would be diffuse and democratic: planning would be decentralised and seen as an activity appropriately carried out by 'ordinary people rather than the preserve of experts'.

(7) It takes account of class and élitist power relationships.

It is interesting that Walker, who is usually regarded as being somewhat to the left of the Fabian socialists, assumes 'that it is possible to establish the foundations for policies leading towards distribution according to need within a capitalist society'.[53]

CONCLUSION

We have now looked at possible alternative futures. Which of these futures is most likely in which countries is largely a matter of guesswork. Prediction at best is a hazardous business, and it is even more hazardous when countries so different as, say, Sweden and the United States are concerned. In Sweden private health and welfare markets are practically non-existent, whereas in the United States private markets are large and growing. Public expenditure as a proportion of GDP is higher in Sweden than in any other Western country. Social expenditure as a proportion of the GDP is well above the OECD average in Sweden and well below it in the United States. Sweden has a comprehensive and still growing range of social services, and provision is generous. The United States has a narrow range of social services and the level of provision is much lower and declining. It is of course difficult to make comparisons between countries so unequal in geographic size and population.

The role of the private market is growing in most welfare states—and faster in Britain and the United States than elsewhere. In the short term this is likely to continue. However, it is difficult to see even the United States going as far as the New Right would wish them to. Friedman and Friedman express disappointment in the scale of the changes made in the United States under Reagan. After an early flurry of changes—some of them considerable—'reform' came to a standstill, and in some areas of government business, policies were reversed:

This was Reagan's honeymoon. It lasted about six to nine months. Then the tyranny of the status quo asserted itself. Every special interest that was threatened proceeded to mount a campaign to prevent its particular governmental sinecure from being eliminated. Government spending continued to rise as a fraction of income . . . Government taxes stayed almost the same as a fraction of income . . . Then in 1982 there was a legislated rise in taxes. Even in the area of regulation, deregulation slowed down and was reversed in some areas.[54]

Friedman and Friedman state that 'the tyranny of the status quo' is a valid political generalisation. If a new administration does not make major changes within its first six to nine months, the opportunity to do so will be lost. As further examples of this generalisation the authors cite Britain, France, West Germany and the province of British Columbia.

Corporatism, which does not commend itself to free-market liberals, is most fully developed in Sweden, Austria and the Netherlands. It is likely to continue in these three countries, and it may make some progress elsewhere. The spread of corporatism will, however, be limited because the conditions in which it thrives are limited. Corporatism requires: (1) an organised and centralised labour movement; (2) a strong, central organisation of capital; (3) the ability of capital and labour to ensure compliance among their constituents; (4) appropriate state institutions. Another problem for corporatism is its reliance on consensus which may be achieved relatively painlessly when times are good, but quickly dissipate during a recession. Finally, there is no 'theory of corporatist democracy to legitimate corporatist intervention'.[55]

Socialism is a possibility within Western welfare states, but realistically it is necessary to take the long view. If anything, events at present appear to be moving in the opposite direction. As France and Australia illustrate, even the election of a socialist government is no guarantee of a sustained socialist programme. However, gradual change in a socialist direction *is* possible. Walker talks of a timescale of at least thirty years:

Instead of violent and decisive change arising out of a workers' revolution, *it is necessary to conceive of structural change in advanced capitalist societies occurring over a long period and involving a wider range of groups than just key groups of industrial workers.* Planning is an integral part of this process of change, but not as a series of blueprints drawn up at the centre and passed to the periphery for action.[56]

Commitment to socialist ideals, argument about socialist principles and demonstrations of socialism in practice are all necessary. Constant working-class pressure ('struggle' if preferred) will have to be organised and sustained. The women's movement will be an important part of the drive towards socialism. McIntosh claims that 'feminist demands are central to any socialist strategy in social policy'.[57] The strategy described by McIntosh is:

to develop a feminist presence in all the places where changes in social policy are fought for. This means within the left political parties, within the labour movement, within all the campaigning and lobbying bodies, and as much as possible in the women's organisations . . . Sometimes this means challenging and transforming their styles of work and approach. Often, though, it means compromises: avoiding taking a line that will lose us the support that we need for other more important battles.[58]

Substitute the word 'socialist' for 'feminist' in the first sentence of this quotation and you also have a sound strategy for socialism in general. All available openings must be used: the labour movement and labour parties, organisations such as the CND and other environmental groups, urban movements, ethnic groups, the poverty lobby and a whole range of reformist pressure groups. Whatever action is taken, however, it is difficult to imagine the United States as a socialist republic, but there may be long-term prospects for socialism in many Western European countries. Revolution seems highly unlikely and it would, anyway, be counterproductive.

Although socialism is a long-term aim, there can be little doubt that welfare pluralism holds centre-stage at the present time. It has the advantage of being apparently based upon a system which is already mixed: the four sectors, already in existence, would now be combined in different proportions. The ingredients would be the same, but the recipe would be different.

Welfare pluralism has also gained by hitching itself to the decentralisation/participation bandwagon, although to be fair it has pushed these arguments further than have other theories. Anti-bureaucratic, anti-professional trends also work in welfare pluralism's favour. Criticisms of government overload and fiscal crisis from the Right and the Left, also serve the welfare pluralist cause because welfare pluralism is claimed to have answers to these problems.

If welfare pluralism means no more than the operation of four sectors in the social services, then obviously it will persist even in the long term. Although in a socialist society there would be no place for private health, welfare and education markets, there is no reason why a voluntary sector should not remain. Traditional service-providing voluntary organisations might no longer be quite so necessary, but self-help and self-management schemes and groups of users of the social services would contribute to, and have a part in implementing, local social plans. The informal sector, too, would continue to play an important role in service provision, although in a socialist society it could no longer rely upon the sexual division of labour. But the underlying ideology of welfare pluralism, as at present propounded, is anti-statist; it wishes to see a substantial shift in the balance of provision from the state to the other three sectors. One of the purposes of this book has been to highlight some of the problems associated with this policy. In the short and medium term the future of the welfare state appears to lie in the direction of welfare pluralism; but even with statutory finance and regulation, serious doubts arise as to the willingness and capacity of the voluntary and informal sectors to substitute for the state. If they cannot respond in the ways and to the extent expected of them by welfare pluralists, then welfare pluralism will merely serve to legitimate cuts in public expenditure and the development of market provision.

For the present the welfare state is under attack in most capitalist countries. Yet, in spite of its undoubted inadequacies, it has brought about improvements in the lives of working people, protecting them from the worst excesses of capitalism. At the same time, the welfare state has aided capital accumulation and legitimated the capitalist system. The dismantling of the welfare state, in spite of this apparent contradiction, however, would result in lower living standards for working people, leaving them totally unprotected in the unrestricted anarchy of the market, and leading to greater inequalities of class, status and power.

This is not an argument for the uncritical acceptance of the welfare state in its current form. It was just such complacency which left the welfare state open to attack in the first place. We do need to look for new ways of organising, providing and financing welfare; but there has been too much talk of 'crisis'; conservative governments are only too happy to accept, and indeed, to promote, the notion of crisis, since it legitimates policies of retrenchment and lowers expectations. Crisis theories also lead to the politics of despair in which the hope, let alone the expectation, of improvement disappears. It we discard the notion of crisis, we can begin to look constructively at new ways of meeting need. If the political will is there, if welfare is given priority, then there will be a future in which the needs of all disadvantaged groups will be fully met: a future in which need is the main distributive principle, in which there is equality between men and women, among different ethnic groups, among different occupational groups and between those in work and those for whom no work is possible. A socialist strategy is the only one which will produce such a future.

Notes

CHAPTER 1

1. W. Temple, *Citizen and Churchman* (Eyre and Spottiswoode, London, 1941), ch. 2.
2. T. H. Marshall, *Sociology at the Crossroads* (Heinemann, London, 1963), p. 279.
3. *Ibid.*, p. 287.
4. D. Wedderburn, 'Facts and Theories of the Welfare State', in *The Socialist Register*, ed. R. Miliband and J. Saville (Merlin, London, 1965), p. 127.
5. The date when most of the British social legislation of the 1940s became operative.
6. D. Fraser, *The Evolution of the British Welfare State* (Macmillan, London, 1973), p. 222.
7. M. Forsberg, *The Evolution of Social Welfare Policy in Sweden* (The Swedish Institute, Stockholm, 1984) p. 7.
8. S. Kuhnle, 'The Growth of Social Insurance Programs in Scandinavia', in *The Development of Welfare States in Europe and America*, ed. P. Flora and A. J. Heidenheimer (Transaction Books, New Brunswick, 1981), p. 126.
9. P. Flora and J. Alber, 'Modernization, Democratization and the Development of Welfare States in Western Europe', in Flora and Heidenheimer, p. 48.
10. For a good critique of this approach, see J. Carrier and I. Kendall, 'Social Policy and Social Change', *Journal of Social Policy*, vol. 2 pt 3 (1973).
11. Fraser, p. 1.
12. Flora and Heidenheimer, p. 22.
13. J. Higgins, *States of Welfare* (Blackwell and Robertson, Oxford, 1981), p. 47.
14. F. G. Castles, 'How Does Politics Matter: Structure or Agency in the Determination of Public Policy Outcomes', *European Journal of Political Research*, vol. 9, no. 2 (1981), p. 121.
15. H. L. Wilensky, *The Welfare State and Equality* (University of California Press, Berkeley, 1975), p. xiv.

16. H. L. Wilensky, 'Leftism, Catholicism and Democratic Corporatism: The Role of Political Parties in Recent Welfare State Development', in Flora and Heidenheimer, p. 355.
17. See, for example, A. J. Heidenheimer, H. Heclo and C. T. Adams, *Comparative Public Policy* (St Martin's Press, New York, 1983); H. Heclo, *Modern Social Politics in Britain and Sweden* (Yale University Press, New Haven, 1974); Castles; F. G. Castles and R. D. McKinley, 'Public Welfare Provision: Scandinavia and the Sheer Futility of the Sociological Approach to Politics', *British Journal of Political Science*, vol. 9, no. 2 (1979).
18. Heidenheimer, Heclo and Adams, p. 210.
19. Castles, p. 168.
20. F. G. Castles, 'Terra Incognita Australis: A Search for New Directions in Public Policy Analysis', *Government and Opposition*, vol. 20, no. 3 (1985), p. 377.
21. J. Alber, 'Some Causes of Social Security Expenditure Developments in Western Europe 1949–1977', in *Social Policy and Social Welfare*, ed. M. Loney, D. Boswell and J. Clarke (Open University Press, Milton Keynes, 1983).
22. Castles, 1985, p. 377.
23. R. Mishra, *Society and Social Policy* (Macmillan, London, 1977), p. 105.
24. H. Heclo, *Modern Social Politics in Britain and Sweden* (Yale University Press, New Haven, 1974), p. 301.
25. See A. J. Heidenheimer, 'Education and Social Security Entitlements in Europe and America', in Flora and Heidenheimer.
26. See E. P. Hennock, 'The Origins of British National Insurance and the German Precedent 1880–1914', in *The Emergence of the Welfare State in Britain and Germany*, ed. W. J. Mommsen (Croom Helm, London, 1981); H. N. Bunbury (ed.), *Lloyd George's Ambulance Wagon: Being the Memoirs of W. J. Braithwaite, 1911–12* (Methuen, London, 1957).
27. Heidenheimer, Heclo and Adams, p. 216.
28. Flora and Alber, p. 63.
29. Castles, 1981, p. 122.
30. Heidenheimer, Heclo and Adams, p. 208.
31. R. M. Titmuss, *Social Policy: An Introduction* (Allen and Unwin, London, 1974), p. 30.
32. H. L. Wilensky and C. N. Lebeaux, *Industrial Society and Social Welfare* (The Free Press, New York, 1965), p. 138.
33. Titmuss, p. 31.
34. R. M. Titmuss, *Essays on 'The Welfare State'* (Allen and Unwin, London, 1963) ch. 2.
35. C. Jones, 'Types of Welfare Capitalism', *Government and Opposition*, vol. 20, no. 3 (1985), pp. 328–42.
36. *Ibid.*, pp. 335–6.
37. D. V. Donnison *et al.*, *Social Policy and Administration* (Allen and Unwin, London, 1965), p. 16.
38. *Ibid.*, p. 23.

39. R. Mishra, *The Welfare State in Crisis* (Wheatsheaf Books, Brighton, 1984), p. xii.
40. Article 40 of the *United Nations Universal Declaration of Human Rights*. The full text of the Declaration may be found in M. Cranston, *What Are Human Rights?* (Bodley Head, London, 1973), Appendix A.
41. Heidenheimer, Heclo and Adams, p. 10.
42. H. Heclo, 'Toward a New Welfare State?', in Flora and Heidenheimer, pp. 383–406.
43. R. M. Titmuss, *Essays on the Welfare State* (Allen and Unwin, London, 1963), ch. 4.
44. P. Thane, *The Foundations of the Welfare State* (Longman, London, 1982), p. 282.
45. See Organisation for Economic Co-operation and Development, *National Accounts: Main Aggregates* (OECD, Paris, 1984).
46. J. Kohl, 'Trends and Problems in Postwar Public Expenditure Development in Western Europe and North America', in Flora and Heidenheimer, pp. 307–8.
47. Jones.
48. Federal Minister of Labour and Social Affairs, *Social Progress in the Federal Republic of Germany* (Bonn, 1985), pp. 7–8.
49. G. V. Rimlinger, *Welfare Policy and Industrialisation in Europe, America and Russia* (John Wiley, New York, 1971), pp. 137–92.
50. Kohl.
51. N. Furniss and T. Tilton, *The Case for the Welfare State* (Indiana University Press, Bloomington, 1977), p. 122.
52. *Ibid.*, p. 123.
53. Wilensky and Lebeaux, pp. xvi-xvii.
54. Mishra, 1977, p. 105.
55. A good account of the War on Poverty can be found in J. Higgins, *The Poverty Business: Britain and America* (Blackwell, Oxford, 1978).
56. G. Myrdal, 'The Place of Values in Social Policy', *Journal of Social Policy*, vol. 1, pt 1 (1972), p. 1.
57. *Hansard*, fifth series, vol. 418.
58. For a thorough treatment of this topic, see V. George and P. Wilding, *The Impact of Social Policy* (Routledge and Kegan Paul, London, 1984), chs. 4 and 5.
59. P. Thoenes, *The Elite in the Welfare State*, ed. J. A. Banks (Faber and Faber, London, 1966), p. 127.
60. J. Nasenius and J. Veit-Wilson, 'Social Policy in a Cold Climate: Sweden in the Eighties', in *The Year Book of Social Policy 1984–5*, ed. M. Brenton and C. Jones (Routledge and Kegan Paul, London, 1985) p. 147.
61. Rimlinger, p. 146.
62. D. Bell, *The End of Ideology* (The Free Press, Illinois, 1960), pp. 402–3.
63. T. H. Marshall, *Social Policy* (Hutchinson, London, 1965), pp. 88–9.

64. T. Parsons, *The Social System* (Routledge and Kegan Paul, London, 1951). See also N. J. Smelser, *Social Change in the Industrial Revolution* (Routledge and Kegan Paul, London, 1959).
65. See J. Carrier and I. Kendall, 'Social Policy and Social Change', *Journal of Social Policy*, vol. 2, pt 3 (1973), pp. 209–24.
66. Mishra, p. 34.
67. Myrdal, p. 3.

CHAPTER 2
1. F. A. Hayek, *The Road to Serfdom* (Routledge, London, 1944).
2. M. Friedman, *Capitalism and Freedom* (University of Chicago Press, Chicago, 1962).
3. J. Saville, 'The Welfare State: An Historical Approach', *New Reasoner*, vol. 3 (1975); D. Wedderburn, 'Facts and Theories of the Welfare State' in *The Socialist Register*, ed. R. Miliband and J. Saville (Merlin Press, London, 1965), pp. 127–46; D. A. Baran and P. M. Sweezy, *Monopoly Capital* (Penguin, Harmondsworth, 1968); R. Miliband, *The State in Capitalist Society* (Weidenfeld and Nicolson, London, 1962).
4. R. M. Titmuss, *Income Distribution and Social Change* (Allen and Unwin, London, 1962).
5. B. Abel-Smith and P. Townsend, *The Poor and the Poorest* (Bell, London, 1965).
6. Central Advisory Council for Education (England), *Half Our Future*, Newsom Report (HMSO, London, 1963); *Children and Their Primary Schools*, Plowden Report (HMSO, London, 1967).
7. See, for example, S. Jenkins (ed.), *Social Security in International Perspective* (Columbia University Press, New York, 1969).
8. A. Doron, 'In Defense of the Welfare State: Some Reflections', in *Social Concerns for the 1980s*, ed. H. Nowotny (European Centre for Social Welfare, Training and Research, Vienna, 1984) p. 21.
9. R. Mishra, *The Welfare State in Crisis* (Wheatsheaf, Brighton, 1984), p. xiii.
10. D. R. Cameron, 'Public Expenditure and Economic Performance in International Perspective', in *The Future of Welfare*, ed. R. Klein and M. O'Higgins (Blackwell, Oxford, 1985), pp. 8–21.
11. *Ibid.*, p. 21.
12. K. Hawkins, *Unemployment* (Penguin, Harmondsworth, 1984), p. 78.
13. V. George and P. Wilding, *The Impact of Social Policy*, Routledge and Kegan Paul, London, 1984), p. 8.
14. J. O'Connor, *Accumulation Crisis* (Blackwell, New York, 1984).
15. *Ibid.*, p. 219.
16. *Ibid.*, p. 1.
17. R. Rose, *Understanding Big Government* (Sage, London, 1984), p. 1.
18. R. Rose and G. Peters, *Can Governments Go Bankrupt?* (Macmillan, London, 1979), p. 6.
19. Rose and Peters.

20. R. Rose (ed.), *Challenge to Governance: Studies in Overloaded Politics* (Sage, London, 1980).
21. A. King, 'Overload: Problems of Governing in the 1970s', *Political Studies*, vol. 23, nos. 2 and 3 (1975), p. 286.
22. *Ibid.*, p. 282.
23. S. Brittan, *The Economic Consequences of Democracy* (Temple Smith, London, 1977), pp. 240–3.
24. *Ibid.*, pp. 247–73.
25. J. Douglas, 'The Overloaded Crown', *British Journal of Political Science*, vol. 6, no. 4 (1976), p. 494.
26. King, p. 287.
27. *Ibid.*
28. *Ibid.*, pp. 294–5.
29. M. Friedman and R. Friedman, *Free to Choose* (Penguin, Harmondsworth, 1980), p. 181.
30. *Ibid.*, pp. 47–54.
31. G. Gilder, *Wealth and Poverty* (Bantam Books, New York, 1982); C. Murray, *Losing Ground* (Basic Books, New York, 1984).
32. N. Blewett, 'The Challenge of the New Conservatism', in *Labor Essays 1982*, ed. G. Evans and J. Reeves (Drummond, Melbourne, 1982), p. 41.
33. C. Offe, *Contradictions in the Welfare State*, ed. J. Keane (Hutchinson, London, 1984), p. 153.
34. *Ibid.*
35. *Ibid.*, p. 77.
36. A. Wolfe, *The Limits of Legitimacy* (The Free Press, New York, 1977), p. 329.
37. J. Kohl, 'Trends and Problems in Postwar Public Expenditure Developments in Western Europe and North America', in *The Development of Welfare States in Europe and America*, ed. P. Flora and A. J. Heidenheimer (Transaction Books, New Brunswick, 1981), p. 327.
38. J. L. Palmer and I. V. Sawhill (eds.), *The Reagan Experiment* (The Urban Institute, Washington, 1982), p. 3.
39. Kohl, p. 334.
40. See OECD, *Social Expenditure 1960–1990* (OECD, Paris, 1985), pp. 16–17.
41. *Ibid.*, p. 15.
42. J. O'Connor, *The Fiscal Crisis of the State* (St Martin's Press, New York, 1973), p. 1.
43. J. Habermas, *Legitimation Crisis*, trans. T. McCarthy (Heinemann, London, 1976), p. 46.
44. *Ibid.*, p. 47.
45. J. Habermas, 'Legitimation Problems in Late Capitalism', in *Legitimacy and the State*, ed. W. Connolly (Blackwell, Oxford, 1984), p. 146.
46. *Ibid.*, p. 145.
47. Habermas, 1976, pp. 74–5.
48. *Ibid.*, p. 75.

49. J. Habermas, 'Conservatism or Capitalist Crisis', *New Left Review*, no. 115 (1978), p. 80.
50. Offe, p. 156.
51. F. Piven and R. Cloward, *Regulating the Poor* (Tavistock, London, 1972).
52. I. Gough, *The Political Economy of the Welfare State* (Macmillan, London, 1979), p. 67.
53. E. Wilson, *Women and the Welfare State* (Tavistock, London, 1977), p. 7.
54. *Ibid.*, p. 39.
55. M. McIntosh, 'The State and the Oppression of Women', in *Feminism and Materialism*, ed. A. Kuhn and A. Wolpe (Routledge and Kegan Paul, London, 1978), p. 255.
56. H. Rose and S. Rose, 'Moving Right Out of Welfare and the Way Back', *Critical Social Policy*, vol. 2, no. 1 (1982), pp. 7–18.
57. *Critical Social Policy*, vol. 1, no. 1 (1981).
58. P. Leonard, 'Restructuring the Welfare State', *Marxism Today*, December 1979.
59. J. Atlas, P. Dreier and J. Stephens, 'A Party for a Change', in *Beyond Reagan: Alternatives for the '80s*, ed. A. Gartner, C. Greer and F. Riessman (Harper and Row, New York, 1984), p. 335.
60. Mishra, p. 123.
61. *Ibid.*, p. 124.
62. N. Gilbert, 'Comment' (on Paper by R. Morris), *Journal of Social Policy*, vol. 13, no. 4 (1984).
63. Department of Health and Social Security, *Inequalities in Health* (DHSS, London, 1980).
64. P. Townsend and N. Davidson, *Inequalities in Health* (Penguin, Harmondsworth, 1982), p. 15.
65. J. Le Grand, *The Strategy of Equality* (Allen and Unwin, London, 1982), p. 128.
66. M. O'Higgins, 'Welfare, Redistribution, and Inequality—Disillusion, Illusion and Reality', in *In Defence of Welfare*, ed. P. Bean, J. Ferris and D. Whynes (Tavistock, London, 1985), pp. 162–79; M. O'Higgins, 'Inequality, Redistribution and Recession: The British Experience', *Journal of Social Policy*, vol. 14, pt. 3, (1985), pp. 279–303.
67. E. C. Ladd Jnr. and S. M. Lipset, 'Public Opinion and Public Policy', in *The United States in the 1980s*, ed. P. Duignan and A. Robushka (Hoover Institution, Stanford, 1980), p. 77.
68. Quoted in 'The Tax Revolt and the Welfare State' (unattributed) *New Society*, 9 October 1980, pp. 72–3.
69. P. Golding and S. Middleton, *Images of Welfare* (Blackwell, Oxford, 1982), p. 5.
70. H. Hankel and F. Pavelka, 'Dismantling Social Welfare by Black Magic', *Eurosocial Newsletter*, no. 22/81.
71. J. E. Alt, *The Politics of Economic Decline* (Cambridge University Press, Cambridge, 1979).

72. H. Heclo, 'Toward a New Welfare State?', in Flora and Heidenheimer, p. 395.
73. *Ibid.*
74. *Ibid.*, p. 396.
75. R. Morris, 'The Future Challenge to the Past: The Case of the American Welfare State', *Journal of Social Policy*, vol. 13, pt 4 (1984), pp. 383–95.
76. R. Jowell and C. Airey, 'British Social Attitudes', *Social Trends 15* (1985), p. 17.
77. L. N. Johansen and J. E. Kolberg, 'Welfare State Regression in Scandinavia? The Development of the Scandinavian Welfare States from 1970 to 1980', in *The Welfare State and Its Aftermath*, ed. S. N. Eisenstadt and O. Ahimeir (Croom Helm, London, 1985), p. 172.
78. P. Taylor-Gooby, *Public Opinion, Ideology and State Welfare* (Routledge and Kegan Paul, London, 1985), p. 51.
79. *Ibid.*, p. 52.
80. A. J. Heidenheimer, H. Heclo and C. T. Adams, *Comparative Public Policy* (St Martin's, New York, 1983), p. 321.
81. R. Coughlin, Ideology, *Public Opinion and Welfare Policy* (University of California Press, Berkeley, 1980).

CHAPTER 3
1. P. Beresford and S. Croft, 'Welfare Pluralism: The New Face of Fabianism', *Critical Social Policy*, no. 9 (1984), pp. 19–39.
2. K. Judge and M. Reddin, 'Notes Prepared for the 1983 Social Administration Conference on the Mixed Economy of Welfare'.
3. S. Hatch and I. Mocroft, *Components of Welfare* (Bedford Square Press, London, 1983), p. 2.
4. J. Wolfenden, *The Future of Voluntary Organisations* (Croom Helm, London, 1978), p. 15.
5. B. Munday, *European Expert Meeting on Established Social Services versus New Social Initiatives* (European Centre for Social Welfare Training and Research, Vienna, 1985), pp. 7 and 27.
6. *Ibid.*, p. 28.
7. See, for example, F. Gladstone, *Voluntary Action in a Changing World* (Bedford Square Press, London, 1979); National Council for Voluntary Organisations, *Beyond the Welfare State* (Bedford Square Press, London, 1980); R. Hadley and S. Hatch, *Social Welfare and the Failure of the State* (Allen and Unwin, London, 1981).
8. Hadley and Hatch, p. 100.
9. Gladstone.
10. N. Gilbert, *Capitalism and the Welfare State* (Yale University Press, New Haven, 1983), p. 184.
11. K. Young, 'The East Sussex Approach', in *Decentralisation and Care in the Community*, ed. S. Hatch (Policy Studies Institute, London, 1985), p. 7.

12. D. Challis, 'The Community Care Scheme: An Alternative Approach to Decentralisation', in Hatch, p. 40.
13. *Ibid.*, p. 42.
14. J. Higgins, *The Poverty Business* (Blackwell, Oxford, 1978), p. 125.
15. Gilbert, p. 169.
16. A. Walker, *Social Planning: A Strategy for Socialist Welfare* (Blackwell, Oxford, 1984), p. 222.
17. Beresford and Croft, p. 35.
18. P. Abrams, 'Community Care: Some Research Problems and Priorities', *Policy and Politics*, no. 6 (1977), p. 125.
19. B. Munday, 'What Future for the Personal Social Services?' in *Social Concerns for the 1980s*, ed. H. Nowotny (European Centre for Social Welfare Training and Research, Vienna, 1984), p. 175.

CHAPTER 4
1. C. Froland, D. L. Pancoast, N. J. Chapman, P. J. Kimboko, *Helping Networks and Human Services* (Sage, Beverly Hills, 1981), p. 19.
2. M. Bayley, 'Helping Care to Happen in the Community', in *Community Care*, ed. A. Walker (Blackwell, Oxford, 1982), p. 179.
3. R. Hadley and S. Hatch, *Social Welfare and the Failure of the State* (Allen and Unwin, London, 1981), p. 87.
4. D. L. Pancoast, P. Parker and C. Froland (eds.), *Rediscovering Self-Help* (Sage, Beverly Hills, 1983).
5. See *Eurosocial Report No. 25* (European Centre for Social Welfare Training and Research, Vienna, 1984).
6. See *Eurosocial Report No. 24* (European Centre for Social Welfare Training and Research, Vienna, 1984).
7. P. Abrams, 'Community Care: Some Research Problems and Priorities', *Policy and Politics*, no. 6 (1977), pp. 125–51.
8. *Ibid.*, p. 128.
9. *Ibid.*, p. 130.
10. *Ibid.*, p. 132.
11. *Ibid.*
12. Walker, p. 4.
13 Ministry of Health, *Health and Welfare: The Development of Community Care*, Cmnd 1973 (HMSO, London, 1963).
14. E. Goffman, *Asylums* (Penguin Books, Harmondsworth, 1968).
15. See, for example, P. Townsend, *The Family Life of Old People* (Routledge and Kegan Paul, London, 1957); M. Young and P. Willmott, *Family and Kinship in East London* (Routledge and Kegan Paul, London, 1957); P. Willmott and M. Young, *Family and Class in a London Suburb* (Routledge and Kegal Paul, London, 1960). A good analysis drawing on a large number of community studies is R. Frankenberg, *Communities in Britain* (Penguin Books, Harmondsworth, 1966).
16. N. S. Hughes and A. M. Lovell, 'Breaking the Circuit of Social Control: Lessons in Public Psychiatry from Italy and Franco Basaglia', *Social Science and Medicine*, vol. 23, no. 2 (1986), pp. 159–78.

17. Commission of the European Communities, *Report on Social Developments Year 1981* (Office for Official Publications of the European Communities, Luxembourg, 1982), p. 119.
18. Commission of the European Communities, *Report on Social Developments Year 1982* (Office for Official Publications of the European Communities, Luxembourg, 1983), p. 127.
19. Abrams, p. 133.
20. J. Campling, 'Editor's Introduction', in D. Gittins, *The Family In Question* (Macmillan, London, 1985), p. ix.
21. E. Shanas, P. Townsend, D. Wedderburn, H. Friis, P. Milhøj and J. Stehouwer, *Old People in Three Industrial Societies* (Routledge and Kegan Paul, London, 1968), p. 180.
22. Reported in N. Gilbert, *Capitalism and the Welfare State* (Yale University Press, New Haven, 1983), p. 121.
23. Division of Social Affairs of the United Nations Office at Geneva, *Informal Action for the Welfare of the Aged* (United Nations, New York, 1980), p. 12.
24. J. Finch and D. Groves, 'Community Care and the Family: A Case for Equal Opportunities?' *Journal of Social Policy*, vol. 9, pt 4 (1980), p. 499.
25. H. Land, 'Who Cares for the Family?' *Journal of Social Policy*, vol. 7, pt 3 (1978), p. 268.
26. Equal Opportunities Commission, *Caring for the Elderly and Handicapped: Community Care Policies and Women's Lives* (Equal Opportunities Commission, Manchester, 1982), p. iii.
27. G. Parker, *With Due Care and Attention* (Family Policy Studies Centre, London, 1985), quoted in *Family Policy Bulletin*, no. 1 (1985), p. 4.
28. A. Charlesworth, D. Wilkin and A. Durie, *Carers and Services: A Comparison of Men and Women Caring for Dependent Elderly People* (Equal Opportunities Commission, Manchester, 1984).
29. Equal Opportunities Commission, *The Experience of Caring for Elderly and Handicapped Dependents: Survey Report* (Equal Opportunities Commission, Manchester, 1980), p. 9.
30. C. Thompson, *Sharing Caring: Caring, Equal Opportunities and the Voluntary Sector* (National Council for Voluntary Organisations, London, 1985), p. 2.
31. M. Nissel and L. Bonnerjea, *Family Care of the Handicapped Elderly, Who Pays?* (Policy Studies Institute, London, 1982).
32. Commission of the European Communities, *Report on Social Developments Year 1982* (Office for Official Publications of the European Communities, Luxembourg, 1983), p. 127.
33. Gilbert, p. 122.
34. Froland *et al.*, p. 40.
35. Charlesworth *et al.*, p. 7.
36. *Ibid.*, p. 18.
37. Equal Opportunities Commission, *Who Cares for the Carers?* (Equal Opportunities Commission, Manchester, 1982), p. 6.
38. Ermisch has produced the fullest analysis of the influence of demo-

graphic trends on the number and proportion of dependants in the population. J. Ermisch, *The Political Economy of Demography* (Heinemann, London, 1983).

39. Gilbert, pp. 119–20.
40. Statistics taken from M. Wicks, 'Community Care and Elderly People', in Walker, pp. 99–117.
41. Norwegian Institute of Gerontology, *Elderly Norwegians* (Norwegian Institute of Gerontology, Oslo, 1984). P. C. Matthiessen, *Factsheet Denmark: The Demographic Situation* (Royal Danish Ministry of Foreign Affairs, Copenhagen, 1981). Swedish Institute, *Old-Age Care in Sweden* (The Swedish Institute, Stockholm, 1984).
42. Gilbert, p. 120.
43. D. E. C. Eversley, 'Some New Aspects of Ageing in Britain', in *Ageing and the Life Cycle Course in a Cross-Cultural Interdisciplinary Perspective*, ed. T. K. Hareven (Guildford Press, New York, 1982). Quoted in Gilbert.
44. J. Martin and C. Roberts, *Women and Employment: A Lifetime Perspective* (Department of Employment/Office of Population Censuses and Surveys, London, 1984).
45. Gilbert, p. 60.
46. The Swedish Institute, *Child Care Programs in Sweden* (The Swedish Institute, Stockholm, 1984), p. 2.
47. Matthiessen, p. 2.
48. L. Paukert, *The Employment and Unemployment of Women in OECD Countries* (OECD, Paris, 1984), p. 10.
49. *Ibid.*, p. 31.
50. J. Ermisch, 'Work, Jobs and Social Policy', in *The Future of Welfare*, ed. R. Klein and M. O'Higgins (Blackwell, Oxford, 1985) p. 63.
51. L. Rimmer, 'Divorce and Lone Parenthood', *Family Policy Bulletin*, no. 1 (1985), p. 7.
52. S. B. Kamerman and A. J. Kahn (eds.), *Family Policy: Government and Families in Fourteen Countries* (Columbia University Press, New York, 1978).
53. R. Münz and H. Wintersberger, *The Austrian Welfare State: Social Policy and Income Maintenance Programmes Between 1970 and 1984* (European Centre for Social Welfare Training and Research, Vienna, 1984).
54. Gilbert, p. 55.
55. R. Stanbridge, *The Guardian*, 28 August 1985.
56. *Ibid.*
57. Gilbert, pp. 103 and 104.
58. The Swedish Institute, *Child Care Programs in Sweden* (The Swedish Institute, Stockholm, 1984), p. 2.
59. N. Questiaux and J. Fournier, 'France', in Kamerman and Kahn, pp. 117–82.
60. H. Land and R. Parker, 'United Kingdom', in Kamerman and Kahn, pp. 331–66.
61. Martin and Roberts.

62. G. Peele, *Revival and Reaction: The Right in Contemporary America* (Oxford University Press, Oxford and New York, 1984), p. 93.
63. F. Mount, *The Subversive Family* (Jonathan Cape, London, 1982).
64. P. West, 'The Family, the Welfare State and Community Care: Political Rhetoric and Public Attitudes', *Journal of Social Policy*, vol. 13, pt 4 (1984), pp. 417–46.
65. Peele, p. 71.
66. *Ibid.*, p. 91.
67. I. Kristol, *Reflections of a Neoconservative* (Basic Books, New York, 1983), p. 77.
68. T. Fitzgerald, 'The New Right and the Family', in *Social Policy and Social Welfare*, ed. M. Loney, D. Boswell and J. Clarke (Open University Press, Milton Keynes, 1983), p. 47.
69. Conservative Political Centre, *The Future of Marriage* (Conservative Political Centre, London, 1981), p. 28.
70. M. David, 'Moral and Maternal: The Family in the Right', in *The Ideology of the New Right*, ed. R. Levitas (Polity Press, Cambridge, 1986), p. 139.
71. Fitzgerald, p. 50.
72. G. Allan, *Family Life* (Blackwell, Oxford, 1985), p. 137.
73. *Ibid.*
74. P. Willmott, *Social Networks, Informal Care and Public Policy* (Policy Studies Institute, London, 1986), p. 47.
75. Froland *et al.*, p. 48.
76. Gilbert, p. 125.
77. P. Abrams, 'Social Change, Social Networks and Neighbourhood Care', *Social Work Service*, no. 22 (1980), pp. 12–23.
78. Willmott, pp. 105–6.
79. Parker, p. 88.
80. M. Bayley and A. Tennant, 'Straight Across: Inter-service Collaboration in Dinnington', in *Decentralisation and Care in the Community*, ed. S. Hatch (Policy Studies Institute, London, 1985) p. 26.
81. *Ibid.*
82. Report of the Barclay Committee, *Social Workers: Their Role and Tasks* (Bedford Square Press, London, 1982), p. 249.
83. *Ibid.*
84. H. Glennerster, 'Decentralisation and Inter-Service Planning', in Hatch, pp. 55–7.

CHAPTER 5

1. *Eurosocial Newsletter*, no. 15 (European Centre for Social Welfare Training and Research, Vienna, 1979), pp. 28–9.
2. L. M. Salamon and A. J. Abramson, 'The Nonprofit Sector', in *The Reagan Experiment*, ed. J. L. Palmer and I. V. Sawhill (The Urban Institute, Washington DC, 1982), p. 221.
3. J. H. Filer, *Giving in America: Toward a Stronger Voluntary Sector*, Report of the Commission on Private Philanthropy and Public Needs (Washington DC, 1975).

4. P. Abrams, S. Abrams and J. Davison, *Patterns of Neighbourhood Care* (Association of Researchers in Voluntary Action and Community Involvement, Wivenhoe, 1979), p. 22.
5. C. Froland, D. L. Pancoast, N. J. Chapman and P. J. Kimboko, *Helping Networks and Human Services* (Sage, Beverly Hills, 1981), pp. 138–9.
6. Abrams *et al.*, p. 6.
7. J. Higgins, *The Poverty Business: Britain and America* (Blackwell, Oxford, 1978), p. 50.
8. Froland *et al.*, p. 116.
9. A. Richardson, *Participation* (Routledge and Kegal Paul, London, 1983), p. 36.
10. J. Atlas and P. Dreier, 'Mobilize or Compromise? The Tenants' Movement and American Politics', in *America's Housing Crisis, What Is to Be Done?* ed. C. Hartman (Routledge and Kegan Paul, Boston, 1983), pp. 166–7.
11. Ministry of Foreign Affairs, *The Kingdom of the Netherlands: Housing and Planning* (Ministry of Foreign Affairs, the Netherlands, 1981), p. 14.
12. A. Twelvetrees, 'Lessons from America: Alinsky's Legacy', *Community Care*, 22 May 1986, pp. 27–8.
13. P. Abrams, 'Social Change, Social Networks and Neighbourhood Care', *Social Work Service*, no. 22 (1980), pp. 12–23.
14. A. Twelvetrees, 'Lessons from America: Corporation Clues', *Community Care*, 15 May 1986, pp. 16–18.
15. P. Davidoff and J. Gould, 'Suburban Action: Advocate Planning for an Open Society', *Journal of the American Institute of Planners* (1970). Quoted in Higgins.
16. J. Benington, 'Strategies for Change at the Local Level: Some Reflections', in *Community Work One*, ed. D. Jones and M. Mayo (Routledge and Kegan Paul, London, 1974), p. 275.
17. D. L. Pancoast, P. Parker and C. Froland (eds.), *Rediscovering Self-Help: Its Role in Social Care* (Sage, Beverly Hills, 1983), p. 17.
18. S. Smiles, *Self Help* (Sphere, London, 1968).
19. R. Sugden, 'Voluntary Organisations and the Welfare State', in *Privatisation and the Welfare State*, ed. J. Le Grand and R. Robinson (George Allen and Unwin, London, 1984), p. 70.
20. R. Wollert and N. Barron, 'Avenues of Collaboration', in Pancoast, Parker and Froland, p. 105.
21. B. Bakker and M. Karel, 'Self-help: Wolf or Lamb?', in Pancoast, Parker and Froland, p. 160.
22. A. Richardson, *Working with Self-Help Groups* (Bedford Square Press, London, 1984), p. 2.
23. Wollert and Barron, pp. 106–7.
24. *Eurosocial Newsletter*, no. 15, p. 21.
25. See R. M. Titmuss, *The Gift Relationship* (Allen and Unwin, London, 1970).
26. Pancoast, Parker and Froland, p. 12.
27. Bakker and Karel, p. 164.

28. R. Lawrence, 'Voluntary Action: A stalking Horse for the Right?' *Critical Social Policy*, vol. 2, no. 3 (1983), p. 26.
29. Ministry of Foreign Affairs, *The Kingdom of the Netherlands: Social Welfare* (Ministry of Foreign Affairs, the Netherlands, 1984) pp. 5–6.
30. Lawrence, p. 16.
31. J. Finch, 'The Deceit of Self-Help: Preschool Playgroups and Working Class Mothers', *Journal of Social Policy*, vol. 13, pt 1 (1984), pp. 17–18.
32. P. A. Morgan, 'Constructing Images of Deviance', in *Marital Violence*, ed. N. Johnson (Routledge and Kegan Paul, London, 1985), p. 66.
33. G. Leene quoted in *Eurosocial Report No. 25* (European Centre for Social Welfare Training and Research, Vienna, 1985), p. 28.
34. B. Munday, *Eurosocial Report No. 16* (European Centre for Social Welfare Training and Research, Vienna, 1981), pp. 56–7.
35. National Council for Voluntary Organisations, *Voluntary Organisations* (Bedford Square Press, London, 1980), p. 4.
36. J. H. Filer, *Giving in America: Toward a Stronger Voluntary Sector*, Report of the Commission on Private Philanthropy and Public Needs (Washington DC, 1975), p. 45.
37. Report of the Wolfenden Committee, *The Future of Voluntary Organisations* (Croom Helm, London, 1978), p. 27.
38. R. M. Kramer, *Voluntary Agencies in the Welfare State* (University of California Press, Berkeley, 1981), p. 231.
39. T. Saasta, 'Tying Charity's Hands', *New York Times*, 2 August 1983.
40. Salamon and Abramson, pp. 219–20.
41. Sugden.
42. P. L. Berger and R. J. Neuhaus, *To Empower People: The Role of Mediating Structures in Public Policy* (American Enterprise Institute for Public Policy Research, Washington DC, 1977).
43. Kramer, p. 69.
44. Ministry of Welfare, Health and Cultural Affairs, *Developments in Social Welfare in the Netherlands* (Ministry of Welfare, Health and Cultural Affairs, Rijswijk, 1983), p. 2.
45. Ministry of Welfare, Health and Cultural Affairs, *Fact Sheet on the Netherlands: Home Help Services* (Ministry of Welfare, Health and Cultural Affairs, Rijswijk, 1985), p. 1.
46. M. Brenton, 'Changing Relationships in Dutch Social Services', *Journal of Social Policy*, vol. 11, pt 1 (1982), pp. 59–80.
47. Kramer, p. 189.
48. R. Hadley, S. Hatch and D. Jones, 'Report on Visit to the Netherlands', in *Report of the Wolfenden Committee*, pp. 275–8.
49. *Report of the Wolfenden Committee*, p. 29.
50. *Ibid.*, p. 41.
51. *Ibid.*, p. 42.
52. *Ibid.*
53. Kramer, p. 153.

54. A. Purkis, *Voluntary Organisations and Government: Reflections from Reagan's America* (National Council for Voluntary Organisations, London, 1985), p. 13.
55. Kramer, p. 53.
56. *Ibid.*, p. 75.
57. S. Hatch, *Outside the State* (Croom Helm, London, 1980), pp. 148–9.
58. F. J. Gladstone, *Voluntary Action in a Changing World* (Bedford Square Press, London, 1979), p. 100.
59. Kramer, p. 157.
60. *Ibid.*, p. 69.
61. M. Brenton, *The Voluntary Sector in British Social Services* (Longman, London, 1985), p. 93.
62. Quoted in *ibid.*, p. 94.
63. Reported in *The Times*, 11 April 1983.
64. L. M. Salamon, 'Nonprofit Organisations: The Lost Opportunity', in *The Reagan Record*, ed. J. L. Palmer and I. V. Sawhill (Ballinger, Cambridge, Mass., 1984), p. 261.
65. Purkis, p. 12.
66. Brenton, 1985, p. 148.
67. Voluntary Organisations Personal Social Service Group, *The Future of the Social Services* (VOPSS, London, 1986).

CHAPTER 6

1. P. Flora, 'On the History and Current Problems of the Welfare State', in *The Welfare State and its Aftermath*, ed. S. N. Eisenstadt and O. Ahimeir (Croom Helm, London, 1985), p. 12.
2. A. J. Heidenheimer, H. Heclo and C. T. Adams, *Comparative Public Policy: The Politics of Social Choice in Europe and America* (St Martin's Press, New York, 1983), p. 27.
3. US Bureau of the Census, *Statistical Abstract of the United States, 1985* (US Bureau of the Census, Washington DC, 1985); H. Birnbaum *et al.*, 'Why Do Nursing Home Costs Vary? The Determinants of Nursing Home Costs', *Medical Care*, xix, 11; S. J. Biggs, 'Bureaucratization and Privatization of Care for Old People', Paper presented at Conference on Bureaucratization and De-bureaucratization of Social Welfare, Zurich, 1986; S. Slavin, 'Privatization and the De-bureaucratization of Social Welfare . . .', Paper presented at the Conference on Bureaucratization and De-bureaucratization of Social Welfare, Zurich, 1986.
4. K. Judge and M. Knapp, 'Efficiency in the Production of Welfare: The Public and the Private Sectors Compared', in *The Future of Welfare*, ed. R. Klein and M. O'Higgins (Blackwell, Oxford, 1985), pp. 131–49.
5. *Ibid.*, p. 139.
6. *Ibid.*, p. 141.
7. D. R. Phillips, J. A. Vincent assisted by S. Blacksell, 'Petit Bourgeois Care: Private Residential Care for the Elderly', *Policy and Politics*, vol. 14, no. 2 (1986), pp. 189–208.